D1406962

critical Links:

Learning in the Arts and
Student Academic and Social Development

Edited by Richard J. Deasy

Studies were selected for inclusion in this Compendium, and summaries of the studies prepared, by James S. Catterall, Imagination Group, University of California at Los Angeles; Lois Hetland, Project Zero, Harvard Graduate School of Education; and Ellen Winner, Project Zero, Harvard Graduate School of Education and Psychology Department, Boston College.

The preparation and contents of this Compendium were financed by funds provided by the National Endowment for the Arts and the U.S. Department of Education under Cooperative Agreement DCA 97-16. However, these contents do not necessarily represent the policies of the National Endowment for the Arts or the U.S. Department of Education, and the reader should not assume endorsement by the federal government.

Contributing Researchers*

Terry L. Baker, *Education Development Center, Inc./Center for Children and Technology (T.B.)*

Karen K. Bradley, *Graduate Studies Department of Dance, University of Maryland, College Park (K.B.)*

James S. Catterall, *Imagination Group, University of California at Los Angeles (J.C.)*

Dick Corbett, *Independent Educational Researcher (D.C.)*

Cynthia I. Gerstl-Pepin, *Department of Educational Policy Studies, Georgia State University (C.G.-P.)*

Lois Hetland, *Project Zero, Harvard Graduate School of Education (L.H.)*

Robert Horowitz, *Center for Arts Education Research, Teachers College, Columbia University (R.H.)*

George W. Noblit, *School of Education, University of North Carolina at Chapel Hill (G.N.)*

Larry Scripp, *Music-in-Education and the Research Center for Learning Through Music, New England Conservatory (L.S.)*

Michael A. Seaman, *University of South Carolina (M.S.)*

Betty Jane Wagner, *College of Education, Roosevelt University (B.J.W)*

Jaci Webb-Dempsey, *Advanced Educational Studies, West Virginia University (J.W.-D.)*

Bruce Wilson, *Independent Educational Researcher (B.W.)*

Ellen Winner, *Project Zero, Harvard Graduate School of Education and Psychology Department, Boston College (E.W.)*

Compendium Advisors

Ann B. Clark, *National Educational Research and Policies Board and Charlotte-Mecklenburg Schools*

Peter H. Gerber, *EdDesigns Group*

Peter McWalters, *Rhode Island Commissioner of Education*

Ann Podlozny, *VFX Producer, ESC Entertainment*

Gerald Sroufe, *American Educational Research Association*

Michael Timpane, *RAND Corporation*

Betty Lou Whitford, *National Center for Restructuring Education, Schools and Teaching, Teachers College, Columbia University*

i

* Each of these researchers contributed to the summaries of studies included in this Compendium. Each summary includes comments from two researchers. The researchers' initials (shown in the list above after their name and affiliation) appear after each section of a summary they authored.

Foreword

In its 1997 report, *Priorities for Arts Education Research*, the Arts Education Partnership's Task Force on Research recommended the creation of this Compendium. The Task Force applauded the National Endowment for the Arts (NEA), in collaboration with the U.S. Department of Education (USED), for commissioning an earlier compendium (*Schools, Communities and the Arts*, published in 1995) and urged that periodic surveys of recent research be regularly produced as a service to researchers, practitioners, and policy-makers. Both the NEA and the USED responded positively to the Task Force recommendation and awarded funding to the Arts Education Partnership (AEP) to commission and publish the next compendium. *Critical Links: Learning in the Arts and Student Academic and Social Development* is the result.

Through a competitive process, AEP commissioned James S. Catterall of the Imagination Group at the University of California at Los Angeles, Lois Hetland of Project Zero at the Harvard Graduate School of Education, and Ellen Winner of Project Zero at the Harvard Graduate School of Education and the Psychology Department at Boston College to assist in the preparation of the document. Their primary tasks were to establish the criteria for the inclusion of studies; examine and select recent research in five art form areas: dance, drama, music, visual arts, and multi-arts; and prepare summaries of the studies, including comments on the contribution of each to the field of arts education and its implications for future research and/or practice.

In light of available resources, a decision had to be made about the focus of the studies to be screened for inclusion in this Compendium, namely, to include either studies of the academic and social effects of arts learning experiences or studies focused specifically on the arts learning experiences themselves. The decision, made with the advice of the Compendium Advisors (listed p. i), was to do the former, in part to identify strong arts education research that would make a contribution to the national debate over such issues as how to enable all students to reach high levels of academic achievement, how to improve overall school performance, and how to create the contexts and climates in schools that are most conducive to learning.

Multiple voices are heard in this Compendium. As Catterall, Hetland, and Winner began their work of summarizing the studies they had selected, the decision was made to engage other reviewers in reading the studies and adding their comments. The field of education research admits of multiple methods and perspectives. It was felt important to enrich the Compendium with a variety of viewpoints on the significance of the included studies. Consequently, each study summary includes comments by two reviewers. Initials identify the commentators on each study.

Subsequent to the completion of the summaries, essayists were commissioned to examine the group of summaries in each art form and to give their views on the implications of that collective body of work. These essays appear at the end of each art form section. Because of the centrality to the Compendium of the issue of transfer of learning, James Catterall, with assistance from Terry Baker of the Center for Children and Technology of the Education Development Center, was invited to address the topic in an additional essay in the Compendium.

Compendia attempt to capture the best work being done at a period in time. We believe this volume has done so. We believe it offers a rich look backward and valuable guidance on future directions for arts education research. And it provides important insights into curriculum designs and instructional practices that will enhance the quality and impact of student learning in the arts.

The Arts Education Partnership urges education decision makers to attend to these lessons. And we urge private and public funding agencies to make substantial investments in further research that builds on the studies and essays included in this volume.

Introduction

Themes and Variations: Future Directions for Arts Education Research and Practice
Richard J. Deasy

A purpose of this Compendium is to recommend to researchers and funders of research promising lines of inquiry and study suggested by recent, strong studies of the academic and social effects of learning in the arts. A parallel purpose is to provide designers of arts education curriculum and instruction with insights found in the research that suggest strategies for deepening the arts learning experiences that are required to achieve those effects.

Rob Horowitz and Jaci Webb-Dempsey in their overview essay on multi-arts studies make a comment that is true of the volume as a whole: "The selection . . . is diverse, both in terms of the arts learning experiences the studies describe and the particularities of the research they report." So their advice to the readers of their essay is good guidance to all: treat the Compendium as a body of work to be explored and mined for commonalities as well as particularities, themes and variations. The insights are layered.

Particularities lie in each of the 62 studies and are probed by the summaries and commentaries written by the contributing reviewers. Five essays then trace common threads found in the group of studies within dance, drama, music, visual arts, or multi-arts. A reader will want to do the same.

A reader also will want to set the essays themselves side by side to search for patterns of analysis and argument. For instance, all of the essayists urge that future research define with greater depth, richness, and specificity the nature of the arts learning experience itself and its companion, the arts teaching experience. They agree that the Compendium studies suggest that well-crafted arts experiences produce positive academic and social effects, but they long for more research that reveals the unique and precise aspects of the arts teaching and learning that do so. Curriculum, instruction, and professional development would benefit greatly from such clarifications.

In his essay on "transfer," James Catterall echoes his colleagues in arguing for a more complete approach to the question of how learning in the arts "transfers" to learning and behavior in other academic and social contexts. While "transfer" is often construed to be a one-way effect in which learning in one domain (e.g., music) causes an effect in another (e.g., spatial reasoning), Catterall reflects the sentiment shared by other essayists in urging researchers to adopt and pursue the more plausible and educationally useful view that transfer involves recipro-cal processes involving multiple interactions among domains and disciplines. He also embraces the perspective recently espoused by John Bransford and Daniel Schwartz that the effects of these interactions perhaps can be known only over time.[1] Longitudinal studies are more likely to reveal the effects of learning across domains and situations than are single snapshots, however empirical and controlled these latter may be.

The essayists also share the view that research is but one form of "usable knowledge" that decision makers should call on as part of a repertoire that includes information drawn from direct experience validated by successful prac-tice. Horowitz and Webb-Dempsey say: "Administrators and policy-makers can be secure in supporting arts pro-grams based on the evidence presented (in the multi-arts studies)." Others might add: "and use the studies to examine, challenge, or confirm the views they have developed through their daily work in schools and classrooms." Good decisions emerge from the interactions among research, practice, and reflection.

1 John Bransford and Daniel Schwartz (2000). Rethinking Transfer. Chapter in Review of Research in Education, Volume 24. Washington DC: American Educational Research Association.

The essayists and the commentators on individual studies find support in the body of work in the Compendium for the role of arts learning in assisting in the development of critical academic skills, basic and advanced litera-cy and numeracy among them. They also offer suggestions, based on the studies, for restructuring curricula and instructional practices. For instance, Catterall and other commentators powerfully detail the use of drama in the preschool and early grades as a technique for teaching and motivating children to develop higher-order lan-guage and literacy skills. Intriguingly, Larry Scripp in his essay and in several commentaries on music studies explores how the skills of learning music relate to comparable skills in language use, both in English and, in a spe-cific study, French. And Karen Bradley, Catterall, and Scripp each discuss studies where linking writing exercises and arts experiences yields deeper and more complex understandings and articulations by students.

The interrelationships between learning in certain forms of music instruction and the development of cognitive skills such as spatial reasoning appear incontrovertible in light of a number of studies in the Compendium. But once again Scripp in his essay urges researchers and practitioners to probe deeply into the particularities of these relationships and argues strongly for the development of new forms of music instruction that he feels will advance at one and the same time both music and related learning.

Another fruitful line of future inquiry would be to build on the studies and the suggestions of commentators and essayists to clarify the habits of mind, social competencies, and personal dispositions that are inherent to arts learning and to explore the application of these qualities in other realms of learning and life. Horowitz and Webb-Dempsey most directly address this issue in their multi-arts essay, but variations on the theme can be found in all layers of the Compendium. In part this is a matter, they say, of continuing to develop "better and more creative research designs" that probe the complexity of the arts learning experience, and also take into account the contexts in which the learning occurs. More richly textured qualitative studies—comparable to many of those in this Compendium—are the necessary prelude to clarifying the questions and directions for subsequent inquiry, including controlled experimental studies. But at issue as well, and well illustrated in the Compendium commentaries and essays, is the need for a lexicon of descriptive terms that authentically capture the arts learning experience while at that same time suggesting an array of interactions with other realms of learning and life—a lexicon that may blunt the debate between "intrinsic" and "instrumental" arts learning. For instance, individual studies invoke terms such as "theorizing" (developing theories to predict the consequences of actions); "persistence and resilience" (the capacity to sustain focused attention and to surmount distractions, setbacks, or frustration), and "respect for authentic achievement" to describe fundamental aspects of arts learning and art making. Terms such as these prompt us to explore the interrelationships between these abilities and attitudes as they are brought into play or produced in the context of arts learning and in other academic, personal, and social contexts and situations. So the term "theorizing" may comprise a "constellation" of mental processes that are cultivated and strengthened by application in disparate contexts including the arts. The essays urge us to explore that possibility.

Bradley, Catterall, and Baker in their separate essays on dance, drama, and visual arts, also have language on their minds, specifically the lack of consistency of usage within the art forms. Bradley in her essay on the studies of dance argues, "a common language from dance theory is critical to the future rigor and robustness of dance research…The grammar of movement is inherent in dance style and technique," but verbal expressions of this grammar need to be codified and used to undergird both instructional practice and research. Her candidate for a useful model is Laban Movement Analysis. Similarly, Catterall urges researchers and practitioners engaged with drama and theater to agree on a basic set of terms; he offers some potential definitions. Baker tackles the vexing question of how "art" itself should be defined and urges researchers to at least adopt and articulate an operational definition in their studies.

Given their perspective that learning in the arts—and its relationship to other learning—is complex and interactive, the essayists also argue strongly, even passionately, for the development and acceptance of forms of assessing teaching and learning that respect and reveal that complexity. They repeatedly make the point that knowing the full range of effects of arts learning requires assessment instruments that can validly and reliably identify and measure the outcomes of arts instruction. Discerning the impact of that learning in other domains requires instruments other than the currently available tests of reading and math achievement. The argument is not just that these tests are not sensitive to the effects of arts learning, but that they also are not adequate to assess the complexity of language and mathematical learning themselves, which, the essayists contend, are interwoven with the cognitive and affective processes of other domains, including the arts. They urge the development of new forms of assessment in all domains. Current forms, which assess only a limited range of content and skill, may divert curriculum and instruction away from more authentic and enriching learning.

Catterall makes a related argument that the technology of achievement assessment current in education, largely centered on reading and mathematics, also defines the educational research agenda and studies that are published. Among the effects, he argues, is a concentration of studies—in the arts and other domains—on young children in the elementary grades where data from standardized tests are most readily available. A corollary is that researchers and evaluators of the arts feel compelled to use these instruments and data, which have professional standing, to determine the impact of the arts—a severe limitation on arts education research of the kind advocated by the essayists.

With these views and perspectives, the essayists place themselves—and the arts—firmly within current discussions and debates about the education policies and practices that will best bring about school reform and improvement and high achievement for students. They make a strong case for the importance of arts learning. And they urge their colleagues in arts research and education to strengthen their contributions to these discussions by following leads and implications found in this Compendium.

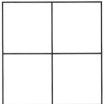

table of contents

critical Links:

Learning in the Arts and Student Academic and Social Development

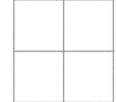

table of contents

Essay:

MULTI-ARTS   63

Summaries:

Essay:

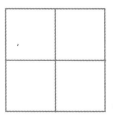

table of contents

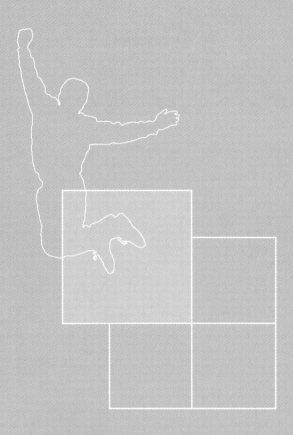

Dance

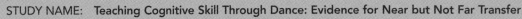

STUDY NAME: **Teaching Cognitive Skill Through Dance: Evidence for Near but Not Far Transfer**
AUTHORS: Mia Keinanen, Lois Hetland, and Ellen Winner
PUBLISHED: Journal of Aesthetic Education, Fall 2000, 34, (3-4): 295-306

Research Questions

Can dance instruction improve reading?
Can dance instruction improve nonverbal reasoning?

METHODS

The authors claim an exhaustive search of computer databases, references in literature, recommendations from primary researchers, and searches through identified journals resulted in 3,714 potentially relevant studies. From these, the authors selected seven studies that could be examined using their meta-analytical technique. Those selected had quantified outcomes in the area of dance and cognition, used control groups, and were conducted on non-impaired populations. All of the selected studies were unpublished. Eliminated were those studies that were primarily deemed to be articles of advocacy, those articles that were teacher testimonies, studies in which students self-selected for dance, any studies that were deemed co-relational, and those studies whose outcomes were affective or physiological.

A first and second coder read the seven studies, with a resulting 12 percent rate of disagreement on 100 coding decisions. Any coding disagreements were subsequently resolved and were coded as to: Year of Publication/Outlet, Outcome, Sample Size, Design, Type of Dance Instruction, Type of Control Instruction, Duration, Intensity, Participant Age, and Participant Characteristics. The studies were analyzed within the two categories of Reading Abilities and Non-Verbal Reasoning. One study (Von Rossburg-Gempton, 1998) tested two populations (senior citizens and young children), and so effects were calculated for each population tested. The meta-analysis conflated the factors across the four studies in each category, with a resulting array of statistics that are extensive but ultimately uninformative.—K.B.

RESULTS

The meta-analysis of the four studies reporting reading outcomes found a small average effect, which increased (doubled) when weighted by sample size. Larger sample sizes produced more positive correlations. However, the range of both effect sizes and the varied tests for significance (there were two) on such a small number of sample sizes provided the authors with the argument for a weak effect overall. The heterogeneity of the studies weakens the validity and reliability of the meta-analysis.

The meta-analysis of the cohort of three studies reporting nonverbal reasoning effects found a much clearer positive correlation between dance experiences and nonverbal reasoning skills. The studies reporting nonverbal effects were more homogeneous than the reading studies. They yielded a greater degree of reliability and validity ($r = .17$, three more studies required to bring results to significance).

Discussion of the results includes the authors' understanding that future dance studies in which cognitive outcomes are part of the desired effect should be more rigorous, should be set up to preclude teacher expectancy effects, should separate out motivational factors, and should be of a sufficient sample size.—K.B.

CONTRIBUTIONS TO THE FIELD

The study is a meta-analysis of seven research projects in dance. The studies span a period of 26 years and vary greatly in sample size, measurement techniques, and dance activities applied as variables.

The use of meta-analysis on a mere seven studies, and the fact that these studies were found in what is described as an exhaustive search of eight databases, journals, bibliographies, and requests to researchers, indicates that the authors believe that research in dance education is in its infancy. Research studies that utilized anecdotal reports or in which students self-selected for dance were eliminated. Recommendations are made for more studies, more empirical studies, and a more uniform use of quantitative research methodology across all studies in the future.

This is the first meta-analysis of the dance education field. In that, its main contribution to the field is that it highlights the limits of meta-analysis on such a small sample size.—K.B.

COMMENTARY

Of the seven studies included in this meta-analysis four examined the effect of dance instruction on reading skills and three on nonverbal reasoning. However, the small number of studies, the variation in dance instruction in each study, and the large gap between early and later studies (16 to 18 years) make it difficult to draw any significant conclusions. This temporal gap is especially worrisome in light of the positive results for the two more recent studies in reading effects (Seham 1997 and Rose 1999); these positive results disappear in the meta-analysis discussion.

Statistical analysis were used to determine the size of the effect as well as whether the effect was positive, null, or negative. Meta-analysis can be more useful than a mere electoral approach (i.e., simply counting up the number of studies with a positive effect, a null effect, or a negative effect) because sample size can be accounted for in determining the probability level for a particular effect. The problem with meta-analysis is that the conflation of numbers ceases to be useful when comparing different types of experiences and variables, especially in small numbers of studies. And, in the end, we only know that any numbers are highly questionable. Guidance for dance educators and researchers is difficult to elicit from such a meta-analysis. Within the meta-analysis, the authors criticize studies where there has been an overt facilitation of transferability by a teacher. The authors ascribe to the belief that if teachers know they are trying to improve reading skills through dance, causality cannot be proven since the teachers may be "signaling" the desired results to the students. Yet good teaching is often about clearly signaling the direction of the expectations. Just such a phenomenon was cited in the meta-analysis discussion as a reason why positive results were suspicious in the Rose study (1999). "…[T]he teachers of the dance group were aware of the hypothesis that dance should improve reading. Thus, those teachers may have taught reading in a more enthusiastic and engaging manner than those teaching the control group." (Keinanen et al., p. 300)

But a more major concern with the meta-analysis, as with a number of other studies in this Compendium, is the failure to distinguish the content of the variable "dance instruction." In the seven studies that met the authors' test for inclusion, the type of instruction was defined under one of three categories: (1) instrumental dance instruction (making letter shapes with one's body, etc.), (2) creative dance instruction (problem-solving, divergent-thinking experiences), and (3) traditional dance instruction (technique class). But that categorization is not meaningful to dance education researchers because often the instrumental use of dance activities is indistinguishable from creative dance instruction. Studies are needed that examine the effects of each of the experiences inherent in dance (technique, improvisation, performance, and composition) and also the interrelationship among their effects. The selection of studies for the meta-analysis does not provide a complete picture of the range of dance instruction and experiences, which would be needed to draw conclusions about the academic and social effects of dance.

Dance education researchers differentiate among experiences in performance, composition, improvisation, and technique. In one study cited (Seham 1997), students at the National Dance Institute (Jacques D'Amboise's school) improved significantly on all scores for cognitive learning against a control group that received no special program, but it is unclear whether the dance classes affected overall concentration and focus as opposed to affecting reading scores. The positive influence of dance technique classes on learning across the board leads the authors to criticize the research rather than encouraging a closer look into the instrumental aspects of a dance technique program. Intensive study in the discipline of dance might lead to increased focus and concentration, and that would be highly instrumental. The error belongs both to the author of the original study (Seham 1997), because the content of the classes was not clearly defined, and to the use of the data within the original study by Keinanen et al. because the meta-analysis is comparing what may be vastly different

types of experiences and drawing conclusions about overall effects on reading scores.—K.B.

CONTRIBUTIONS TO THE FIELD

The value of this work is its careful and comprehensive review of the entire research field (including published and unpublished work), uncovering 3,714 studies that investigated the effects of dance on student learning in nondance areas.

The research used a widely accepted technique, meta-analysis, allowing the authors to assess the aggregate contribution of multiple studies that employed a range of student reading and reasoning measures, as well as varied statistical techniques.

The most important contribution, beyond the fact that this is the first systematic review across all the research on this topic, is simply that only a handful of studies met the researchers' standards for acceptable scientific rigor. The clear message is that the field needs more research.—B.W.

COMMENTARY

The researchers found only four studies meeting their strict standards of acceptable research that investigated the relationship between dance instruction and reading skills and three studies that assessed reasoning skills. The former group of four studies included a total sample of only 527 students while the latter group of three studies involved only 188 students. So, in almost 50 years of research only 715 students have been exposed to carefully designed experimental treatments on the learning effects of dance. One obvious response is to decry the lack of controlled research in this field. It is also not unreasonable to argue that such a small sample hardly qualifies for such sophisticated quantitative analysis.

The more appropriate point is, perhaps, that the medical/agricultural model upon which these standards for meta-analysis are derived is not necessarily the best one from which to understand the complex endeavor of education or more specifically dance education. The varied contexts in which instruction is delivered, even from classroom to classroom in the same building, make it difficult to meaningfully transfer successes in controlled experimental settings to messy classrooms.

While it is important to understand the value that dance can add to students' cognitive skills, it is just as important (if not more so) to know the how and why dance contributes to learning, as well as the organizational and instructional conditions that allow arts learning to help students become more successful students. Thus, the 3,714 studies should also be mined to learn what the many qualitative studies can add to these important questions.—B.W.

"…a more major concern with the meta-analysis…is the failure to distinguish the content of the variable 'dance instruction.'"

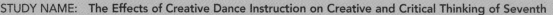

STUDY NAME: The Effects of Creative Dance Instruction on Creative and Critical Thinking of Seventh
Grade Female Students in Seoul, Korea
AUTHOR: Juja Kim
PUBLISHED: Unpublished Doctoral Dissertation, 1998, New York University, NY

Research Question

What effect on creative and critical thinking abilities does a program of creative or traditional dance instruction have on seventh-grade girls?

METHODS

Seventy-eight seventh-grade girls without previous dance experience took 45-minute classes in either creative (n = 38) or traditional (n = 38) dance twice a week for eight weeks (total of 15 sessions). Groups were intact classes from one neighborhood middle school (heterogeneous SES) in Seoul, Korea.

The programs are described in detail in the text and in appendices. The traditional program was taught in three five-week blocks of modern, ballet, and Korean traditional dance, by teachers who selected the style, and who designed and taught the segments consecutively. The creative program was designed and taught by the researcher for all 15 sessions.

The study employed a quasi-experimental, pre- and post-test, nonequivalent control group design. The Torrance Test of Creative Thinking (TTCT) Figural Forms A and B (counterbalanced by group and test administration) were used as pre- and post-tests for creative thinking. Raven's Standard Progressive Matrices were used as pre- and post-tests for critical thinking. The tests were selected for their high reliabilities, long histories, and nonverbal forms (to match the nonverbal dance medium). Tests were administered by trained proctors blind to group and hypothesis and scored by a psychologist. In addition, students responded to a pre-course interview and in three written reflections after the fifth, 10th, and last class sessions. Qualitative data were analyzed by procedures outlined by Miles and Huberman, Weller and Romey, and Yin, including creating data arrays, constructing categorical matrices, making flow charts of relationships, constructing frequency distributions, and ordering data chronologically.

Analysis of quantitative results checked assumptions and employed independent t tests on gain scores (post-test – pre-test) and ANCOVAs (covarying pre-test scores). Bonferroni adjustments were made to control Type I errors (i.e., erroneously finding a positive effect), and alpha level was set at $p < .01$. Clear tables report descriptive and inferential data, and text reports exact ts and ps for some comparisons, although not for non-significant ones (which are important, since $p = .02$, a high probability, is a very different finding from $p = .49$, which is a probability essentially equivalent to chance).—*L.H.*

RESULTS

Of four hypotheses, three were supported by the quantitative analysis: (1) subjects in traditional dance instruction did not make significant gains in creative or critical thinking, (2) subjects in creative dance did make significant gains in creative and critical thinking, and (3) subjects in creative dance had significantly greater gains in creative thinking than subjects in traditional dance. The fourth hypothesis was not supported: (4) subjects in creative dance did not gain significantly more in critical thinking than subjects in traditional dance instruction. However, the trend in critical thinking was toward the creative group (Creative Mean gain = 2.02; Traditional Mean gain = .97, equivalent to a moderate effect size of $r = .21$, equivalent to $d = .42$). Thus, while the hypothesis was not supported, the creative dance program did enhance subjects' abilities to think critically to a moderate degree.

The qualitative analysis demonstrated that students' assumptions about dance changed, depending on the type of dance instruction they experienced. This suggests the importance of program type and quality, because these factors affect learning. Thus, decisions about program goals need to be made carefully to support the intended aims of the program.—*L.H.*

CONTRIBUTIONS TO THE FIELD

This study combines rigorous quantitative and qualitative methods to explore a relatively unstudied and important question about transfer from dance instruction to higher-order thinking skills.

Quantitative analysis showed gains on four components of creative thinking (originality, elaboration, flexibility, and fluency) for subjects in creative dance instruction. These same students did not improve in critical thinking from pre- to post-test (but see Results section). A control group who studied traditional dance (modern, ballet, and Korean traditional) made gains only in the "fluency" component of creative thinking and not in critical thinking skills.

Qualitative analysis provided insight into students' perceptions of their dance experiences. Students in the creative dance instruction saw dance as requiring thought, intelligence, and problem-solving and as related to everyday life, while those in traditional instruction made none of these connections and saw dance as a means to a beautiful body and health.—*L.H.*

COMMENTARY

This study suggests that when dance is taught as creative problem-solving, students' creative thinking skills improve.

When it is taught as a series of steps to be replicated, creative thinking skills do not develop. In other words, the type of dance instruction appears to affect both what is learned in dance and what transfers to higher-level thinking.

Future research should compare programs of creative dance in which one group receives a program focused on creative problem-solving, similar to the program described here, and another employs creative problem-solving with the addition of deliberate bridging to the critical thinking used in a target subject.

This study would be an excellent model to replicate because of its rigor, focus on higher-order thinking, and clear reporting (numerous descriptions and appendices offer details about programs, methods, and data). Replicating within the United States would be informative, especially with subjects of various ages and abilities (gifted in dance, gifted in academics, at risk, or behaviorally disordered). Varying subjects' ethnicity and socio-economic backgrounds, and matching traditional dance forms to subjects' cultural backgrounds, would also provide useful information.—L.H.

CONTRIBUTIONS TO THE FIELD

The study is vastly comprehensive, including a fairly complete review of the literature of the early theorists in dance education from Laban to Murray to Mettler to Fleming to Russell to Anne Green Gilbert. But the author does not recognize the relationships of some of the theorists to Laban—particularly Russell, Boorman, and Preston-Dunlop. The author does not take into account that these approaches are based on Laban's theories and that Laban's theories permeate many of the other approaches as well. Therefore, while the review of the literature is broad, it is not organized into any meta-theory of creative dance. The author does not discuss how these theories informed her own creative dance classes (described later in the study), nor does she distinguish between teacher-centered and child-centered approaches to creative dance. She assumes that all creative dance approaches are child-centered, which is not necessarily the case.

Both quantitative and qualitative analyses of data provide a complete view of what was accomplished over the 15 sessions in creative movement and traditional dance forms. The results revealed that creative dance classes could indeed foster creative thinking, but not necessarily critical thinking skills. The permutations of the quantitative analysis are impressive, but the qualitative analysis actually reveals more specific information about what worked and what didn't work over the eight weeks. The content of both sets of classes is scrupulously documented, providing the opportunity to replicate the study in places other than Korea, with different age groups and utilizing different forms of traditional dance.

The author reports the responses of the participants in honest detail, including the remarks the participants made about being bored and embarrassed by the creative dance classes. She goes on to aggregate the responses demonstrating that ultimately, the creative dance group had a more positive and subjective appreciation of dance and the traditional dance group a more objective and detached view of dance.—K.B.

COMMENTARY

It is not unreasonable that the creative dance classes yielded an increase in creative thinking skills. The long shot was that creative dance classes would improve critical thinking skills. While Kim does not explore the body of literature on transference of learning from one modality to another, she was seduced by the claims that early theorists and scholars made about the potential for dance to influence or develop critical thinking skills. These early scholars did not do rigorous investigation of their claims, but wrote rich and broad descriptions of what it appeared was happening when children moved creatively. As cognitive science and the scholarship of teaching and learning have uncovered more about the brain, mind, and body connections, the theorists Kim based her thesis on appear quaint and naïve.

Kim also fell into a dichotomy within the field of dance education that the field needs to move beyond. The notion that traditional, teacher-centered dance classes will not yield creative or critical thinking skill development, while creative dance (which is "student-centered") will bring all good things is a trap. In this study, the traditional dance group did increase in one of the four categories of creative thinking skills: that of fluency of thinking. There are indications in this and other studies relating dance to creative thinking skills that movement or dance alone may enhance fluency.

The conflation of creative and critical thinking processes leads her to expect that creative dance experiences would enhance both and dance technique classes would enhance neither. The weakest part of the study occurs early in the dissertation, when she infers that because "thinking always involves both creative and critical processes," these functions must therefore always work together. However, in testing for the two kinds of thinking, she was compelled to utilize two different pre- and post-tests; suggesting that so far we haven't figured exactly how the two functions work together, or even if they do.

It is important to eliminate the dichotomous thinking about the content of dance classes and determine what dance technique, dance improvisation, dance composition, and dance performance do influence in regard to creative and critical thinking skills. One can imagine that composing a dance piece, refining it, and performing it might foster more closed-ended cognitive activity than explorative and open-ended improvisation. Kim had the creative dance students compose a dance in the last week of the classes, but there was no time to refine or perform it, much less test for effect.

The age and culture of the students clearly influenced the results, something Kim does explore in her paper. The seventh-graders were shy and withdrawn and therefore tentative about the creative process. Seventh-graders would bring a particular self-consciousness to any process, no matter what their culture of origin. The value of respect for authority that is more ingrained in Korean culture may have aided the research. Even though the girls felt comfortable enough to share their negative feelings with the teacher-researcher, they were cooperative and willing. One might imagine different results from a population of ninth-grade boys or second-grade mixed-gender groups.—K.B.

STUDY NAME: **Effects of a Movement Poetry Program on Creativity of Children with Behavioral Disorders**
AUTHORS: Martha C. Mentzer and Boni B. Boswell
PUBLISHED: Impulse, 1995, 3, 183-199

Research Questions

Can a program that integrates poetry-making with creative movement enhance creativity (originality, fluency, and flexibility) in children with behavioral disorders?

What are the unexpected outcomes of a program that integrates poetry-making with creative movement for children with behavioral disorders?

METHODS

Two boys participated, aged 7 and 10 years. The boys were selected from a pool of five children living at a residential treatment home. Selection was based on their 90 percent participation in the program. The boys' individual diagnoses and behavioral disorders were described, but no references were made to the cultural contexts of their families (e.g., race, ethnicity, SES).

The program integrated creative movement and poetry stimuli, and the boys participated in 16, 50-minute sessions over a period of 10 weeks. Sessions had a consistent, three-part structure, each part of which was described clearly: (1) an introduction and warm-up, (2) movement to a poem ("the heart of the lesson"), and (3) closure. The movement and poetry segment involved reading the poem aloud twice while the boys read along, the boys creating individual movement sequences for lines they each selected, and then sharing their movement sequences. By the fourth session, the boys began writing and creating movement for original poetry they "spontaneously spoke" and recorded on cassettes, which was later compiled into a booklet for each child. A behavior management reward system (tokens) that was used throughout the residential program was also incorporated into the program.

The study design was qualitative, and it was well conducted, analyzed, and reported.

Data were collected and analyzed from four sources:

(1) Anecdotal Recordings by two observers, trained prior to data collection. The observers alternated which child they observed for each session. They recorded observations chronologically within sessions to capture program information (progression of content) and the children's behaviors and verbalizations. Observations were summarized collaboratively by the principal investigator and observers after each session and then coded for (a) creative behavior (operationalized as originality, fluency, and flexibility, after Torrance), (b) unexpected outcomes, and (c) external factors. Originality = number of movements unique to the individual. Fluency = number of movements. Flexibility = number of definite changes in movement quality (force, direction, level, or shape).

(2) Observational Checklists. Sessions were videotaped, and two observers were trained prior to viewing by clarifying definitions and concepts and completing the creativity checklist (which tracked originality, fluency, and flexibility, as defined above) for a child from the home who was not one of the two subjects. Each observer's agreement with the principal investigator was $r \geq .85$. Then the observers completed checklists for eight (50 percent) randomly selected and ordered sessions of one child, which they viewed independently until satisfied about accuracy.

(3) Questionnaires/Interviews. Open-ended questionnaires were conducted with four staff members and the two observers, one week after the study. The questionnaires examined four general areas: (a) program success, (b) learning, (c) behavior changes, and (d) needed program changes. Open-ended interviews with the subjects, conducted and audiotaped by the principal investigator one week after the study, included the same general areas as the questionnaire (through the question: What does poetry mean to you?) and an additional supplementary area, feelings: (a) how feelings about poetry had changed from beginning to end of the program, (b) how the boys felt about moving with other children, and (c) what feelings arose when the boys moved to their favorite poem. Data from both sources were transcribed, coded, and summarized by the investigators into the four categories plus a "miscellaneous comments" category for comments that did not otherwise fit.

(4) Children's Original Poems. From the fourth session on, children created and spontaneously "spoke" their poems into an audiocassette. The poems were transcribed into booklets for each child. They were analyzed as "unexpected outcomes" and described according to creativity variables, representative topics, and overall characteristics.

Data sources contributed uniquely and also reinforced each other through triangulation, which affords verification and clarification of results. Anecdotal records were most helpful in understanding program outcomes.—*L.H.*

RESULTS

Three general results were reported for these two behaviorally disordered children: (a) the boys demonstrated all three creativity variables to varying degrees, (b) growth was both shared and individual: both boys gained interest in poetry, one gained social behavior skills, the other gained motor coordination skills, and (c) both boys enjoyed the program.

The study generated the foundation for testable hypotheses (along four dimensions) for further study of this research question.

(1) Areas of Learning: (a) independent thinking skills, (b) motor coordination, (c) body and spatial awareness, (d) verbal and physical expression of thoughts and feelings, (e) body knowledge, (f) awareness of dance elements;

(2) Behavior Changes: (a) willingness to participate in new activities, (b) positive group participation, (c) appropriate participation, (d) overcoming inhibited expression;

(3) Program Changes: (a) extend over longer time, (b) increase importance of token system, (c) increase time for poetry writing per session, (d) focus more on reflection of feelings in both movement and poetry;

(4) Study Design: (a) interview more frequently during the program (at least three times) to develop trust earlier, (b) continue to emphasize detailed anecdotal records.—*L.H.*

CONTRIBUTIONS TO THE FIELD

This study is exemplary in its qualitative methods and reporting. The article describes the program and study clearly, and it offers both program modifications and hypotheses to test in future research.

The study suggests that, when combined, poetry and movement may contribute to engagement, development of creativity, and social and/or motor learning in children with behavioral disorders.—*L.H.*

COMMENTARY

The study is a model of qualitative work. It affords a fine-grained analysis of two children by triangulating four sources of data for validity: anecdotal records, observational checklists from videotaped sessions, questionnaires and interviews; and student work (poetry produced by the subjects). The authors report their findings in multiple formats (text, graphs, lists of hypotheses for future qualitative or quantitative research), and specify that their results apply only to these two boys and to future research questions. The authors are also careful to ensure and assess reliability and reduce bias by defining terms in measurable ways, by training observers, by randomizing session selection and order for coding, and by alternating which child is observed by which observers for each session.

Future research should explore the categories defined as outcomes by this study and replicate its careful methods and judicious reporting.—*L.H.*

CONTRIBUTIONS TO THE FIELD

This case study of two boys is quite complete and revealing about creative thinking and the particularities of the two boys' learning styles. Qualitative data collection is well documented and supported with citations from previous studies using similar techniques. Both boys were able to develop a portfolio of poems written from movement, indicating that improvisational dance from a linguistic stimulus can generate original thoughts with a degree of fluency.—*K.B.*

COMMENTARY

The study adds to the growing body of literature about creative thinking and what characterizes it. There are specific descriptions of behaviors associated with the creative thinking attributes of fluency, flexibility, and originality with both movement and writing examples.

A statement in the Discussion section of the study raises an area for further exploration in the field of dance education research. The authors reflect on the lack of emotional or affective images in the poems written by the two boys and speculate that greater attention on identifying and applying feelings to the process of writing poetry might extend creative output. More studies that address the inclusion of affective variables in cognitive skill development are needed, especially in dance, where the cognitive, affective, and psychomotor domains are so well synthesized. The authors go on to conclude that since one boy improved more in social behavior and the other in motor coordination, the union of creative movement and poetry writing provided a "stronger fabric" for development, especially for children of different and challenging learning styles.

The authors also state that the most useful data for understanding the outcomes the boys achieved came from the anecdotal records. The field needs to recognize that movement analysis may offer the clearest depiction of what cognitive or behavioral changes occur through involvement in dance.—*K.B.*

> "The study suggests that, when combined, poetry and movement may contribute to engagement, development of creativity, and social and/or motor learning in children with behavioral disorders."

7

dance

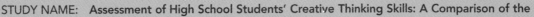

STUDY NAME: **Assessment of High School Students' Creative Thinking Skills: A Comparison of the Effects of Dance and Non-dance Classes**
AUTHOR: Sandra Minton
PUBLISHED: Unpublished Manuscript, 2000, University of Northern Colorado, Greeley, CO

Research Question

Is there a relationship between dancing and creative thinking?

METHODS

Two hundred eighty-six high school students (15 years old, on average) who were enrolled in dance (experimental group) and non-dance (untreated control group) courses participated. Students studied under six dance teachers in beginning and advanced courses for a wide range of dance forms. Dancers participated for about five to eight hours a week, in and out of school, for a semester. Controls attended classes in business accounting, English, health, interpersonal communications, and psychology.

Experimental and Control subjects were pre- and post-tested in groups on the three parts of the Torrance Test of Creative Thinking (TTCT), Figural Form A: picture construction, picture completion, and creation of recognizable objects. The test is fairly reliable: inter-rater reliability ($r = .66 – r = .99$); retest reliability ($r = .60 – r = .70$). TTCT is norm-referenced on five factors: fluency (number of ideas), originality (novelty of ideas), abstractness of titles (imaginative titling that captures the essence of a drawing), elaboration (detail identification), and resistance to premature closure (completing figures in non-simplistic ways). Because subjects were assigned random identification numbers by instructors, responses were scored blind by the investigator, which is a strength of the study. Group equivalence at pre-test was determined by a t test. Repeated measures of ANOVA on change scores were computed for experimentals vs. controls for all subjects and by school for each of the six schools. Finally, pre- and post-test scores were correlated with four indices of commitment and experience with dance: previous dance training, current dance instruction outside of school, total dance experience, and hours dancing per week.—L.H.

RESULTS

Elaboration, originality, and abstractness of titles correlated with higher levels of dance experience (results are presented in bar graphs, without specific values). It is puzzling that patterns of effect across factors of the TTCT are inconsistent, with different schools demonstrating significant differences ($p < .05$) for different creativity factors. The author reasonably suggests that the variation may result from differences in teachers or in school cultures—variables that should be assessed in future studies. Although results are compromised by potential selection bias (and can only be generalized to high school students who choose dance classes), there is evidence against an interpretation that higher creativity scores resulted because those who took dance started out more creative: dancers scored lower, on average, on pre-tests for all five creativity factors. Thus, it is not likely that the creativity gains resulted from a more creative group in the dance treatment but, rather, from the dance instruction itself.—L.H.

CONTRIBUTIONS TO THE FIELD

This study suggests a possible relationship between dancing and improved ability to consider multiple perspectives. Such flexible thinking is useful in a range of disciplines.

The study finds that high school students who studied a variety of styles of dance for a semester scored better than non-dancers on the elaboration, originality, and abstractness of titles factors of the Torrance Test of Creative Thinking.

This study also models an experimental design that allows reliable conclusions about transfer to be drawn. Experimental designs establish the direction of effect, in this case, from dance instruction to the outcome measure of creative thinking.—L.H.

COMMENTARY

Dancers in this study are more likely than students who did not receive dance instruction to employ creative thinking of the type measured by three factors assessed by the Torrance Test of Creativity. The study thus supplies empirical support for a belief that dance teaches divergent thinking.

The study does not assess or assert, however, how likely the dancers would be to use these thinking skills in, for example, history or science classes. That is possible, but not likely, since cognitive transfer across subjects is difficult to achieve (see Salomon, G. & Perkins, D. N. [1989], Rocky roads to transfer: Rethinking mechanisms of a neglected phenomenon. *Educational Psychologist.* 24[2], 113-142). Generally, skills are employed in contexts similar to those in which they are learned. In this case, the tests were administered at the start of a dance class, which may have helped subjects use what they had learned in dance more readily in the testing context than they would in other subjects or classes.

Future research should investigate whether creativity in specific disciplines (e.g., science, history) can be fostered through dance programs, explore how teacher behaviors affect the creativity factors enhanced (what makes a quality dance teacher or experience?), and employ multiple, situated measures of creativity, rather than just paper-and-pencil tests.—*L.H.*

CONTRIBUTIONS TO THE FIELD

The study indicates that dance is a valid way for students to develop creative thinking skills, especially in the categories of originality and abstract thinking. The data are well decoded, and the study is a model for quantitative analysis in the field.—*K.B.*

COMMENTARY

The dance students studied an array of dance styles and approaches. Further research needs to tease out whether movement improvisation and/or choreography affect creativity to a greater or lesser degree than a dance technique class, where expectations are much clearer and the teachers directly model outcomes.

Whether dancers can utilize their original and abstract-thinking skills in other disciplines is an additional area of exploration for future researchers. Studies such as the Minton study show a correlation between a variety of dance activities and some creative thinking skills, but we need to demonstrate transferability as well as correlation in order to demonstrate the full value of dance activities. Studies that also test for skill development of creative thinking skills in writing and other creative problem-solving disciplines would be useful, especially if such studies demonstrate either that dance allows for deeper and more pervasive learning or that some dance activities are more transferable than others.—*K.B.*

"This study suggests a possible relationship between dancing and improved ability to consider multiple perspectives."

STUDY NAME: **The Impact of Whirlwind's Basic Reading Through Dance Program on First Grade Students'**
Basic Reading Skills: Study II
AUTHOR: Dale Rose
PUBLISHED: Unpublished Evaluation Study, February 1999, 3-D Group, Berkeley, California

Research Question

Can first-graders' reading abilities be improved through a dance program in which children learn to use their bodies to physically represent letters?

METHODS

In 1998-1999, a Basic Reading through Dance (BRD) program was implemented in three Chicago public elementary schools. The goal of the program was to improve first-graders' reading ability through dance. The program lasted over 20 sessions. Each session was led by three dance specialists. The heart of each session consisted of teaching students to physically represent sounds by making shapes with their bodies to represent letters and letter combinations. Nine schools served as control schools. All 12 schools served predominantly African-American poverty-level children. A total of 174 BRD children and 198 control children were pre- and post-tested in reading using the Read America's Phono-Graphix Test. The test assesses the ability to recognize sounds for letters as well as phoneme segmentation ability. The study compared gain scores in the BRD and control children over three months.—*E.W.*

RESULTS

While both groups improved significantly in reading, those in the BRD group improved significantly more than those in the control group on all measures assessed by the reading test. They improved more in their ability to relate written consonants and vowels to their sounds, and to segment phonemes from spoken words, including nonsense words, compared to the control children.—*E.W.*

CONTRIBUTIONS TO THE FIELD

This is a well-designed study that shows that a three-month program in which children learn to physically represent letters with their bodies works to improve basic reading skills in these children.—*E.W.*

COMMENTARY

This study offers an innovative way to teach basic reading skills to at-risk children. Future research should examine whether the same kind of methods can help children improve in higher-level reading skills beyond basic decoding. It is important to recognize that the activities that helped children to learn to read were ones closely tied to reading: putting one's body in the shape of letters. This study does not allow the conclusion that dance leads to reading, but rather that putting one's body in the shape of letters improves basic

reading skills in young children. Whether or not this activity is "dance" (a matter dancers could debate), we can conclude that this activity is an innovative and enactive way of helping children master sound-symbol relationships.—*E.W.*

CONTRIBUTIONS TO THE FIELD

The method used in this study can be easily replicated for different age groups and more advanced skills—and should be. The study is rigorous in design, and the results have validity. Clearly, it demonstrates that movement can reinforce cognitive skill development—in this case, early reading skills. With a sample size of 174 in the experimental group and 198 in the control group, the evaluators have done a great service by demonstrating that quality research can be done easily and with direct application to the actual classroom.

The results should be disseminated widely.—*K.B.*

COMMENTARY

One of the most compelling aspects of the study is the use of improvisational movement exploration to discover how sounds can combine into words. The development of linguistic abilities mirrors the development of dance phrase making. Therefore, the study reveals that, more than merely reinforcing letter-shape recognition, dance can help children discover the "music" of language. Both auditory and visual stimuli were used to cue the kinesthetic. Students

"This study offers an innovative way to teach basic reading skills to at-risk children. Future research should examine whether the same kind of methods can help children improve in higher-level reading skills beyond basic decoding."

learned the shape of letters as well as the sounds of letters and were able to blend both sounds and letters into meaningful words. The use of a divergent approach, where children have a choice of multiple correct solutions, as opposed to the convergent approach such as a simple imitation of shape, is an example of the kind of active learning that will improve young children's skills. In the study, the experimental group scored lower on the pre-test, and therefore came further along using dance movement as the modality for reading skills.—*K.B.*

"One of the most compelling aspects of the study is the use of improvisational movement exploration to discover how sounds can combine into words. The development of linguistic abilities mirrors the development of dance phrase making."

Dance

STUDY NAME: **Art and Community: Creating Knowledge Through Service in Dance**
AUTHOR: Janice Ross
PUBLISHED: Paper presented at the meeting of the American Educational Research Association, April 2000, New Orleans, LA

Research Questions

How does dance instruction affect self-perception and social development for at-risk and incarcerated adolescents?

How does participant/observation research by undergraduates in a dance-centered service-learning project affect perceptions of the purposes of arts generally and dance specifically in the undergraduates' and the lives of others?

METHODS

Sixty 13- to 17- year-old at-risk and incarcerated adolescents participated in 45-minute jazz and hip-hop dance classes twice weekly for 10 weeks. Eleven college students, all with dance experience but only one dance major, engaged in participant/observation research. They observed, danced, and interviewed the teens and produced a "collective meta-portrait" (one student's contributed portrait is an appendix). The principal researcher gathered data weekly from three sources produced by student researchers: reflection journals, in-class discussions, and written syntheses building toward students' final portrait. The principal researcher summarized and gave examples from these data sources but did not produce a portrait of the college students. Thus the relationship between the data and conclusions are not unequivocally clear.—*L.H.*

RESULTS

The first study produced hypotheses about why dance may be a medium particularly well suited to fostering positive self-perception and social development for disenfranchised adolescents. Hypotheses include the influence of teachers and teaching styles generally employed in dance (charismatic, physically powerful instructors, individualized instruction); the synergy of certain dance forms (jazz, hip-hop) with culturally valued leisure activities; the release of physical and psychological stress in which "expression, not conquest" is the activity's goal (in contrast to team sports); the focus of instruction on practicing non-linguistic bodily expression, which is a primary vehicle through which maladaptive social behaviors are conveyed; and the need and opportunity in dance to express individuality within a group, which provides practice with issues central to developing positive social identity and adaptability.

The second study suggests that the congruence of dance, service (providing data to prison administration about the dance program's effectiveness), and research (which placed college dance students in a social/therapeutic context and required reflection about impact and uses of the discipline) is an effective tool for advancing college students' understanding about how dance can be used and how reflection necessary in the method of portraiture fosters learning.—*L.H.*

CONTRIBUTIONS TO THE FIELD

This study used a qualitative methodology (portraiture) to explore a provocative and under-researched relationship between arts (dance) and social and community service. Its goal was to generate a conceptual framework and potentially testable hypotheses for future research.

The study found that incarcerated and low-income, non-English-proficient middle school students reported gains in confidence, tolerance, and persistence related to dance instruction. It resulted in hypotheses that may explain why dance is particularly well suited to promoting such gains.

The study also found that college student researchers reported an expanded view of dance as a tool for fostering social values instead of serving solely as a medium for performance or as recreation.—*L.H.*

COMMENTARY

The study focuses on non-traditional outcomes of dance instruction. It posits artists as social activists and positions dance as a tool for social interventions, in this case, for at-risk and incarcerated adolescents. Its two-level structure

models a way that college teachers might expand their students' views of the purposes of their disciplines to include potential social impact.

Future research should investigate the hypotheses generated by this study about dance as an intervention for juvenile offenders and other disenfranchised adolescents. Such research could be qualitative or quantitative. Studies might compare the social effects of team sports with jazz and hip-hop dance instruction, or of different styles of dance instruction, with each treatment analyzed along the dimensions hypothesized by this study. The group-research model could be extended to groups of teachers in action-research projects.—*L.H.*

CONTRIBUTIONS TO THE FIELD

Three major contributions to the field arise from this study: (1) The methodology used (portraiture of the incarcerated students by the student-researchers from self-reflective journaling, contextualized and framed observations, interviews and presentations with feedback from the other student researchers) is brilliant, rich, and allows the process of learning to be revealed in its multifaceted components.

(2) The secondary level of the study (the self-reflective journaling by the student researchers) reveals a tool for expanding students' understanding of the value and range of the field of dance beyond technical proficiency and performance. Student researchers began to understand how dance could be a tool for progressive social and psychosocial growth.

(3) The conclusions by the author are profound and clearly make the case for why dance works so well with disadvantaged youth. Because she (Ross) had so much rich information to draw from, there are several stunning insights, including her statement, "Patience, and sometimes even compassion, can be social by-products of aesthetic engagement, and new regard for the human body (is what) dance can introduce."—K.B.

COMMENTARY

Ross has defined the best approach this writer has come across to understanding and unpacking what happens in a dance class. By using self-reflective observations, journaling, rich discussion, interviews, and a consensus-building approach to drawing conclusions, the author fosters understanding of both the value of and the constraints on dance-informed learning. The study is a model for dance education researchers. Field observation requires a selection of stances, which, if their techniques embrace elements from the value system of the event or culture being studied, can truly portray the breadth and details of the event.

While the longitudinal value of dance classes for incarcerated youth may be difficult to deduce, requiring large expenditures of energy and time, the fact that several of the student researchers are continuing their involvement with the arts and underserved populations means there will be a small cadre of "anthropologists" who can continue to observe, reflect, critique, suggest, and develop projects such as this one in the future.

For the future, dance education researchers need to look at other forms of dance (in this case, jazz and hip-hop were the delivery system for dance technique) and to other dance experiences such as choreography, improvisation, and performing.—K.B.

"…the best approach this writer has come across to understanding and unpacking what happens in a dance class."

dance

STUDY NAME: **Motor Imagery and Athletic Expertise: Exploring the Role of Imagery In Kinesthetic Intelligence**

AUTHOR: Anna Margaret Skotko

PUBLISHED: Unpublished Bachelor's Honors Thesis, March 23, 2000, Harvard University, Cambridge, Massachusetts

Research Questions

Is motor imagery a core operation of kinesthetic intelligence?

Does motor imagery ability increase with dance expertise?

Do kinesthetic and visual-spatial intelligences rely on similar or distinct cognitive processes?

critical links

METHODS

Participants were healthy, English speaking, right-handed females with normal or corrected-to-normal vision. Thirteen were novice dancers (9- to 12-year-olds with two years or less of ballet training), 12 young non-athletes (9- to 12-year-olds with no history of routine athletic training), 16 professional-level dancers (aged 18 to 25 with at least 10 years of routine ballet training), and 16 adult non-athletes (aged 18 to 25 with no history of routine athletic training). All subjects were recruited by posters and did not know the purpose of the study. Dancers and non-dancers in each age group were matched on socio-economic status.

Subjects completed Raven's Standard Progressive Matrices (as an index of general intelligence) and four experimental tasks: (1) decisions about biomechanical constraints (e.g., "If your right palm is put on your right knee, your thumb is on the left side of your knee.") and mental rotation of (2) hands, (3) feet, and (4) cube figures.—*L.H.*

RESULTS

Young dancers made significantly fewer errors on the biomechanical constraints tasks than their age-mate non-athletes. No other comparisons were significantly different statistically ($p = .05$), although the trend was that dancers performed the biomechanical tasks and tasks requiring rotation of hands and feet faster and more accurately than non-athletes. Interestingly, the opposite (though still non-significant) trend occurred with mental rotation of objects (cube figures): non-dancers tended to perform these tasks faster and more accurately than dancers. Because these tasks may index two different skills (kinesthetic versus visual-spatial intelligence), and because the standard intelligence test (Raven's) did not predict performance level on the imagery tasks, the results support the idea of discrete and specialized cognitive abilities (multiple intelligence theory).—*L.H.*

CONTRIBUTIONS TO THE FIELD

This study demonstrates the complexity of questions about transfer from arts (e.g., dance) to non-arts domains (e.g., mental rotation).

The study found no statistically significant differences between dancers and non-athletes on motor imagery ability. In addition, professional-level dancers were not significantly better at motor imagery than novice dancers. However, the effect sizes were positive and of moderate size. However, a considerably larger sample would be required to achieve statistical significance.—*L.H.*

COMMENTARY

This was a rigorous, initial study of a complex and understudied research domain—the effect of dance training on the ability to mentally rotate objects and/or pictures of body parts (hands and feet).

The author suggests that (1) future research should use larger samples, (2) longitudinal experimental, rather than correlational, designs would control varia-

"...the entire area of kinesthetic intelligence is under-explored..."

tion in subject characteristics that may obscure any experimental effect, (3) experimental tasks should be redesigned to look more realistic (i.e., color photographs or videos of feet and hands), and (4) task difficulty should be made equivalent for tasks using objects or body parts.

Finally, the author suggests reframing the research questions as "Does motor imagery ability generalize from one domain to another?" or "Can motor imagery ability be improved with athletic or cognitive training?"—*L.H.*

CONTRIBUTIONS TO THE FIELD

Since the entire area of kinesthetic intelligence is under-explored, especially in terms of the relationship of kinesthetic intelligence to cognition, this impressive study by an undergraduate initiates a dialogue that should continue. The author begins with an excellent discussion of motor planning and practice and the role of imagery in the development of kinesthesia. She includes interviews with elite athletes discussing how imagery makes a significant difference, subjectively, in performance. Since she uses ballet dancers as her subjects for the elite athlete group, the study makes the case for expanding research in the area of kinesthetic intelligence to include dancers. Ultimately, when and if the case is made for the role of kinesthetic intelligence in developing the "whole child," how dance facilitates the process should be included.—*K.B.*

COMMENTARY

The author, in her discussion, divides the tasks (there were four) into two categories: egocentric motor imagery (tasks one-three, which involved translating written and visual depictions of body-part relationships to the core of the body) and visual-spatial imagery tasks (task four, which involved a paired depiction of a series of cubes in various states of rotation). There was no real significant difference among the experimental groups; athletes did not do better than non-athletes. The author has several wonderfully reflective insights into why the results were not differentiated, but misses the most obvious: that the athletes were performing these tasks at a computer and were disengaged from their kinesthesis while performing the tasks. It would be a worthy study to replicate everything about the study but allow the groups to move before responding. Therefore, the time on task may vary somewhat (and speed was a variable measured for this study), but results may be more accurate. Ballet dancers learn visually, with some auditory coaching for phrasing and musicality, but they also learn by "marking" the movement—doing a kind of scaled-down-and-back version of the patterns in their hands and legs.

In addition, modern dancers, particularly modern dancers who have had exposure to Laban Movement Analysis or Laban notation, or who have studied Laban-based dance techniques, would make an intriguing subject group for such kinesthetic tasks. Laban's approach to movement develops body-part awareness and spatial acuity directly, and such analytic skills may test differently from elite ballet dancers who, the author points out, are highly specialized and "domain-specific." Since Laban's theories of movement permeate elementary-level creative movement curricula in the United States and Canada, such a population may provide more useful data for understanding the role that kinesthetic intelligence plays in overall cognitive abilities.—*K.B.*

Informing and Reforming Dance Education Research

Karen Kohn Bradley

The purpose of research in education is to improve the learning environment, learning processes, and teaching practices in schools and classrooms. As examples of how dance might help in these areas, the dance studies collected in this Compendium offer important initial insights into the best practices in the field and their effects. Educational researchers will find these studies a useful step on the longer journey to developing more, better, and more useful research on dance education. These studies also demonstrate the need for a common language to describe and analyze dance and its effects.

Dance Education and Transfer to General Learning

The seven studies in this Compendium suggest what directions dance researchers should pursue. They also provide important positive indications of exactly what young people learn in dance that relates to skills and attitudes applicable in other academic settings. Implications for curriculum and instruction are apparent as well.

The most consistent indication across the seven studies is the finding that dance is effective as a means of developing three aspects of creative thinking: fluency, originality, and abstractness. Mentzer & Boswell, Minton, and Kim all had positive correlations with at least one of these three areas of creative thinking. The results suggest that, at the least, physical activities specific to dance support development of fluency by actively engaging students. This is not surprising when one considers that fluency of thinking is essentially a facility and mobility of mind and involves the ability of the student to turn ideas around and look at them from different angles. In dance, the body does the same thing and reflection on that process is a valuable aspect of dance-making. Originality and abstractness, likewise, are valued modes of dance education, especially where improvisation and composition are taught.

The studies thus suggest that dance instruction may provide a means for developing a range of the creative thinking aspects of critical thinking skills. More study of programs where creative thinking is valued by the school and assessed in regular classroom settings will reveal further insights into how dance activities support such development.

The studies by Ross and Mentzer & Boswell also provide indications of how students engaged in dance develop and are able to express new insights and interpretations. The two studies probe how moving, and reflecting on that movement through writing and drawing, can lead to shifts in how students view dance experiences and how students view themselves through dance experiences. Both studies are qualitative analyses. Nevertheless, the new insights are observable as behavioral changes and offer a rich direction for future research.

Ross's study demonstrated the process of journaling as a means of tracking changes in attitude of college dance students toward dance education. Her findings showed that journaling and rich discussion can broaden and deepen students' understanding of, and attitude toward, dance as a means of social change. The college students observed and reflected upon a dance program held in a juvenile prison facility. Mentzer & Boswell's study demonstrated the effects of a creative movement program on the writing and drawing of two learning-disabled boys. Specifically, one wonders whether the general effects of dance itself, the process of moving, the thinking/reflection upon moving, or the writing/drawing/dance-making products are all equally necessary in order to effect the kind of rich shifts in perception these two studies suggest. Dance, as is suggested about other art forms in the essays in this Compendium, is in need of research that explains the interrelation of its specific dimensions as an arts experience and cognitive processes.

The Rose study is a quantitative study that provides a deep and rigorous look at a dance program that strives to use dance to improve the reading skills of students in three Chicago public elementary schools. The findings showed that the experimental group of first-graders improved significantly in the three areas of reading skills measured: consonant sounds, vowel sounds, and phoneme segmentation abilities. As difficult as empirical studies can be to carry out on a public school population and across two disciplines (dance and reading, in this case), Rose has established groundwork for additional studies in this area and has provided a basic approach to experiments that reveal a great deal about how a typical dance program can affect cognitive development.

Proving causality between variables is difficult enough when those variables are confined to a sterile environment in a petri dish. While we desire predictability in education, children are complex and slippery learners. In education research, we are trying to understand the underlying processes of learning. Our goal is not replicability in the laboratory but improvement in the classroom, a different kind of replicability. Rose's larger sample size (174 in the experimental group and 198 in the control group), timely pre- and post-testing, and rigorous analysis of test scores provide an integrity of process that makes the

"The use of a common language from dance theory is critical to the future rigor and robustness of dance research..."

impressive positive outcomes (the experimental group started out lower in reading skills and finished higher) exciting and provocative.

Rose, Mentzer & Boswell, and Ross provide important guidance on the future of dance education research and instruction. All three studies view dance experiences as more than simply learning to dance or learning about dance. Dance is defined as a full and powerful modality for interacting with the world of ideas. In addition, in these studies, teachers' goals for the students were overt, supplying clear directions for student learning and facilitating transference. While such practices may not provide the sterility of context that is required by some research methods, they are part of good teaching and can lead to a fuller understanding of how real children learn in real schools.

"Educational researchers will find these studies a useful step on the longer journey to developing more, better, and more useful research on dance education."

Most of the studies included are instructive in their procedural assumptions but do not clearly define the specific dance activity under study. Future research needs to delineate what the dance variable is (technique, improvisation, performance, or choreography), what the intended outcomes of that specific dance experience are (improved critical thinking skills, increased fluency or abstractness of thinking, better technique, more original choreography, etc.), and how the movements are assessed in relation to the intended outcomes. The impact of such informed, specific, and rich data on classroom practice and student learning would be powerful.

The Need for a Common Language

In order for dance teachers to improve and disseminate their best methods and content, even more research and reflection on effective classroom practice are needed. Both quantitative and qualitative studies should incorporate dance theory as a way of noting and analyzing instructional content and practice and student learning. Dance theory will fill an important gap visible in this collection of studies, the lack of a common language by which to discuss dance and the changes that take place during the course of learning dance.

The use of a common language from dance theory is critical to the future rigor and robustness of dance research, whether it is empirical or descriptive. Getting at the details of movement change, describing shifts in attitude and expression, facilitating the expansion of movement vocabulary, and accurate measurement of such growth are the essence of a sound and useful body of research. The grammar of movement is inherent in dance style and technique, and various methods of analysis have been developed, one of which is Laban Movement Analysis (LMA). LMA is a system of movement analysis that has been used to document elements of movement change in athletes, actors, politicians, and in various cultures, as well as with dancers.

In several of the studies, noting or eliciting specific components of the movement might have allowed for more detailed analysis of the learning. The potential of the level of detail LMA provides could be demonstrated in studies (e.g., Rose) where children made letter shapes with their bodies and moved to the sounds of letters in order to develop early reading skills. By providing language that orients children in space, allows them to articulate (nonverbally) specific configurations of pathway and line, delineates qualities of movement and sound, and relates parts to wholes, LMA could provide data not only on whether the children learned their letters and could form words from them but also on the individual approach each child took. Learning styles and the preferred modalities of each child can be noted through the movement observation.

In addition to delineating specific approaches to learning and providing a means for perceiving the details of change, users of LMA adopt a particular stance toward analysis of the movement components of an event. The trained observer notes no more than what has changed in the mover's configurations. Therefore, the analysis and subsequent interpretation of the data reveal what the mover does, not what he/she does not do. LMA provides a map of the individual child's learning style as well as a way of documenting the evolving content of the child's learning.

The case study of Mentzer & Boswell, in which two boys were studied for creative thinking growth via creative movement experiences, could be enriched by observation of specific movement changes, in addition to the study's analysis of the poetry they wrote and drawings they made. Skotko could have observed the movement changes both the "dancers" and "non-athletes" she studied went through to organize for the motor planning tasks she analyzed. Dale Rose could have recorded the specific aspects of movement that best reinforce language acquisition and early reading skills. And Ross' college students could have written more descriptively and critically about the dance classes they were observing, providing more informed and richer data to track attitude changes.

Aligning Curriculum and Instruction in Dance with Research: Implications for Future Research

Beyond the need for a common language to discuss the changes that take place through dance, and more and better research, the dance studies in this Compendium illustrate a need for dance curricula in public schools to reflect current research so that educators and researchers can conduct informative assessments. In order for research to be useful and applicable to real classrooms, teachers and researchers need to share the common goal of reflecting on practice with integrity and insight. Teachers need to know various processes of inquiry and terms of discourse in the field of dance and need to field-test approaches to capturing specific information about how well students are utilizing dance for cognitive development. Researchers need to know the breadth and depth of dance content and open up to the methods of observation embraced within the discipline itself.

The research also suggests that for transfer of cognitive development from dance to other areas of learning and application to be more powerful, teachers should explicitly support transference so that it is more strongly incorporated into meta-cognitive activities, especially activities such as mapping and other such theoretical constructions. Lots of rich evaluative and reflective activities—writing, drawing, discussion, applied projects, product-making within the field (dance-making, performance building) and thoughtful, not rote, practice—are also indicated as productive reinforcements.

Conclusions

Clearly defined, discipline-embedded studies in dance need to be encouraged, supported, and disseminated. With good statistics and in-depth studies of the specifics of particular processes, educators will be able to replicate, amend, and develop the best practices dance education can offer. Educators, parents, and administrators will learn just how potent and effective dance can be with children, intrinsically and instrumentally. And finally, educators can design rich, effective dance experiences with the needs of real children in mind.

Drama

STUDY NAME: **The Effects of Creative Drama on the Social and Oral Language Skills of Children with Learning Disabilities**
AUTHOR: Rey E. de la Cruz
PUBLISHED: Doctoral Dissertation, 1995, Department of Specialized Educational Development, Illinois State University, Bloomington, IL

Research Question

Can a creative drama program with an emphasis on specific social and oral language skills lead to increases in the social and oral language skills of children with learning disabilities?

METHODS

Existing research pointed to two developments important to the success of children with learning disabilities. One was the centrality of linguistic skills, variations in which account for most placements of children into special-needs status. The second was consensus in research that children with learning disabilities typically lack social skills necessary for effective peer-to-peer and student-teacher interactions—relations that contribute generally to success in school. While the use of drama to promote linguistic and social development in special education had a history of scholarly advocacy, no one had put the idea to a concrete test.

The study was developed with the assistance of 70 special and regular education teachers who helped define the most important and problematic social skills for children with learning disabilities. What essentially amounted to a factor analysis identified four clusters of behaviors and skills as critical for success in the classroom: (1) courtesy to others—apologizing when actions have injured or infringed on another, (2) self-control—finding acceptable ways of using free time when work is completed, (3) focus—ignoring distractions from peers when doing classroom work, and (4) social compliance—following written directions.

Thirty-five students with learning disabilities were selected from two urban schools with speech centers. They ranged in age from 5 to 11 and had diverse ethnic and cultural backgrounds. There were 21 students in the experimental group and 14 in the control group, apparently divided by school. The main design was a pre- and post-test model with two groups.

The treatment group engaged in 12 weekly 40-minute creative drama activities, three of the 12 sessions aimed at each of the four skill clusters. Separate drama programs with common goals were designed and run in parallel for the students with learning disabilities receiving primary- and intermediate-level instruction respectively. The dramatic activities were designed with the four critical social skill clusters in mind—e.g., one three-week segment emphasized mutual courtesy and recognizing when one's actions hurt another child. The dramatic action in this segment reinforced apologizing.

Comparison-group children received their normal routine of weekly language therapy.

Student language skills were assessed before and after the intervention using the Test of Language Development (TOLD). The Walker-McConnell Scale of Social Competence was used to gauge social skills, along with the Test of Specific Oral and Language and School Adjustment Skills (SLS). Scales within these social skills assessments were matched to the four primary social behavior clusters outlined above. Post-test measures were taken in the two weeks following the program and also eight weeks later to test for sustained effects. In addition to pre- and post-test measures, interviews probed the experiences and conclusions of students in the drama group.—J.C.

RESULTS

The researchers used analyses of variance for testing group differences on various post-test measures and pre- to post-test gains. The children who participated in the creative drama program increased their social skills in all four clusters of social behaviors more than students in the control group. They also significantly improved in their oral expressive language skills when compared with the control group. Receptive language skills (acts of interpreting oral speech of others) were not comparatively affected by the drama program. While these results provide indicators of the helpful effects of dramatic activities on the social and language skills of students with learning disabilities, the follow-up test might be considered to be the most critical element of the research design. In comparison to so many studies that halt operation at the post-assessment, this study tests for sustained effects two months later. All post-measures of language and social skills for the drama group held up over time.

When asked about what they learned in the experiment, children most frequently mentioned aspects of courtesy and general peer-to-peer relations—getting along with their classmates. Students also reported that the drama lessons helped them listen and speak better.—J.C.

CONTRIBUTIONS TO THE FIELD

The main contribution of this study is that it is the first reported sizable experimental test of creative drama concerning academic and social development of children with learning disabilities. Historically, research studies focusing on children with learning disabilities used linguistic deficits as the main distinguishing characteristic of children in this group. In addition, numerous studies agree, according to the authors, that students with learning disabilities need adaptive social skills to interact with others more effectively, to be accepted by their peers, and to work effectively within heterogeneous, mainstreamed school classrooms.

This experiment contributes relatively "hard" quantitative evidence that both linguistic and social skills increased through a program of creative drama.—J.C.

COMMENTARY

The importance of this study, and of research generally that relates learning in the arts to developments of special-needs populations, is underscored by the fact that about eight percent of all elementary and secondary education students are enrolled in special education programs. Among these children, a majority has designated learning disabilities (2.2 million out of 4.3 million special education students).

The research enlisted 70 regular and special education teachers to help identify important and difficult social skill needs of students with learning disabilities, which grounded the main questions and instruments used in this study. The study used experimental and control groups assessed with standard, scaled tests of social and language development; the work also enlisted systematic interviews to gauge the meanings and conclusions that subjects drew from the experiment.

The study includes detailed appendices describing the various dramatic activities and the inclusion of supplemental interviews. These appendices are helpful windows into this study.—J.C.

CONTRIBUTIONS TO THE FIELD

This study makes a unique contribution in its focus on the effect of drama on the expressive and receptive oral-language abilities of students with learning disabilities. It is appropriately grounded in the rich body of claims and research on the effects of drama as a stimulus for growth in the development of oral language for all students, not just those with learning disabilities.

De la Cruz went to great lengths to compare the views of special education and of general education teachers in terms of the social skills they considered both important and difficult for students with learning disabilities, and focused on only those skills that both groups of teachers agreed on. Thus, her findings pertain to the interest of both groups of teachers.—B.J.W.

COMMENTARY

De la Cruz's finding that drama training can improve the social skills of students with learning disabilities is a significant finding for a society concerned about the escalation of violence in schools and the need to balance pressures for accountability with realistic and effective approaches to the social development of students.

An interesting aspect of this study, though not its main purpose, is the comparison between the social skills special education and regular teachers consider important and difficult. An ethnographic study of the ways these two groups

of teachers view their students who have learning disabilities, and the ways they relate to them in facilitating the improvement of their social skills, might be revealing. The more teachers understand the challenges of students with learning disabilities and know effective ways to facilitate social and language development the better.—B.J.W.

"This experiment contributes relatively 'hard' quantitative evidence that both linguistic and social skills increased through a program of creative drama."

STUDY NAME: The Effectiveness of Creative Drama as an Instructional Strategy to Enhance the
              Reading Comprehension Skills of Fifth-Grade Remedial Readers
AUTHOR: Sherry DuPont
PUBLISHED: Reading Research and Instruction, 1992, 31(3): 41-52

Research Question

Does a program of creative drama integrated with children's literature contribute to the growth of reading comprehension skills of fifth-grade remedial reading students?

METHODS

The study looked at three groups of fifth-grade students in remedial reading classes that demonstrated comparable skill levels in both the California Achievement Test and the Reading Diagnostic section of the Metropolitan Achievement Test (MAT6). Each group had 17 students. Groups One and Two received a structured remedial reading program for six weeks using six selected children's stories. Group One used creative drama to support story comprehension. Group Two used "traditional," non-remedial methods to support story comprehension—they read the same stories as Group One, followed by vocabulary exercises and teacher-led discussions. Group Three was the control group and continued the ongoing remedial program.

Group One was taught by the researcher; Groups Two and Three were taught by their regular teachers. The study acknowledges the challenge of having the researcher provide the creative drama intervention. The researcher worked closely with the other two teachers to ensure that the teachers used similar and detailed lesson plans and common learning outcomes. This helped to validate inferences about observed instructional outcomes.

The study used the MAT6 for pre- and post-study assessments of reading comprehension. Groups One and Two also used a weekly criterion-referenced test (CRT) to assess story comprehension, since these two groups focused on children's literature as part of their instructional designs. (A CRT asks factual or inferential questions, which have right and wrong answers, and sometimes better and worse answers. Higher scores indicate higher comprehension of a story). A team of three reading teachers/specialists and the researcher designed the CRT linked to the stories used in this research; an independent panel also reviewed this test.—J.C.

RESULTS

The study finds that "…when children have been involved in the process of integrating creative drama with reading they are not only able to better comprehend what they've read and acted out, but they are also better able to comprehend what they have read but do not act out, such as the written scenarios they encounter on standardized tests." This is an important finding that warrants scrutiny and additional research—that drama not only contributes to the immediate subject of a dramatic enactment but also associates with comprehension of written stories unrelated to the drama activity. This is an instance of transfer of skills in one arena to skills useful more generally, albeit a closely related transfer. The observation suggests that some sort of disposition in a child's approach to reading may be influenced by the connection between dramatic enactment and reading. Comparisons across all three groups show that the group using creative drama achieved significantly higher scores on the CRT than the traditional group (Group Two); the creative drama group also outscored Groups Two and Three on the MAT6 reading achievement test. Analyses of variance show that Group One is the only group showing a significant increase from pre- to post-test scores. Group Two actually displays a significant decrease in the MAT6 test scores—perhaps because the test-retest protocol can turn children off to retests following too soon on the heels of a first test. Group Three also shows a decrease in mean scores from pre- to post-tests, but this decrease is not significant.

The research has some design limitations and interpretation puzzles linked to factors such as the use of intact classes rather than random assignment to groups, the rather small size of the respective groups studied (17 students in each), and the use of the researcher as a teacher. The study, however, is designed to minimize these impacts through careful pre-testing and coordination between the researcher and other participating teachers.

There remains the possibility that children in the researcher-led class using creative drama knew that something important was up and gave the post-test more effort than did the other two groups. This raises the possibility that an unknown combination of at least two conditions propelled the positive results—the positive impact of creative drama linked to reading, and the positive impact on motivation brought by a guest drama teacher bringing something new to reading lessons in the classroom.—J.C.

CONTRIBUTIONS TO THE FIELD

This study finds that fifth-grade remedial reading students engaging in a six-week course of literature-based "creative drama" show significantly greater gains in story comprehension than students in a discussion-based program and a control student group. An important contribution of this work is that it involved fifth-graders, in comparison with a majority of literacy-related drama studies, which experiment with preschool or early-primary-grade children.

Another contribution is that the entire study population suffered shortfalls of reading skills for their grade level and thus all were at high risk of subsequent difficulties across the school curriculum. Moreover, this study found skills gained through drama *transferred* to skills in comprehending literature not presented as part of the program, a claim that must be taken seriously and scrutinized carefully.—*J.C.*

COMMENTARY

DuPont uses the term "creative drama" to indicate the practice of reading non-illustrated story text, followed by children's invented (or created) scenes prepared for enactment, along with "oral and pantomimed" extensions of their stories. She anchors the label in a 1975 term defined by the Children's Theatre Association of America to mean "…an improvisational, non-exhibitional, process-centered form of drama…(where children)…imagine, enact, and reflect upon human experience."

This is a thoughtful study with results worth attending to. The author suggests that "…merely reading and discussing children's literature is not an effective means for enhancing reading comprehension as measured by standardized tests," at least for remedial readers. This is a strong claim, since reading and discussing are the bread and butter of traditional reading instruction at the upper-elementary-school level. An extension of the main work within this study leads to suggestions that creative drama can improve children's *attitudes* toward reading by associating reading with a fun activity; such engagement, as theory should hold, encourages more reading and may also enhance mental imagery of written material. Such imaging skills and dispositions have been found to associate with comprehension of written text.

The study's findings suggest areas where additional research might pay off, including extending the study to students with higher levels of reading skills and assessing the effectiveness of creative drama in substantive content areas such as social studies and science. That is, research could test the idea that one can learn more science (or about a particular theme or unit within a science course) through creative drama than through other modes of instruction.—*J.C.*

CONTRIBUTIONS TO THE FIELD

This research was carefully planned and executed, with every attempt made to make the three groups of studied children (each group involved two classes of eight to nine remedial reading students) as comparable as possible. In addition, instructional strategies during the specified reading lessons were strictly adhered to. This lends more credence to the finding that integrating creative drama with children's literature produces better reading comprehension than just using the same literature without creative drama or basic skills instruction.

The study also calls attention to the intriguing, yet untested possibility that creative drama assists students in developing "mental images" of stories, which in turn helps with comprehension.—*B.W.*

"…when children have been involved in the process of integrating creative drama with reading they are not only able to better comprehend what they've read and acted out, but they are also better able to comprehend what they have read but do not act out, such as the written scenarios they encounter on standardized tests."

COMMENTARY

The research, while illustrating the power of combining drama with literature as a reading technique, still suffers from the fact that the researcher was the teacher of that experimental condition. While there were steps taken to ensure fidelity of instruction during the specified reading lessons, what remains unresolved without qualitative research is the influence of differential instruction during the rest of the school day. We know nothing about who the teachers were during the remainder of the day or their pedagogical style. Students don't learn comprehension skills just during reading class. How much of an impact did that other instruction have on students' reading comprehension?

The research points to some important and interesting unresolved questions. First, it remains unknown why students with creative drama instruction performed better, both on the criterion test and on transferability to a standardized test of comprehension. Second, the author asks whether the power of dramatic acting as a tool for comprehension might be used in other areas of learning such as mathematics or science. And, finally, are most poor readers inclined toward kinesthetic-tactile learning styles? What implications might that have for teachers in carefully assessing students' learning styles and in tailoring instruction that ensures an optimal match between learning styles and instructional practices?—B.W.

STUDY NAME: **Role of Imaginative Play in Cognitive Development**
AUTHOR: Robert S. Fink
PUBLISHED: Psychological Reports, 1976, 39: 895-906

Research Questions

Does training in imaginative play influence the imaginativeness of subsequent unstructured free play among kindergartners?

What is the impact of adult-led training in imaginative play on specific cognitive developments of kindergartners in contrast to two alternative conditions: (1) supervised but unguided free play and (2) routine attendance in a kindergarten class?

METHODS

This study addresses the potential roles of imaginative play (or creative role-playing) on two foundational cognitive abilities of children—referred to as "conservation" and "perspectivism." Conservation refers to an individual's understanding that attributes of persons or objects in their environment may remain constant when these persons or things take on additional attributes: a father who becomes a doctor would still be a father. Two types of "perspectivism" are also examined. "Physical perspectivism" refers to an understanding that the physical arrangement of the environment remains the same even though one moves among different vantage points. "Social perspectivism" refers to an ability to sustain understanding of kinship relations or social relations within a group: is this father also a brother, and how would you justify this? The kindergartners examined in this work were relatively weak in both conservation and perspectivism at the start of the study.

The study involved 36 kindergarten children randomly assigned to one of three groups: (1) adult-structured group training in imaginative play processes, (2) free-play activity in the non-directive presence of the experimenter, and (3) a control group. Each child was observed before, during, and after the experiment by each of five trained observers.

For the experiment, one group was assigned to a training condition in which groups of four children met twice weekly for four weeks of coached imaginative play. The investigator introduced a theme, encouraged the children to create props using materials provided, and initiated imaginative play. The second group was also divided into groups of four children who met with the investigator on the same schedule as the training group. Their intervention consisted of a free-play period with no structured training. The control group continued regular kindergarten activities. After one month, all children in the three groups were again tested for conservation and perspectivism.—J.C.

RESULTS

The pre and post observation-of-play results provide evidence that higher levels of imaginative play can be taught to young children through teacher-initiated activities and modeling. Moreover, these behaviors are retained after the completion of the training. The study found that "…the children in the (imaginative play) training group demonstrated a significant improvement in play imaginativeness during the post-training observation."

The training in imaginative play was also linked to developmental gains associated with social roles. While all three groups improved on conservation and perspective-taking tasks over time, the training group, coached in imaginative play, consistently improved on both measures more than the two comparison groups.

"…coached imaginative play contributes to important social developments of children."

These results suggest that coached imaginative play contributes to important social developments of children. As Piaget described, the passage of children between very young ages—"pre-operational" (2 to 3 years) to a more mature period (7 to 8 years)—is marked by significant differences in the way children understand the world around them. At the pre-operational stage, the child "assimilates" events and conditions around him or her, making events, people, and places fit his or her preconceived views of the world. This egocentric stance gradually gives way to a more accommodating stance by the child toward his/her own environment—one in which the child shows evidence of a more generative and plastic take on the world. This is a stage in which the child begins to understand the world around him both in his or her own terms, as before, but also *in the terms of the other players on the stage*. It is in this transition that children grow in their skills at conservation—of social roles particularly in the case of imaginative play, and in perspectivism—a set of skills permitting accurate and consistent comprehension of social situations through different vantage points.—J.C.

CONTRIBUTIONS TO THE FIELD

This early (1976) study differs from others in the Compendium mainly because it examines very specific cognitive functioning impacted by imaginative play, rather than more holistic skills such as reading comprehension or story sequence recall, which are assessed in many drama/academic skills studies. The author finds that kindergartners who engage in imaginative play training sessions show significant improvement in two important Piagetian developmental measures—conservation and perspectivism. Conservation and perspectivism are critical building blocks allowing children to make physical and social sense of the world around them.—*J.C.*

COMMENTARY

The study provides evidence that given appropriate modeling and resources, the imaginative play of young children can result in important developmental gains in contrast to play under a mock training experience (meeting with the investigator who merely supervised free play) or in the typical routines of the kindergarten classroom. This study offers useful guidance for classroom activities, and supports the existing research on the ability of imaginative or dramatic play to enhance psychological and intellectual development.—*J.C.*

CONTRIBUTIONS TO THE FIELD

This study highlights the importance of imaginative play in a young child's cognitive development. In particular, the study calls for a modification of Piaget's theory, which suggests that imaginative play experiences do not aid in cognitive development. Instead, the research suggests that, contradictory to Piaget's assertions, imaginative play can help a child develop cognitive abilities.—*C.G.-P.*

COMMENTARY

This study suggests that more research is needed that pays attention to how a child's playtime is structured. This has implications for practice, in that it suggests that teachers can facilitate the development of imaginative play by suggesting possible themes and using appropriate props to support play.—*C.G.-P.*

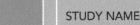

STUDY NAME: **A Naturalistic Study of the Relationship Between Literacy Development and Dramatic Play in Five-Year-Old Children**

AUTHOR: Jennifer Ross Goodman

PUBLISHED: Unpublished Ed.D. Dissertation, 1990, George Peabody College for Teachers, Vanderbilt University, Nashville, TN

Research Questions

How is literacy used within dramatic play and why?

What factors influencing how literacy is used within dramatic play are important?

METHODS

This study was carried out in a school serving a college campus. Subjects were children of college employees representing a wide range of income and education levels. The research was carried out in an intact preschool classroom with 17 children (one African-American, one Asian, 15 white; 12 girls, five boys; ranging between just under 5 to 6 years of age). The class used dramatic play on a nearly daily basis over five months. Ninety-seven play episodes were observed. Themes within dramatic play ranged from the very common (house, family, school, stories) to the occasional unique subject (farm, fishing, concert).

The researcher used traditional ethnographic methods to categorize themes of the children's drama and to explore the literacy activities of children during dramatic enactment. The researcher worked to minimize the intrusiveness of the research on classroom behavior by taking on a routine role of assistant teacher over the entire five months. Data collection included participant observation, informal interviews, and document analysis. As the study progressed, tape recording and videotaping were introduced to support analyses. The researcher focused on a variety of literacy-related phenomena: functional uses of literacy; the ability of children to translate familiar stories into play texts; use of play to establish physical setting and to present stories; the use of personal themes; and modes and degrees of social interaction.—J.C.

RESULTS

"Literacy" was the primary focus of this research—the use of reading skills, decoding written materials and drawing inferences, and translating narrative and sequence into dramatic text. The study finds that one common form of literacy served to organize children's play—namely that children's favorite stories often become the basis for many play scripts. Children also used literacy skills in composing their play scripts. Both teacher/student and student/student interactions influenced children's choices about the importance and use of literacy within their plays. The settings of literary texts appeared in varying degrees in their dramatizations.

Through play, the children exhibit important facets of their literacy—their ability to read texts and materials (even artifacts) related to their play, their use of written artifacts within their play, and their efforts at composing scenes and plays. Within the "risk-free" atmosphere of dramatic play, children are also able to expand their use of literacy skills. The researcher notes a positive relationship between creating stories and translating stories into play texts. Such translation includes establishing settings, characters, character relationships, and plots.

In the words of the study's author: "This study supports the use of dramatic play in literacy learning in that children are frequently using literacy on their own as well as with teacher direction." The use of literacy by children in drama suggests a significant "opportunity benefit," namely supplanting non-learning, self-directed time with the literacy-rich activities of drama.

The dramatic play examined in this study also exposed an aspect of literacy internal to dramatic enactment apparently important for the motivation of children to gain literacy skills. Literacy objects were perceived as giving power to the possessor (the child with the map was allowed to direct play). Moreover, literacy in the form of detailed understanding of texts appeared to give power to playwrights. And the ability to direct play also reflects the children's "storying" skills and appears to elevate their social status within the classroom.—J.C.

CONTRIBUTIONS TO THE FIELD

The main contribution of this study to the body of research on drama and learning is its singular focus on the use of reading, writing, and written artifacts within the dramatic activities of pre-kindergartners. Literacy refers to reading and writing skills. Literacy is *used* in drama when children decode texts or scripts for enactment, use written or symbolic documents (such as a ticket or a map) within a play, or when they write scripts. We include a number of studies of reading comprehension and story understanding linked to dramatic enactment in this Compendium, but only in this study do we see an inquiry into the effects of using reading, writing, and written objects within dramatic activities. What results is a refined portrait of critical cognitive developments occurring through drama. The researcher finds that "dramatic play is a vehicle whereby children can both practice and learn about literacy skills and begin to develop 'storying' skills which might be used in story writing."—J.C.

COMMENTARY

This study provides a thoughtful analysis of how dramatic play among pre-kindergartners fosters the development of literacy skills and how the specific use of literacy activities and artifacts within dramatic play can reinforce reading and writing development. Because 5-year-olds are at fairly early stages of "literacy" development, dramatic play may be all the more important for these children if the dramatic form provides a motivating context for learning about literacy, using literacy skills, and exploring new and abstract concepts. In the findings of this study, drama provides that context.

The relationship between creating play texts and writing abilities was not addressed in this study, but would be a good candidate for extended work with this sort of program—specially for somewhat more mature readers and writers such as fourth- and fifth-graders.—*J.C.*

CONTRIBUTIONS TO THE FIELD

This qualitative investigation makes a distinct contribution from most of the other studies in this Compendium in that data were collected in a naturalistic setting (a regular kindergarten classroom) over an extended period of time (five months). Furthermore, the purpose was not to test a pre-determined hypothesis to explore the effect of arts on student learning. Rather, the research describes the relationship between dramatic play and literacy and then goes on to explore some of the critical factors that influence that relationship by using richly textured qualitative data.

The research provides powerful evidence that dramatic play is an important vehicle whereby children can both practice and learn about literacy skills and knowledge.—*B.W.*

COMMENTARY

The biggest shortcoming of this type of research is the lack of generalizability to other settings. To what degree are the findings only applicable to the Caucasian, middle-class students in the study? In addition, the sample included a preponderance of females (12 females and five males). While some examples were offered from the boys, most of them were from the girls. Might the relationships look different in a predominantly male or balanced-gender context? The richness of findings from the detailed observations however, generally outweighs concerns such as these.

The research highlights three messages that transcend age and content. That is, the findings apply not only to young learners but also older ones and not only to literacy but also other aspects of learning. These have important implications for classroom practice. First, the physical setting in which learning takes place is critical; it is important to have it be both rich and ever changing if learning is to be maximized. Second, the learning environment needs to take advantage of students' personal interests. To de-contextualize learning from what students know and understand restricts the learning potential. And, finally, learning is highly relational. Quality learning requires extensive opportunity for student-student and teacher-student interaction.—*B.W.*

"The research provides powerful evidence that dramatic play is an important vehicle whereby children can both practice and learn about literacy skills and knowledge."

STUDY NAME: **An Exploration into the Writing of Original Scripts by Inner-City High School Drama Students**
AUTHOR: Jeanette Horn
PUBLISHED: New York, NY: National Arts Education Research Center. National Endowment for the Arts/United States Department of Education, 1992 (ERIC: ED366 957)

Research Question

How do ethnically diverse students in an urban theater magnet high school work collaboratively to conceive of and write original theater pieces regarding topics of interest to them?

critical links

28

METHODS

This study took place over a school year in the "theater institute" at a New York City high school—a magnet school within the school. While there is an audition process for admission to the school, all students who express a genuine interest are accepted. The teacher/researcher (T/R) conducted the double-period, daily theater class for the seniors in the school. As part of their theater magnet school experience, the students had studied various aspects of theater an hour per day as 10th- and 11th-graders. Even with this background, the students entered the senior year theater class with common, doubting feelings: traditional theater was "not for people like us," "no one looks like us on stage," and "no one writes about the dreams and problems we share."

In the senior-year class, students were encouraged to write and perform an original play addressing something of relevance to themselves. The T/R coached and facilitated the student work but did not tell the students what to write. She led the students through various activities designed to engender creativity (e.g., visual awareness), sense of ensemble (e.g., listening skills), and playwriting skills (e.g., character sketches). The T/R used a variety of strategies to document the class. Instruments included interviews, tape recordings of student discussions and scene rehearsals, observations of audience reactions, and reports of other teachers and the school principal. The T/R also administered pre- and post-questionnaires; the T/R and students maintained logs. The students ultimately chose to write and perform plays of their own, although as described below, the start-up phase proceeded with great hesitation.

Several students left the researcher's program during the course of the school year, mainly at the semester break when students are reviewed for overall progress in school. Thus the researcher obtained a full set of observations and other data for 29 students.—J.C.

RESULTS

The program established guidelines and training aimed at student playwriting, but the students began the program with little sense of just how to proceed. Initial, exploratory writing exercises showed that the students struggled even with what to write about, much less about how to conceive of an issue or interest area that might become a play. But the challenge (and the teacher) kept a spark of interest alive and students slowly became more pro-active. They looked less to the teacher and more to themselves for ideas and were more responsible for their ideas. They collaborated in discussions of each other's evolving scripts. Attendance improved over the year. Students began using the school and local libraries regularly. And in contrast to the early weeks, when students could find nothing to write about, they ended up writing far more than they could address in their dramatic productions. All students who began the program did not get this far, but for the 29 who remained for the entire year, the impacts of the theater institute were unmistakable.

Students provide evidence of important growth in self-perception and behavior over the year. Students increasingly saw themselves as leaders and as important members of the class. Library registration increased from 25 percent to 85 percent of the class over the year; and the percentage of students agreeing that they knew how to put on a play went from 25 percent to 57 percent. (In a theater magnet school program, this last development seems an important accomplishment; but it seems an excessive responsibility for a capstone course. What did these students learn about theater in grades 10 and 11?)

The resulting story is one in which incipient halting, nonproductive struggles with a problem give way to sustained activities, informed through the use of multiple outside resources. This outcome evokes Bransford's notion of "unsequestered" problem-solving outlined in his recent review of research on the "transfer" of skills.[1] (See the essay on *transfer* in this Compendium). Unsequestered (*freed-up*) problem-solving refers to acts of stretching toward a quality product or performance through identifying and seeking out helpful resources and taking time to do so—as opposed to stopping at ready solutions and refusing to take risks of being wrong.—J.C.

CONTRIBUTIONS TO THE FIELD

This study makes more than one valuable contribution to the domains of theater/drama and academic and social development. First, it focuses on writing dramatic scripts and setting up productions by students—and not solely on dramatic story re-enactment and fantasy play, which dominate the literature. Second, the study's subjects are high school seniors—only a handful of Compendium drama studies involve students beyond the elementary school level. Third, this study focuses on collaborative creative processes in the making of dramatic art—the program became a laboratory for spontaneous and guided cooperative learning. And finally, this study uses a teacher/

1 John Bransford and Daniel Schwartz (2000). Rethinking Transfer. Chapter in Review of Research in Education, Volume 24. Washington DC: American Educational Research Association.

researcher model in which the teacher serves two hours per day, all year as the instructor for the students. Researcher engagements as teachers in other studies in the Compendium are typically low intensity, occasional, and active for no more than a few days or weeks.—*J.C.*

COMMENTARY

This is a year-long, non-experimental study. Although a variety of instruments are used and specific data collected, most of the data from interviews and questionnaires take a fairly minor supporting role in the conclusions drawn by the researcher. The most important findings of this study relate to the arc of the students' lives in this classroom over the school year. The portrayal comes as much from the researcher's sense of what went on and how things changed over the school year as it does from changes in student answers from pre- to post-program questionnaires.

This is a study of playwriting and performance. But clearly it is also a story of adult mentorship. Individual attention or connection can sometimes turn an indifferent academic career into a productive and positive experience. These students ultimately benefited from writing and enacting their plays; but a dogged coach interested in their welfare seemed to serve as a necessary catalyst.—*J.C.*

CONTRIBUTIONS TO THE FIELD

This study makes a significant contribution to understanding how the dramatic arts—coupled with a collaborative pedagogical approach focused on continual improvement—can improve student engagement in learning as well as higher-order thinking skills. The teacher/researcher in this case provides a comprehensive case example of how action research can be used to improve practice and motivate an ethnically diverse group of inner-city high school drama students.—*C.G.-P.*

COMMENTARY

In this study, dramatic writing is used as a curricular vehicle to assist students in developing critical thinking and collaboration skills. The study documents that it is not just dramatic writing but also the process through which students are taught that is important (e.g., dramatic writing requires critical thinking skills). The researcher-teacher used a collaborative/democratic approach to instruction requiring the class to write a play together; thus, they were dependent upon each other. With the current push for higher test scores nationally, this study points to the importance of valuing higher-order thinking skills.—*C.G.-P.*

"…provides a comprehensive case example of how action research can be used to improve practice…"

STUDY NAME: A Poetic/Dramatic Approach to Facilitate Oral Communication
AUTHOR: Larry Kassab
PUBLISHED: Unpublished Doctoral Dissertation, August 1984, Department of Speech Communication, Pennsylvania State University, State College, PA

Research Question

What is the effect of a six-week poetry/drama workshop on: the willingness of students to communicate orally; their oral communication skills; their feelings at the time of oral presentation; and their self-confidence and self-image?

METHODS

This study involved 27 sophomores in a rural public high school in Pennsylvania. A workshop was implemented in an intact classroom with 22 academic, one business, and four vocational students (15 females and 12 males). The intervention consisted of 28 sessions over a six-week period led by the researcher—a relatively intense program in a domain where twice-weekly drama sessions or a few days of dramatic enactments are more the mode. The workshop was voluntary, but the entire class agreed to participate and no one withdrew.

In the first segment of the study, students were introduced to the basic form and conceptions of poetry and encouraged to write poems emphasizing personal feelings and thoughts. Once the poetry-writing segment was completed, the researcher provided oral presentation skills instruction and coached students toward oral interpretations of their poems. The final segment entailed rehearsals and presentations.

Data were gathered from seven sources: two assessments by the regular teacher (*Pre-Workshop Student Assessments and Assessments of Final Presentations*), four student self-reports and questionnaires (*Profile Questionnaire, Initial Self-Report, Interim Reaction Report, Final Questionnaire*), and the researcher/instructor's log of *Daily Observations and Interpretation*. The questionnaires were designed to capture student behaviors and student learning from three different vantage points.—*J.C.*

RESULTS

The study found that the workshop on the oral interpretation and dramatic presentation of personal poems improves oral skills, increases comfort with oral communication, and enhances self-esteem and self-image. The first two results seem straightforward—speaking before classmates over time cultivates speaking skills and increases self-confidence. The likely causes of observed and reported advancements in self-esteem and self-image are open to alternative explanations presenting personal poems in a supportive environment might have such an effect; so might increased confidence in oral communication more generally. No data were collected on the students' willingness to engage in, or their effectiveness in speaking in, their other classes or in other settings—something the researcher might have done as part of the experiment or during the weeks and months after the program. The limitations of the study do not detract, however, from the apparent core effectiveness of this pedagogical design.—*J.C.*

CONTRIBUTIONS TO THE FIELD

One contribution of this study is the unique set of behaviors drawn into its lens. Kassab's experiment differs from others in the drama section of the Compendium in three ways. One is that it involves student-composed poetry at the core of the dramatic act, and not the commonly utilized stories by other authors or student-created fictional narratives. The second difference is that the emphasis is on the personal, self-reflective, nature of the "play"—or poetry enactment in this case. And the third difference is that the enactment balances the poetic composition with effective oral delivery as the essential dramatic art of the program. The study also contributes positive findings about the effects of drama on both academic and social development—namely, increased oral communication skills as well as increased self-confidence noted below.—*J.C.*

COMMENTARY

Improving oral communication skills and student comfort with oral communication has strong implications for classroom success. The use of reading poetry aloud to encourage and support oral communication is well established in the therapeutic community and holds relatively untested promise for school-based use. This study begins to examine this link.

The study's design is too limited to draw broad conclusions, but it does provide evidence that this approach brings benefits to students. This study makes a good case for the promise of further research into the effectiveness of poetic interpretation accompanied by oral presentation in supporting both academic and social growth. The study perhaps serves best as a first step in establishing a classroom program and a set of data collection protocols around which a more rigorous investigation could be designed. The study offers many areas where spillover benefits and/or transfer might be probed: these include whether there are any residual results from such an intervention over time, whether the types of writing undergirding dramatic enactment (e.g., poetry vs. expository prose) produce different results, and whether the skills gained in this type of program (or in other programs aimed at the same oral communication goals) impact academic achievement.—*J.C.*

CONTRIBUTIONS TO THE FIELD

The importance of this study centers on its suggestion that poetry writing and oral presentation can improve communication skills. Of equal importance is that the study's findings are dependent upon the particular pedagogical approach used by the instructor, namely that the workshops served as a supportive learning environment (free from criticism and judgment) for the students. The author suggests that a supportive learning environment coupled with a poetic/dramatic approach can improve a student's oral expression. Thus, the study highlights one possible way of improving oral communication skills.—C.G.-P.

COMMENTARY

This study highlights the importance of examining the process by which the arts are taught to students. Studies often assume that adding art instruction will lead to improved student outcomes. What these conceptualizations miss is how the structure of the classroom environment can influence how the arts impact student learning. In this case the author of the study created an environment in which students worked in groups and their input and concerns were valued. So it is difficult to disentangle the impact of the use of poetry and drama from the noncompetitive and nonjudgmental learning environment created by the instructor/researcher. Additionally, the study also suggests that the lack of emphasis on public speaking in high schools leaves many students with weak oral communication skills.—C.G.-P.

"...makes a good case for the promise of further research into the effectiveness of poetic interpretation accompanied by oral presentation in supporting both academic and social growth."

drama

31

STUDY NAME: Drama and Drawing for Narrative Writing in Primary Grades
AUTHORS: Blaine H. Moore and Helen Caldwell
PUBLISHED: Journal of Educational Research, November/December 1993, 87(2): 100-110

Research Questions

What are the effects of thought-organizing activities involving drama on narrative writing in comparison to traditional pre-writing-planning activities?

What are the effects of thought-organizing activities involving drawing on narrative writing in comparison to traditional pre-writing-planning activities?

METHODS

This was a reasonably large-scale study by the standards of research in educational psychology, involving 63 students. The students were randomly chosen from the second- and third-grade classes in a single school. The study was conducted in a rural area, predominantly populated by lower-middle-class Caucasians. The study took place over 15 weeks, mid-length among studies commonly seen.

Three groups were compared. One group focused on drawing activities, one group on drama activities, and the third served as a control group experiencing a traditional question-and-answer approach to developing narrative writing skills. The drama activities focused on individuals' ideas for stories. Students in the drama group used poetry, pantomime, games, movement, and improvisation to develop their narrative writing. Students in the drawing group used figure, action, and setting drawings to develop their narratives. A third group used no special intervention to promote narrative writing skills. The teachers had two 2-hour training sessions to learn how to lead and facilitate these sessions. Teachers were rotated among groups to ensure that teacher differences would not unevenly influence the quality of the writing. This was a thoughtful and validating feature of the design.

All three student groups began each week together in a 15-minute session discussing the various aspects of narrative writing. This included issues, characters, settings, dialogue, endings, and other aspects of narrative writing. Then each experimental group broke off on its own to continue a 45-minute session of either drawing or drama exercises followed by a 30-minute session of writing. The control group followed with a traditional lesson plan from a school text.

The writing exercises were rated every week. The researchers developed the rating scale based on both holistic and analytic scoring plans. They first registered overall impressions and then scored individuals on overall writing skills, ideas, organization, style, and context. The multiple assessors in this study attained an inter-rater reliability of .96.—J.C.

RESULTS

This study found that when the curriculum is designed to develop specific writing skills and the teachers are trained on the substance and implementation of the planned exercises, drama and drawing can significantly improve the quality of narrative writing for second- and third-graders. This is consistent with a limited number of other studies that have used drawing to enhance writing, and a more abundant array of studies that connect dramatic activities with verbal skills and writing proficiency.

Repeat-measure Analyses of Variance (ANOVAs) were used to test for significant differences in narrative writing skills across the three groups. In general, the differences between the program and control students were substantial and significant at $p > .001$ (i.e., the chance that the true differences were zero was less than 1 in 1,000). The authors conclude that drama and drawing are an effective method to warm up or rehearse students in ways that boost narrative writing performance.—J.C.

CONTRIBUTIONS TO THE FIELD

This study makes significant contributions to our understanding of roles dramatic activities can play in the development of writing skills. The results show statistically significant differences between the overall narrative writing scores of both the drama and drawing groups in comparison to the control group. Drama and drawing were equally effective, but since writing was assessed weekly, the authors were able to observe that the drawing group started out more slowly in effectiveness before its participants caught up with the drama group. The design of the study itself is also a contribution to this area of research, particularly its attention to the dynamics of learning over the 15 weeks and its clear descriptions of the tested activities. The authors do more than most researchers to explain the study's specific drama and interactive activities.—J.C.

COMMENTARY

The authors present a very anchored study. Their review of the literature displays an exceedingly comprehensive list of resources and references. Moore and Caldwell are working with an understanding of the existing knowledge and theories in their field. The design of the study is very high in quality. The pre- and post-testing and analytic designs are well conceived; scale reliability tests are strong. Although the authors designed the tests and evaluation criteria, independent assessors analyzed the results. What is being measured is very clear. The study applied to second- and third-graders, but seems to have implications for a wider group of students. The overall clarity of description would permit this study to be used as model for other programs.—J.C.

CONTRIBUTIONS TO THE FIELD

The study's results support the ideas that pre-writing planning activities are important for second- and third-graders and that the multi-modal work—drama and drawing—contributes to development in a third communication area—writing. It is important work the results of which should be recognized.

Staff development work with teachers in preparation for this study was extensive and, over time, seems to have been both persuasive and effective. The primary conclusion that such time is needed for the implementation of practices that link disciplines and activities is an important one for others who do this work to consider. As time for staff development becomes less and less available in our crowded school schedules, such a lesson should not be forgotten.—T.B.

COMMENTARY

The authors of this study place their work in the context of a growing body of research by scholars in other fields who have documented the effects of "planning" or pre-writing on student writing and who have developed support for multi-modal approaches using drama and drawing that have the process of composition in common with a third communication system (writing). This multi-modal instructional characteristic is one that others seeking to relate or integrate instruction from different domains should consider. The strength of the multi-modal approach cannot be judged from the abbreviated presentation used in this paper, but the expanding number of such studies suggests that the topic is an important one to those engaged in studying and teaching writing processes.

The fact that this study is a large-scale one, conducted over several weeks of time and involving a varied group of teachers, just as you would find in a real school system, makes the research especially important. The control group is significantly like a traditional language arts group so few should question the results of the study. Every opportunity seems to have been provided for all the groups to be successful.

Similar work with students of different ages would be interesting. The positive results need to be highlighted in more widely read journals than the *Educational Researcher*. The linkages to studies in other areas—modalities—are important to note and to point out to those in schools who question the value of integrated work. Arts-in-education personnel who use integration or infusion approaches should know that there are others doing work with similar concepts in other disciplines and are finding research that supports their efforts. A little transfer to arts in education would be nice.—T.B.

"...drama and drawing can significantly improve the quality of narrative writing for second- and third-graders."

drama

33

STUDY NAME: **Children's Story Comprehension as a Result of Storytelling and Story Dramatization: A Study of the Child as Spectator and as Participant**

AUTHOR: Anita Page

PUBLISHED: Doctoral Dissertation, 1983, University of Massachusetts, University Microfilms International

Research Question

Does story dramatization enhance story comprehension among first-graders?

METHODS

This study tests for differential effects on story understanding brought through dramatizing stories versus listening to adults reading stories. A traditional experimental approach to such a question would be random assignment of subjects to two groups, exposing one to dramatization and one to listening, and comparing effects for the two conditions. This study takes an added step to boost the validity of claims made on behalf of either treatment. The study is carried out in two phases so that any pre-existing advantage to either group in a paired comparison is essentially nullified. In the first phase, one of the two first-grade groups listens to a story read by a teacher. The other group listens to an audiotape of the same story and proceeds to engage in a dramatic enactment of the story. The same routine is carried out for the two second-/third-grade groups. Children are tested for story understanding through a 10-item test of comprehension, a picture sequencing instrument, and a telling of the story by each child to an interviewer. In the repeat phase, the same procedures and measures are carried out, but the groups who listened to a teacher-read story now hear the audiotape and proceed with an enactment—and vice versa. The author reports careful attention to the vocabulary, structure, plot, and complexity of the two stories involved in the respective phases of the study. As described, the stories were equivalent in potentially important respects such as length, structure, and vocabulary level.

In addition to testing for several main effects across each pair, the author examines effects at the first-grade level versus the second-/third-grade level. The author attends to the basic reading levels of subjects by referencing student files.—*J.C.*

RESULTS

This study reports several significant results. One is that children are more engaged during dramatizations than when just listening. Another is that several key ingredients of story understanding are better conveyed through drama: main idea, character identification, and character motivation. These are essential elements of comprehension. Both modes are effective in promoting recall of story sequence, story details, and story vocabulary.

Beyond the main treatment versus comparison group effects, drama had more effects on the younger (grade one) students than the older students (grades two and three). The author draws a reasonable inference that drama in this study was more beneficial for less developed readers than for more developed readers, signified at first by the grade-level distinction. When outcomes are compared for students within groups by reading level, this inference is reinforced. Story understanding effects are greatest for first-graders reading below grade level.—*J.C.*

CONTRIBUTIONS TO THE FIELD

This study offers firmly grounded evidence of certain benefits of using drama in the classroom to enhance children's story understanding. One result, a finding seen commonly in drama and the arts in education more generally, is that children are "more engaged and involved through drama" than they are through storytelling by teachers reading from books. Another result is an indication that drama is more effective in promoting story understanding for very young children (first-graders) than it is for second- and third-graders. A corollary is that children with lower reading skills, and those reading below grade level, are the greatest potential beneficiaries of enacting stories in order to understand them.—*J.C.*

COMMENTARY

Many studies link dramatizing text to enhanced understanding, particularly increased story understanding and reading comprehension. Such studies receive much attention in this Compendium. Story understanding through spoken and written presentations was also featured in the Podlozny meta-analysis summarized in this volume, an analysis that examined the effects of 109 studies of classroom drama published since 1950.

This study could be considered an anchor study in this domain. One reason is its very strong and appropriate experimental design; a second is that its focus on story comprehension represents the modal work in the area of drama and academic learning. But its influence on the literature surrounding learning through drama may have been limited because it is available as a doctoral dissertation and not through a more widely accessible outlet such as a book chapter or journal article.

The study's research methods are of particular value and worth comment up front. The study went beyond a simple treatment and control group design to test its hypotheses. The author used randomization to establish two pairs of comparison groups (a first-grade pair and a second-/third-grade pair) and followed a clever design, which repeated the intervention so that both groups at each level received the drama treatment once as part of the experiment.—*J.C.*

CONTRIBUTIONS TO THE FIELD

This study makes an important contribution to thinking about how drama can be used to teach reading. It suggests that the dramatic arts (storytelling with dramatic effect and story dramatization by students) can improve reading comprehension. Additionally, it highlights how children are more engaged and involved in learning when participating in story dramatization rather than listening to storytelling by the teacher. Rather than being passive receivers of knowledge, students who make dramatic presentations of stories may reach a deeper involvement in a story, particularly students who are reading below grade level. In the current political climate, which emphasizes the importance of basic literacy, this study shows how the dramatic arts can contribute to and improve basic skills.—*C.G.-P.*

COMMENTARY

As the author notes, one of the most common approaches to teaching reading is having a teacher read a story to students. The study suggests that the dramatic arts could be a useful addition to reading programs and assist students with story comprehension, particularly when students are active participants in story dramatization. The deeper implication of this, as the author suggests, is that while elementary teachers are supportive of creative dramatics, many do not actually use classroom drama in their classrooms. This points to the need to understand why many teachers do not use dramatic arts to increase literacy.—*C.G.-P.*

"...children with lower reading skills, and those reading below grade level, are the greatest potential beneficiaries of enacting stories in order to understand them."

drama

35

STUDY NAME: **The Impact of Whirlwind's Reading Comprehension through Drama Program on 4th Grade Students' Reading Skills and Standardized Test Scores**
AUTHORS: Michaela Parks and Dale Rose
PUBLISHED: Unpublished Evaluation, 3D Group, 1997, Berkeley, CA, 25

Research Questions

What is the impact of a collaboratively developed reading comprehension/drama program on reading skills, standardized test scores, and drama skills?

How does collaboration among teachers, principals, artists, and researchers to develop the curriculum, assessment tools, and the goals of a drama-skills and reading program play out?

METHODS

This was a development and evaluation project. After establishing the four project and control classrooms, the principals, teachers, artists, and evaluators met to develop goals, agree on assessment criteria, and train teachers and artists for implementing what resulted as this version of a Whirlwind curriculum. (Since Whirlwind works with teachers and schools to develop programs, it might be said the Whirlwind Program is a program development process. It is not Whirlwind that is being evaluated or researched in a given setting, but rather the specific product of the collaboration in that setting—a customized and implemented design).

After an initial planning and design period, the teachers from each participating class collaborated with an opera singer and an actor from Whirlwind for 20 one-hour sessions over 10 weeks. The 20 sessions each focused on a reading and dramatic-presentation exercise designed in a collaboration between the teachers and artists. The dramatic exercises began simply—with solo short enactments—and became more complex and involved more children over time. The activities grew from the planners' collective sense of particular drama exercises that would enhance particular reading skills. The performance assessment sessions were audio- and videotaped as well as scored on a protocol with 23 agreed-upon criteria. The evaluation report contains information describing the drama activities and exercises that were used in each session. The report appendices include a description of the exercises used for the performance assessments and the evaluation criteria as well as other statistical information.

Four elementary schools representing diverse mixes of student race/ethnicities and differing geographic areas served by the Chicago Public School System were chosen for participation. All four schools had hosted Whirlwind programs in previous years and thus had established working relations with the sponsor. Within each of the four schools, all fourth-grade teachers were invited to participate and all teachers accepted the invitation. Within each school, two classrooms were chosen randomly for inclusion in this study, and between each of these pairs of classes, one was chosen randomly for participation and the other enlisted as a comparison classroom, receiving no special program.

What resulted was a 10-week drama program, two hours per week, which engaged four classes of fourth-grade students in each of four schools, which were then compared to four control classes, one in each of the respective schools. Ninety-four fourth-graders participated (classes of 21, 24, 24, and 25 students) and 85 students made up the control group (classes of 22, 28, 25, and 10). Professional artists worked together with the classroom teachers. The three components of each session included "Game Time" for physical and vocal warm-up and getting focused, "Acting" for advancing acting skills and applying these to specific narratives, and "Observation/Conversing" for writing in journals and discussing the work of the session. At the end of the 10 weeks there was a specific theater presentation exercise along with a performance assessment. In the spring prior to the program year and in the spring at the close of the program year students were given a section of the Iowa Test of Basic Skills designed to measure reading comprehension.—J.C.

"This study supports general rationales for including drama programs in the reading and communication curricula for elementary schools."

RESULTS

Participant students' reading comprehension scores on the Iowa Test of Basic Skills (ITBS) improved three months more (in the standard grade-level metric) than the control group, with high statistical significance. ITBS scores improved the most with respect to student ability to identify factual information from written text. On the formal performance assessment created by the collaborating team, the program students improved significantly more than control students in reading comprehension, drama skills, and nonverbal expression of information inferred from a written text. Participants also improved three times more than the control group in nonverbal ability to express factual material. Program students did not improve relative to controls in reading ability measured through verbal expression in contrast to a *written* assessment.

The design of this study supports contentions that the program did in fact promote subject developments in both reading skills and nonverbal communications skills. This study supports general rationales for including drama programs in the reading and communication curricula for elementary schools.—J.C.

CONTRIBUTIONS TO THE FIELD

This study is a good illustration of strong evaluation/research design, execution, and reporting. There are many attractive elements in this study, apart from the substantive student educational experiences involved. This rendition of the Whirlwind program involved: (1) good numbers of subjects (four participant classrooms plus four control classrooms—about 180 students in all); (2) sensible, purposeful selection of four diverse Chicago schools from which to randomly choose classrooms; (3) random selection of both participant and control classrooms among teachers expressing a desire to participate; (4) a full year between nationally recognized pre- and post-measures of reading comprehension skills; and (5) an outside evaluation team. Perhaps the strongest component of the study design is that all classroom teachers, program and control alike, had self-selected in favor of participation in advance.

The study offers a useful model of multi-outcome assessment within a program evaluation, and a sound model for the creation of the program and assessment design by multiple program constituents. The study adds to a general body of literature connecting drama interventions to verbal skills and adds novel contributions in its design, use, and results of systematic performance assessments.—*J.C.*

COMMENTARY

The collaboration process among the teachers, artists, principals, and researchers designing the program, well described in the study report, can serve as a model for other programs because of the detail of program elements presented. This is a good example of reporting both program development and operation and also the results of the work. This is a high-quality study amidst a field of programs combining arts and education. There is enough accessible information about the various aspects of the design, implementation, and evaluation process for most educators, artists, and researchers to use this information as the foundation for their own projects.—*J.C.*

CONTRIBUTIONS TO THE FIELD

This study adds to the literature that documents the positive effects of drama on reading performance. It is noteworthy because of the careful effort to draw comparable control and comparison classrooms, matching both student and school characteristics.

The findings are made more robust by including not only standardized test scores but also more tailored performance assessments.

The sample of low-income, urban students of color exposed to drama showed impressive gains in grade-equivalent terms of three months more than the control group.—*B.W.*

COMMENTARY

There are two notes of caution about interpreting these generally positive findings. First, while classrooms were ran-domly assigned to control (no drama) and experimental conditions (twice weekly instruction for 10 weeks), there was no assessment of the general quality of reading instruction received by the control and experimental classrooms. An alternative hypothesis may be that the impressive Iowa Test of Basic Skills (ITBS) score increases were more a function of differential instruction. Second, while it was impressive to see a performance assessment that complemented standardized test score measures, the results from this test were more ambiguous than the authors portrayed. The performance assessment was divided into five subscales. The three subscales related to reading (verbal fluency, factual recall, and verbal inference) revealed no difference between the control and experimental classrooms. The two nonverbal drama subscales (acting out factual recall and dramatizing inferences) did show important differences. This latter finding should not be surprising because the control groups had no drama instruction.

The positive findings for this population of students, who often do poorly on standardized tests of achievement, may offer some hope for schools struggling to reduce the achievement gap between poor urban schools and their more wealthy suburban counterparts. More research needs to be undertaken to address the role the arts may play in this.

While the research provides adequate information for replication (with the exception of drama curriculum), the research leaves open the important question of whether students would do even better on reading assessments if they had regular, ongoing classroom drama instruction (as opposed to a special 10-week treatment) in an environment where drama instruction was regarded as an important core subject rather than an extra, add-on class.—*B.W.*

"The sample of low-income, urban students of color exposed to drama showed impressive gains in grade-equivalent terms of three months more than the control group."

STUDY NAME: The Effects of Thematic-Fantasy Play Training on the Development of
              Children's Story Comprehension
AUTHORS: Anthony D. Pellegrini and Lee Galda
PUBLISHED: American Educational Research Journal, Fall 1982, 19(3): 443-452

Research Question

What are the relative effects of three modes of story reconstruction training—thematic-fantasy play, teacher-led discussion, and drawing—on the development of children's story comprehension?

METHODS

This study engaged 108 children in grades K-2 from a rural school in northeast Georgia (18 boys and 18 girls in each of the three grades). The children were read three books by adults, one each, on three separate occasions. After each reading the children were exposed to one of three conditions for processing and exploring what they heard: thematic-fantasy play, discussion, or drawing. The first two story listening and processing episodes were considered training sessions; the third story reading was used for a formal test. Story comprehension was measured by a criterion-referenced test gauging story recall and student judgments about the story or its characters. Story understanding was also measured through the use of a scaled story-retelling task.—J.C.

RESULTS

Kindergartners and first-graders who participated in thematic-fantasy play scored significantly higher in *story comprehension* than their peers in both the discussion and drawing groups. There were no significant differences in *story comprehension* across training conditions for second- graders. Separate analyses explored total *story recall* and *recall of sequence of events*. The thematic-fantasy play groups recalled a significantly higher number of the events from the stories that they heard than both the discussion and drawing groups. The thematic-fantasy play groups also scored significantly better on sequence recall than did either the discussion or drawing groups, and were more successful in answering judgmental questions. Finally, for kindergartners, the centrality of the role played in the thematic-fantasy play event was positively linked to story recall (e.g., being the wolf in "Little Red Riding Hood" was about twice as effective in producing story recall as playing the grandmother).—J.C.

CONTRIBUTIONS TO THE FIELD

How we come to *understand* things we hear or read is a crucial question in education and human development. There are many different strategies used for processing and developing an understanding of new material. In graduate student seminars, for example, lectures or readings are usually followed by discussions as a strategy for processing information and furthering understanding. This study looks at the various ways in which children in kindergarten through second grade process information. The analysis finds that "thematic-fantasy play," or taking on a role and acting out all or part of a story, contributes more to measured story comprehension than two familiar alternative "information processing" activities in grade school, namely adult-led discussion and drawing exercises. This study concludes that children become more active, interactive, and effective information explorers when acting out a story than when reviewing the story through adult-led discussions or when drawing to illustrate a scene or theme from a story.—J.C.

COMMENTARY

Pellegrini and Galda suggest through this study that thematic-fantasy play requires children to accommodate the views of others in order to initiate and sustain play and that this gives them broader information recall than those children who are limited to discussion or drawing activities. They also find that children engaging in fantasy play are more successful in answering judgmental questions (questions requiring a critical stance) posed about the characters and situations. These questions require children to "take on simultaneously the role perspectives of the actor and the ideal (i.e., portrayed character) role." The findings of this study are consistent with other research cited by the authors, which holds that fantasy play, in asking children to conserve their own identity as well as take on a fantasy role, facilitates the ability to take a critical stance toward the meaning of the story and the identity of its characters.

This study is well designed and moderately extensive in scale (using 108 subjects and three iterations of the experiment before taking final measurements). The work involved a tight experimental design including randomization of children to groups and adults to facilitative and training roles. The researchers used systematic content assessment tests and formal guides to assess stories told by subjects and to measure outcomes.

This study, but no more than most, might be criticized for what it does not explore—particularly for not considering specific aspects of fantasy play that could impact story comprehension. For example, research on the importance of kinetic activity in language development, especially for kindergartners, suggests that purposeful movement may play a part in the effectiveness of fantasy play for this group. Future studies could look at how different aspects of thematic-fantasy play, such as social interaction or kinetic play, may account for the measured impacts. Studies could also explore different modes of discussion activities or different levels of skills of the adults leading discussions—certainly a variable that could prove important to the generalizations suggested by this study.

As described in this Compendium's summary of another Pellegrini study (Pellegrini 1984), both studies draw from the same experiment, but frame and measure different outcomes for the children and groups involved.—*J.C.*

CONTRIBUTIONS TO THE FIELD

The results of this small (108 children) study outline a very brief intervention where young children were read a story by an experimenter other than the classroom teacher. Students then engaged the story either by drawing a picture, talking about the story with an adult, or acting out the story with three peers and an adult. Students were then tested using both a criterion-referenced test and a test of recall. The results highlighted the fact that higher comprehension occurs when students can reconstruct a story through thematic-fantasy play than through either discussion or drawing. This research illustrates the value of using dramatic play to enhance students' story comprehension.—*B.W.*

COMMENTARY

These results, while exploring the value of different reading recall interventions, are limited for several reasons. First, the 10-item criterion-referenced test is divided into two factors: story-related and judgmental intelligence. Inadequate information is provided about the validity of these two constructs. Second, the presentation of the findings leaves out many important statistics. For example, analyses of variance (a statistical technique used to assess the effect of different variables) were discussed for the two factors with details by grade level for the first factor but not for the second. Likewise, detailed results were presented by grade for a separate assessment of total recall and sequencing recall (the second outcome measured in this study). Yet, discussion of the analyses of variance collapsed these grade-level distinctions. Finally, the authors incorporated student gender into the analysis but did not include that variable in another published study of the same students with the same experimental intervention. Why not?

The research begins to explore some important issues and points to questions to be addressed by future research: What would be the effect of a more naturally occurring fantasy-play intervention (e.g., in a regular classroom setting) on student comprehension? To what degree does regular, routine fantasy play—as a central part of the curriculum—impact student comprehension? How significant is the role of an adult as a catalyst to stimulate fantasy play? How important is age or developmental readiness to the issue of comprehension for older students?—*B.W.*

"How we come to understand things we hear or read is a crucial question in education and human development."

STUDY NAME: **Symbolic Functioning and Children's Early Writing: Relations Between Kindergarteners' Play and Isolated Word Writing Fluency**
AUTHOR: Anthony D. Pellegrini
PUBLISHED: EDRS Number ED 201 407 (1980): 1-15. Early Childhood Education, University of Georgia, Athens, Georgia

Research Question

What is the relationship between kindergartners' use of symbolic expression (mainly the use of spoken words) in free play and their ability to generate isolated written words an inquiry with implications for success in writing)?

METHODS

Sixty-five kindergartners (37 males and 28 females) took part in the study. All kindergartners in the rural school involved were invited to participate, and those whose parents gave permission joined the study. The investigators first administered Robinson's Test of Writing Fluency to assess student ability to write isolated whole words—the development of central concern in the research.

Beginning two weeks following the writing fluency test, researchers observed all children during their free-play periods over four weeks. Each student was observed five times, with each observation lasting 20 minutes. The observers recorded descriptions of play episodes according to a typology or hierarchy of play considered to involve differing levels of "cognitive/ symbolic" functioning. These include functional play (exercising muscles/movement), constructive play (creating something), dramatic play (using language in the service of a pretend role), and games with rules (play subordinated to a pre-arranged set of rules). The latter two types of play—drama and games with rules—are more cognitively demanding because they involve using language for socially shared symbols that allow children to sustain play.

The researchers conducted analyses of variance to test whether observed play-style differences among the four categories were associated with different levels of measured writing fluency.

The researchers also used several individual-level variables in a regression model to test the influences of gender, age, and socio-economic status, as well as observed type of play, on writing fluency.—*J.C.*

RESULTS

The analyses of variance showed that among the play styles observed, dramatic play had the strongest effect on isolated word writing. The regression analysis showed that of the four factors examined (gender, age, SES, and play style), only differences in *play style* (to be more specific, play styles using more symbolic functioning) had a significant main effect on isolated word writing fluency. (Note: the author uses the term "main effect," a standard attribution to significant correlations (actually *partial coefficients*) in a regression model. "Association" would be a more accurate term than "effect" in this study's regression analysis, since direction of influence cannot be inferred from the data).

The author provides a concise theoretical framework through which these observations might be understood. As children discover that individual letters bear meaning and that individual words represent things, they increase in their abilities and dispositions to use symbolic expression. Such developments would show up on tests of isolated word writing. Researchers exploring play prior to this study took interest in the levels of symbolic functioning during children's play. Building on that tradition, this study found that the more a child engaged in dramatic play, a type of play demanding symbolic functioning, the better that child tended to perform in writing words, an action implying the use of symbolism.—*J.C.*

CONTRIBUTIONS TO THE FIELD

Most research on the influence of drama on academic performance addresses verbal skills at or above the beginning reading levels typically shown by first-graders—that is, an ability to decode simple words and to read very simple sentences. This study broadens the literature through its focus on very early and simple individual word fluency in writing. The research finds positive relations between level of "symbolic functioning" (witnessed across a variety of play styles including dramatic enactment) and word fluency. Symbolic functioning refers to using "…symbols, or signs [to] represent other classes of objects or concepts."

A second important contribution of this study is that it differentiates among types of play and assesses the relative effects of each form within the study. The question explored by this study was not play versus no play, nor dramatic play versus some "control" activity. The research investigates differences in effects of what are defined above as functional play, constructive play, dramatic play, and games with rules. These types of play are considered to involve different levels of symbolic expression (or symbolic functioning) and thus are expected to associate with different levels of writing fluency. The study finds that

"This study adds to the body of research focusing on early childhood literacy."

among the forms of play explored, dramatic play had the strongest association with word writing fluency.—*J.C.*

COMMENTARY

This study adds to the body of research focusing on early childhood literacy. Much of the existing research focuses on the study of writing competency at the higher end of the continuum for developing writers, i.e., children writing words organized into phrases or sentences. In this study, Pellegrini specifically targets isolated word writing fluency with the understanding that this is a crucial beginning component in the process of becoming literate. He then looks at the possible contributions that certain factors make to such emerging literacy in order to suggest what might be incorporated into the curriculum to help augment the process of literacy development for young people.

In linking fantasy play and very young children's abilities to write words through close observation, Pellegrini assumes that the symbolic processes used in dramatic play are similar to the symbolic processes used to write individual words.

This hints at a critical limitation of this study. All measures were essentially simultaneous, and the research question thus became—what sorts of play styles *associate* with what sorts of word fluency? No firm claims can be made about which causes which. There is reason to believe that play styles would contribute to written word fluency; it is also reasonable to think that children with higher levels of written word fluency might play in different styles.—*J.C.*

CONTRIBUTIONS TO THE FIELD

This study adds to the literature on the contribution of free play (as an expression of artistic endeavor) to writing fluency. Sixty-five kindergarten students were each observed during five 20-minute play sessions over the course of a four-week period. The findings suggest that more complex play (i.e., dramatic play) is strongly associated with higher achievement in writing.—*B.W.*

COMMENTARY

Through some unspecific process, each child's 100 minutes of play were reduced to a single number: 1=functional, 2=constructive, or 3=dramatic. It seems questionable that such play can accurately be reduced to a single number. These scores were then included in a series of regressions to test the relationship between categories of play, other potentially important predictive factors (age, gender, and SES), and the ability to write isolated words. The small sample size pushes the limits of being able to meaningfully apply multiple regression techniques.

Assuming that the numbers can be meaningfully interpreted, the author ends the report with an important discussion about the implications of the findings for teaching. The significance of viewing students as active, not passive, learners cannot be underestimated. Furthermore, helpful suggestions of how teachers might assist students actively choose objects to be symbolically transformed serves as a good model for translating complex theoretical issues into the domain of classroom practice.—*B.W.*

drama

STUDY NAME: **Identifying Causal Elements in the Thematic-Fantasy Play Paradigm**
AUTHOR: Anthony D. Pellegrini
PUBLISHED: American Educational Research Journal, Fall 1984, 21(3): 691-701

Research Questions

Does thematic-fantasy play training facilitate children's immediate and maintained story recall?

Does thematic-fantasy play contribute to conflict-resolution skills?

Does adult participation in thematic-fantasy play activities influence the outcome of thematic-fantasy play training?

METHODS

One hundred and ninety-two children in kindergarten and first grade from a predominantly African-American, high-poverty school in rural northeast Georgia took part in this study. The children were randomly assigned to one of four groups: adult-directed play, peer-directed play, accommodation questioning (facilitated discussion), or control. An adult read a story to the children on three separate occasions, and after each reading the children "processed" the story according to their assigned treatment or control (no additional organized story processing) condition. Corresponding to other Pellegrini study designs, the first two sessions were essentially carried out for practice. The third session provided the opportunity for data collection and analysis. After the third story-reading session, the children carried out their respective processing activities and then were tested in three different ways. First, the children were given a 10-item criterion-referenced test for recall of narrative details. They were then asked to retell the story to an experimenter who audiotaped and later scored the retelling according to a formal scoring guide. Finally, the children were asked to lay out the sequence of the story by placing a set of pictures in order according to their recall of the story's plot. The children were given repeat testing on the CRT and the retelling task one week later to assess sustained story recall. Analyses of variance were conducted to test for score differences across the four groups.—J.C.

RESULTS

This study finds that the thematic-fantasy play condition generally (whether adult or peer directed) was more effective for *immediate story recall* than was assistance through accommodation questioning or no assistance at all (the control group). But thematic-fantasy play was more effective than other groups in promoting *sustained story recall* in only one of six sustained-recall tests (the CRT for kindergartners). The fact that an impact on sustained recall was seen only for kindergartners aligns with Page's study (summarized in this Compendium), where the effects of dramatic enactment on story understanding were strongest for younger children (K as opposed to grades one or two)—and for weaker readers. The observation that effects are limited in duration raises some caution in leaping to grandiose conclusions from the very large majority of studies that do not test for sustaining effects.

In teasing out behaviors within dramatic enactment that contribute to story recall, the authors find that verbal interaction among peers, which to varying degrees is characteristic of fantasy play, enables children to construct narrative structures and thus to demonstrate better story recall. This study also found that both adult-directed and peer-directed play were equally effective in facilitating children's story recall, indicating that adult assistance did not play an important role in thematic-fantasy play training.

This study further suggests that fantasy play may assist children in developing conflict-resolution skills. Fantasy play often results in disagreements regarding plot development and the role each child is allowed to play. In order to sustain play, children often resolve these conflicts themselves. This conflict/resolution cycle allows the children to broaden their perspectives of an event by seeing through the eyes of their peers. This process deepens their understanding of a story as well as fosters a cooperative learning environment.

Finally, this study implies but does not grapple with an interesting problem of generalization. Since the study population was reported to be very homogeneous—predominantly African- American and low-SES—can we say that its results are confined to such populations or should they be considered more widely? There is no ready answer to this question, other than to find or generate replication studies with other populations. When examining studies with other populations, a few important questions should be explored: Is the adult assistance phenomenon in some way related to culture? Are the results of this study tied to the base-line reading and narrative-recall proficiencies of the study population, which are not described? And finally, are the observations about conflict resolution influenced by the homogeneity of this study school's culture, and would things work differently in a school populated by highly diverse cultures or home languages?—J.C.

CONTRIBUTIONS TO THE FIELD

This study builds on previous work in understanding the positive roles that fantasy re-enactment can play in facilitating cognitive development, especially language-related skills. (See for example, Pellegrini & Galda, 1982, summarized in this Compendium). This study informs an important question left largely unaddressed in previous studies: Does adult involvement influence the outcome of play experiments? The results of this part of the study may interest teachers, classroom aides, and parent classroom volunteers. By age 5, children do not appear to need adults to sustain play and both peer-directed and adult-directed play groups can be equally effective in facilitating story recall.

The study also contributes as one of few experiments measuring sustained as opposed to relatively immediate effects. (Drama modestly influenced sustained recall for the youngest subjects only). The study also embraces a little-studied potential effect of drama—the impact of story enactment on conflict resolution. The verdict on this effect is yes.—J.C.

COMMENTARY

The results of this experiment add significantly to the research on the benefits of thematic-fantasy play as an instructional practice. The study also illustrates, along with others reviewed in this Compendium, the traditions of careful research design and thoughtful question generation by Pellegrini and colleagues during the early 1980s. These works were published in top educational psychology journals, in contrast to much (but certainly not all) of what we are able to find in research on drama and theater in education.

A characteristic of this and the other Pellegrini studies is that they formally test for the effects of conditions within dramatic enactment, and not only for the effect of using drama versus no drama. That is to say, this research attempts to tease out conditions within the use of drama in the classroom, which may influence its success. The researcher explores the effects of particular factors on the outcome of the interventions examined (e.g., the effect of adult involvement on children's fantasy play), as well as the interaction of multiple factors within the intervention (e.g., the relationship between grade level and treatment). In addition, there are two related details in the results that are worth highlighting here. One is that the research largely found no sustaining effects of thematic-fantasy play on story recall, in assessments only one week later. Another is that the sustaining effects that were observed were found only for kindergartners and not for first-graders. This aligns with the Page, Pellegrini, and Wagner studies (summarized in this Compendium), which found story understanding effects through drama stronger or present only for their younger subjects.—J.C.

CONTRIBUTIONS TO THE FIELD

What is intriguing about this study is that it suggests that for kindergartners peer-directed play can be as effective as adult-directed play at facilitating a student's immediate and maintained story recall. For kindergartners, not only is the dramatic use of thematic-fantasy play a more effective method for immediate story recall than accommodation questions, but the students themselves can be important effective facilitators of this method. This approach suggests that kindergartners can independently aid in their own learning through fantasy play.—C.G.-P.

COMMENTARY

The study suggests that children in kindergarten, regardless of whether they are middle class or of lower socio-economic status, do not need an adult to assist them in maintaining fantasy play. However, the school in which the study was conducted was identified by the authors as "a predominantly LSES (lower socio-economic status) black school in rural northeast Georgia". It appears the sample was not representative of LSES Caucasian students or middle-class students. Thus, questions remain about its generalizability to these groups.—C.G.-P.

"…fantasy play may assist children in developing conflict-resolution skills."

STUDY NAME: **The Effect of Dramatic Play on Children's Generation of Cohesive Text**
AUTHOR: Anthony D. Pellegrini
PUBLISHED: Discourse Processes, 1984, 7: 57-67

Research Questions

To what extent does the informational status of a listener (whether familiar or not familiar with a story) affect a student's use of oral language to retell the story? (Do students use effective and appropriate language when told in advance the knowledge base of the listener?)

With what relative effectiveness can children's use of oral language (retelling stories to non-familiar listeners) be facilitated through the use of alternative interventions, namely discussion, drawing, and dramatic play?

METHODS

This study involves 108 students (54 girls and 54 boys) ranging in educational level from kindergarten to second grade. The students were divided into same-age groups of four (two boys and two girls) and then randomly assigned to one of three conditions describing the activities that they would engage in prior to retelling a story to an adult: social dramatic play, discussion, or drawing. There were two experimenters, one male and one female, who were also randomly assigned to different groups and conditions.

An adult read a children's book to each group on three separate occasions. After each reading session, the children were separated into their treatment conditions to process the story by the means assigned. Individual children were then asked to retell the story to an experimenter. One-half of the children retold the story to the experimenter who had read the story to them (i.e., an "informed" listener). The other half retold the story to the other experimenter, who claimed not to have heard of the story (i.e., a "naïve" listener). Retelling sessions were audiotaped, and student responses were analyzed. The first two reading, processing, and retelling sequences were done for practice. Data were collected on the third rendition.

In order to analyze the students' ability to convey meaning during story retelling, the researchers looked for and marked elements of cohesion within the students' narratives, noting particularly the level of cohesion generated by gestures and language that recognized the comprehensive informational needs of the unfamiliar listener.—J.C.

RESULTS

Pellegrini found that students using dramatic play to think about, review, and otherwise process the story they had just heard were more likely to use explicit language when retelling their stories than students in either the discussion or drawing groups. That is, they were better at producing a retelling that would be coherent and make sense to a listener who did not already know the story. Pellegrini makes a critical point, that conveying meaning explicitly is an important skill and one that is traditionally valued and rewarded, both in school and in later-life instances of communication.—J.C.

CONTRIBUTIONS TO THE FIELD

This is an important study as it focuses on intriguing aspects of literacy: how an individual *conveys* meaning, and the importance of the knowledge base of the listener (as told to the child in advance) in how children retell stories. This study concludes that students' oral language varies according to listener status and that dramatic play is an effective preparation instrument for fostering the use of explicit language (i.e., conveying stories effectively to those who do not know anything about the stories in advance). It is crucial to foster these language skills, particularly in school settings, where children are expected to use explicit language in most written and oral language activities.—J.C.

COMMENTARY

It should be noted that this study is based on the same sample of children and cluster of experiments reported two years earlier in Pellegrini & Galda (1982) (also summarized in this Compendium). It is not uncommon in academia, as is done here, for experiments to be mounted with two or more differing effects assessments in mind—including the use of separate instruments to compare differing outcomes attained by treatment versus control groups. This 1984 study reports on the effects of alternative strategies impacting student ability to retell stories, while the 1982 study reports the impact of alternative story-processing strategies (discussion, drawing, and dramatic play) on the development of children's story *comprehension*.

The specific target of this study is more subtle than the direct measures of comprehension and language skills assessed in most of the studies we include in this section of the Compendium. Effective reading, writing, and oral-language production require more than what we might call first-order skills—decoding words and sentences or crafting grammatically correct oral or written declarations. At a higher order, words, sentences, and paragraphs are understood in context, and listeners and readers as well as speakers and writers succeed in some proportion to this realization. This study recognizes that an effective retelling of a story should account for what the listener may already know about it and, more specifically, should take into account situations where an audience is uninitiated. Dramatic play appears to increase tendencies of children to be thorough and explicit in their narratives in situations where this is needed.—*J.C.*

CONTRIBUTIONS TO THE FIELD

This research, based on listening to 108 students retell stories (as relayed to students in an experimental setting), makes an important contribution to the understanding of how students make meaning from what they learn by listening to adults. This research demonstrates that acting out a story produces better understanding than either just talking about it or drawing a picture of what was learned. This meaning-making, through hands-on learning opportunities, is a significant piece of the knowledge-base puzzle on literacy.—*B.W.*

COMMENTARY

A couple of research shortcomings limit interpretation of this study. First, an incomplete explanation of the outcome measures (i.e., what students learned after listening to a story) makes it difficult to interpret the findings. For example, students' meaning-making was defined by endodorphic and exodorphic elements (author's language). These two elements were further subdivided into reference and ellipsis categories, each of which was further differentiated by three different subcategories. Thus, 12 different outcome measures were constructed. But the reader was given no explanation of how to interpret the quantitative score for any of these. What does it mean to produce a score of 9.15 for the exodorphic category in response to the informed listener? Second, the one table of results for this study presents means and standard deviations for each of the 12 outcome measures, broken out by story reconstruction training and condition of the adult listener. Yet most of the analysis of effects, using the statistical technique of analysis of variance, collapses many of these subcategories. This approach makes it difficult to follow and interpret the results. Finally, the authors incorporated the status of the adult listener into the analysis but did not include that variable in another published study of the same students with the same experimental intervention. Why not?

The research helps identify important conditions (i.e., more active learning environments where students use the arts to engage content) where students' literacy might be enhanced. But it leaves unanswered the effect of a more naturally occurring drama intervention (e.g., in a regular classroom setting) on students' oral language. To what degree does regular play-acting—as a central part of the curriculum—impact students' use of oral language? The research also poses a real challenge for teachers because typical classroom environments often permit implied, shared assumptions that naturally foster more exodorphic explanations. Because enhanced literacy relies heavily on students' offering more explicit meaning from what they are learning, what specific steps might teachers take to design better learning environments? It is more complex than just fostering dramatic play.—*B.W.*

drama

45

"Effective reading, writing, and oral-language production require more than what we might call first-order skills—decoding words and sentences or crafting grammatically correct oral or written declarations."

STUDY NAME: **Strengthening Verbal Skills Through the Use of Classroom Drama: A Clear Link**
AUTHOR: Ann Podlozny
PUBLISHED: Journal of Aesthetic Education, Fall 2000, 34(3-4): 239-276

Research Question

Does classroom drama help students develop verbal ability? (The researcher created seven meta-analyses that considered nine related hypotheses related to type of plot, role of leader, degree of transfer, amount of drama instruction, age, type of population, study design, publication status, and publication date).

METHODS

Podlozny framed her review of instructional practices in three dimensions of drama: enactment, plot, and the leader's level of involvement. Within these framing or defining categories, she set seven verbal outcomes to be examined: story understanding (oral measures), story understanding (written measures), reading achievement, reading readiness, oral language development, vocabulary, and writing. Two hundred studies conducted since 1950 were identified, from which 80 were selected according to criteria that included having at least one measure of verbal achievement, being experimental in design, and having sufficient information for an effect size to be calculated. The researcher and one assistant coded all studies. A five percent rate of disagreement in the coding was resolved in rechecking texts. After calculating average effect sizes across the groupings, the nine hypotheses were tested regarding the influence of specific factors associated with the hypotheses. These included substantive variables related to type of treatment or type of participant, method variables related to research methods, and extrinsic variables such as date of publication or publication status.—*T.B.*

RESULTS

For the first meta-analysis of 17 studies assessing the effect of drama on story understanding and recall measured orally, the effect sizes ranged from $r = .00$ to $r = .66$. The confidence interval range of $r = .16$ to $r = .34$ does not span zero—the necessary condition for establishing statistical confidence, allowing a finding that there is a relationship between drama and oral story understanding/recall. The finding that the effect sizes for this meta-analysis were significantly heterogeneous led to the testing of possible relationships with a variety of other variables.

With an effect size range of $r = .00$ to $r = .96$ and a confidence interval range of $r = .37$ to $r = .73$, it was concluded that there is a relationship between drama and story understanding as expressed in the form of written measures (meta-analysis 2). Further analysis of variables stimulated by the heterogeneous nature of the effect sizes for this group led to the surprising conclusion that drama instruction might be more effective for *low-SES populations* and remedial readers. Previous meta-analyses found that *average populations* benefited more from drama study.

The third meta-analysis examined reading achievement using standardized tests. The range of effect sizes was $r = .15$ to $r = .56$, and the confidence interval ranged from $r = .11$ to $r = .29$, allowing a conclusion that there is a relationship between drama instruction and reading achievement.

Meta-analysis 4 studied reading readiness and had a range of effect sizes of $r = -.03$ to $r = .66$. The calculated confidence interval of $r = .15$ to $r = .36$ supported the conclusion that there is a relationship between drama instruction and reading readiness.

The text of the report for meta-analysis 5 on oral language development states that the range of effect sizes was from $r = -.04$ to $r = .73$. The calculated confidence interval of from $r = .20$ to $r = .41$ allows the conclusion that there is a relationship between drama instruction and oral language development.

Meta-analysis 6 was the only one to find no relationship with effect sizes ranging from $r = -.20$ to $r = .37$ and a confidence interval of $r = -.07$ to $r = .19$. The results show that there is no reliable relationship between drama instruction and vocabulary development.

Meta-analysis 7 examined eight studies of writing achievement. The confidence interval on the effect sizes ranged from $r = .09$ to $r = .52$ and supported the conclusion that there is a relationship between drama instruction and writing achievement.

Overall, the results of this rather massive meta-analysis are "very encouraging for educators who use drama in the classroom in expectations of achieving greater verbal development." The author also notes that the studies indicate that there is evidence of transfer to new material in these reports, perhaps indicating that "…transfer of skills from one domain to another is not automatic; it needs to be taught."—*T.B.*

CONTRIBUTIONS TO THE FIELD

This report makes substantial contributions to the fields of drama education and arts education research. Because it includes information confirming positive correlations, the report will encourage teachers, teaching artists, and school administrators to include drama in their classroom practice. In the same way, the report also makes a contribution to the expansion of instructional practice in the everyday classroom.

The report's contribution to researchers is at least

twofold: it uses a meta-analysis procedure that is properly based on grouping comparable studies, and it identifies a rich variety of weaknesses in the studies while making recommendations for corrective steps and future research strategies that could deepen the research base in drama education. The discussion of weaknesses such as a lack of conversation among researchers, the rare replication of studies, an absence of consistence of measures, and the lack of set operational definitions of such labels as "drama," "socio-drama," and "creative dramatics" does not condemn the effort but encourages renewed research conducted with greater care and precision. Such a stance can be viewed as a very positive contribution in light of the practice of many researchers to interpret weaknesses as signs of failure or as contraindications.—*T.B.*

COMMENTARY

Podlozny's work places the often-questioned practice of meta-analysis in the arts on much firmer ground. She carefully groups the 80 studies (she selected from among the 200 possible reports) in categories based on seven types of recognizable drama outcomes and compares sets of studies within each group rather than across the total set of studies. She is interested in specific outcome results rather than in "drama" as a singular field. This specificity establishes greater confidence in her work and makes it easier for drama educators to make connections to specific aspects of their own classroom work.

As part of her setting up of the context for this study, she reviews four separate, previous meta-analyses of drama studies and thereby establishes the need for the creation of the "finer sieve" of her own study. Her tone here, as always, is strong and clear without being condescending.

Methodologically, her effect size calculations and especially the additional analysis of other variables when the sizes were heterogeneous, gives further credence to the report and helps identify subtleties that could help teachers. For example, the surprising result that enacting a text makes a new text more comprehensible is interpreted as demonstration of the power of drama to develop text comprehension skills that transfer to new material.

The fact that eight of the nine hypotheses were supported, all but the vocabulary connection, is remarkable, given the usually negative reports of the study of positive correlations in arts education studies of transfer.—*T.B.*

CONTRIBUTIONS TO THE FIELD

This is a powerful meta-analysis presenting a synthesis of research on classroom drama. The contribution to the field is unparalleled. Positive effects are shown in six areas related to language development: written and oral measures of story recall, reading achievement, reading readiness, oral language development, and writing. The author's test for effects on vocabulary revealed a very weak influence.

Podlozny also examines the effects of specific characteristics of drama programs and types of participating students. These analyses cut across the body of studies independent of the various outcomes listed above. Programs involving structured plot or low-SES students show larger effects. So do studies using non-experimental research designs as well as studies that were published in academic journals or books.

Podlozny reports an important element of the studies she reviewed. This is that drama shows influences not only on children's understanding of enacted stories but on understanding of subsequently experienced unrelated texts (read or heard). She describes this as an instance of transfer of skills or knowledge.—*J.C.*

"…the report will encourage teachers, teaching artists, and school administrators to include drama in their classroom practice."

COMMENTARY

The portrait of drama in education advanced in this Compendium bears strong resemblance to that shown by Podlozny. Even though our selection process (biased toward rigorous comparison group designs and adding more recent works) distilled the field to 19 studies (Podlozny examined 80), the effects we report are quite similar. The lone apparent departure was our not identifying drama as a positive influence on reading readiness. Few studies claim to focus on reading readiness, even if they are related to early language development. For example, of the 80 studies referenced by Podlozny, only two include reading readiness in their titles. A close examination of the studies we include shows influences of drama activities on very early language development by 5-year-olds and kindergartners that could be considered developments in reading readiness.

Five Compendium studies show mild indications of transfer effects consistent with Podlozny's conclusions about reading—namely effects on reading comprehension, thoughtful writing, and on certain social skills outside the purview of Podlozny's review.

We also found good evidence that drama's effects are larger for students who get out of role to direct, provide leadership, or otherwise reflect on the process. (Meta-play is one term for these actions). In contrast, Podlozny did not find a substantial effect for students taking leader roles in drama.—*J.C.*

STUDY NAME: **"Stand and Unfold Yourself" A Monograph on the Shakespeare & Company Research Study**
AUTHOR: Steve Seidel
PUBLISHED: Project Zero, Harvard Graduate School of Education, Cambridge, MA, 1998; also in E. Fiske (Ed.), Champions of Change: The Impact of the Arts on Learning, The Arts Education Partnership and the President's Committee on the Arts and the Humanities, Washington, DC, 1999: 79-90

Research Questions

How do participants (in the Shakespeare & Company program) identify the value of their participation for themselves?

What elements of the programs seemed most critical to creating those benefits?

METHODS

A team of researchers studied two full seasons of the Shakespeare & Company's National Shakespeare Institute. A season consisted of a one-month teacher training experience in the summer and an associated Fall Festival of Shakespeare, where teams of trained artist-teachers work over two months with over 400 students in 10 schools to study and perform Shakespeare plays. The research staff visited the school programs, observed sessions, attended student performances, interviewed teacher and student participants, reviewed written materials, and talked with program faculty and administrators. The design was to look closely and systematically at the elements of the program in order to consider what made this program so successful and to consider the prospects for transferring such a program to other settings. The research staff and participants held team meetings throughout the year and retreat meetings each spring to focus intensively on what they were seeing and learning.

Students and staff usually participate in the National Shakespeare Institute for three or four years; this study captured a two-year slice of this cycle. A set of questions was developed around authenticity, academic rigor, applied learning, active exploration, adult relationships, and assessment practices. Numerous quotes from students and teachers in response to these questions are included in this study as evidence of the impacts and success of the program. The methods could best be described as lying in the regions of ethnography and case study. The most important methodological ingredients were up-close interactions and observations, and sustained involvement during two seasons of paired summer and fall sessions.

The scholars focused on learning in four fields—the language itself, acting, working in creative communities, and learning about oneself and linking that to social and intellectual development.—J.C.

RESULTS

The researchers found much to like in their assessments of the impact of these programs on their participants.

1. Participants engage in Shakespeare's plays in ways that respect (rather than short-circuit) the complexity of the plays; it is precisely this respect for complexity that engages these learners.
2. Once engaged and with adequate support, guidance, and resources, participants do embrace and meet the challenges that had seemed difficult or overwhelming (and that often steer readers and theater-goers alike away from Shakespeare).
3. The Shakespeare & Company programs created caring and creative communities; caring and creativity seem explicitly linked to each other and to the development of deep understandings.
4. Feelings and emotions are linked to achieving deep understandings of Shakespeare's plays and are often a critical entry point to engagement with the plays.
5. Teachers made transitions from didactic teaching styles to "teacher as player" and "teacher as facilitator or catalyst" during this program; these transitions were experienced as transformative and profound by both teachers and students.
6. Participants gained information and skills: studying Shakespeare and his language, approaching dramatic action, acting, working with others, and seeing themselves as learners.
7. Playfulness and seriousness do not conflict with each other in the Institute and Fall Festival learning environments.
8. The highest levels of professional training are wholly consistent with the principles, structures, and pedagogy of these programs.

The report also suggests ingredients desirable for replication of such a program in other locales: (a) a supportive local agency such as a theater company or school, (b) an adequate pool of artists and educators inclined to do this work, (c) a community interested in the arts, (d) financial support, and (e) ongoing conversations among the players to negotiate commitment to such a program.—J.C.

CONTRIBUTIONS TO THE FIELD

This study supports a growing body of research showing that dramatic study and enactment can produce a rich learning environment. This work shows that Shakespeare's plays can be particularly effective because of their life-like complexity (that is, when care, patience, and skill interact to invite participants to engage such complexity). The complexity of issues and emotions in the plays promotes word-by-word, emotion-by-emotion, thought-by-thought investigation of meaning. This step-by-step approach invites those who study Shakespeare to go deeply into their own experience, a process that is linked to all types of learning.

This study does not just document the impacts of Shakespeare & Company's summer teacher training and fall student productions on the understanding and interpretation of Shakespeare's plays, or on acting and stage direction skills. The study illustrates a whole approach to teaching and learning, including assumptions about teachers and teaching and learners and learning, that has implications across a wide spectrum of educational situations. The implications concern not only what is taught and learned but also who we are as teachers and learners.—*J.C.*

COMMENTARY

This study is not standard issue from education journals. It is a long-term study examining two seasons of summer teacher development and fall play production in 10 schools. Shakespeare & Company offers much more than many research studies can get their arms around, overcoming many common challenges—including those of time, resources, or the rigors of conceptual creativity and clarity needed for a study like this.

We should wish this sort of program on all teachers and students willing to engage this work. It may seem to readers that this program lies in a dream world where teachers can spend a full month in the summer with a professional company, and work intensively with groups of engaged students during the following fall. But the prospects for replication at a meaningful level may be better than they first appear. The crux of the challenge is the first-rate training of teachers. This study provides a sense of what is required for this.—*J.C.*

CONTRIBUTIONS TO THE FIELD

This study provides an example of how an arts organization can work with schools to extend the traditional curriculum. Specifically, the program provides a model of how arts-based, project-based learning can assist students in developing higher-order thinking and problem-solving skills.—*C.G.-P.*

COMMENTARY

"Unfolding" is used to describe how students open themselves to learning processes through the study of Shakespeare: acting, working in creative communities, and linking self-knowledge to social and intellectual development.—*C.G.-P.*

"...caring and creativity seem explicitly linked to each other and to the development of deep understandings."

49

STUDY NAME: **Nadie Papers No. 1, Drama, Language and Learning. Reports of the Drama and Language Research Project, Speech and Drama Center, Education Department of Tasmania**
AUTHORS: Megan Schaffner, Graham Little, and Heather Felton
PUBLISHED: National Association for Drama in Education, Education Department of Tasmania, August 1984

Research Questions

What are the effects of drama (defined in this study as "being and doing within an imaginary situation") on fifth- and sixth-graders' language development?

What are the impacts of drama on the development of informational language, expressive language, and interactional language?

What are the effects of drama on the development of moral values?

METHODS

The authors selected nine schools for this study to represent city, suburban, and rural areas, different socio-economic backgrounds, and varied organizational contexts (public and private schools in Tasmania). Eleven classes of fifth- and sixth-graders were included in the study on the basis of teacher interest. Even though some teachers had no previous classroom drama experience, they still self-selected to participate in the study. The teachers had continuous access to speech and drama coaches, whom they worked with at the outset of the program and called in from time to time.

After a two-day initial workshop, the teachers were invited to engage children in dramatic activities of their own design; there was no standardization of length of sessions, frequency of drama activities in the classrooms, or continuity of themes. The amount of data collected implies that most or all participating teachers became actively involved in the use of drama over the school year. The one restriction placed on the teachers and students was that they had to use "imaginary" drama, and not work from written texts. This model reinforced the project's interest in "expressive" language, as opposed to decoding text. As the authors describe the design of the study, "Within this frame of reference the children and the teacher can explore relationships, attitudes and values in a vivid and immediate way…attitudes, relationships and significant moments are explored from 'the inside' rather than through discussion alone."

After permitting teacher experimentation and trials during the first three months, researchers spent two school terms documenting dramatic activities in all of the classrooms by audio taping every session in all participating classrooms. Teachers were instructed to gather samples of language and verbal exchanges from all of the children, with even attention to each child in the classroom over time. From all transcripts, a total of 280 language samples containing drama in action, planning discussion, and post-improvisation reflection were obtained—representing all classrooms evenly for each type of language sample.

The researchers analyzed the resulting "word samples" using formal criteria for classifying and describing the children's use of language. The main classifications of interest concerned the predominant purpose of the sampled language: expressive, interactional, or informational. Expressive language reflects the speaker's individual thoughts, feelings, ideas, and personal viewpoint. Interactional language reflects a speaker's focus on the person(s) being addressed through attempts to persuade, control, or command. And informational language involves the speaker's focus on neither him/herself nor the listener, but is concerned with giving information.—*J.C.*

RESULTS

The author claims that language use in imaginary drama exercises not only differs from language use in regular classrooms but also encourages desirable types of thinking and cognitive development. The reasons are the observed characteristics of language in drama: speculation, reflection, explanation, and evaluation. The author considers the overriding difference between children's language in normal classroom activities and language in their dramatic work is that regular classroom language is overwhelmingly informational; in contrast, the language of imaginary drama is only half informational, and half expressive and interactional. (The author provides no confirming data on the purposes of regular classroom language, but a predominance of informational purpose seems plausible).

Drama provides opportunities for children to use language for a wider variety of purposes than otherwise typically occurs in classrooms. Drama provides an opportunity to develop expressive language, which, as heard in the reflections segments, helps uncover feelings as well as develop opinions and thoughts. The authors found that drama encourages critical child-to-child exchanges and reflection on social interactions. The reflection phase had tendencies to bring up issues related to moral values in the otherwise information-based curriculum. As the authors maintain, "Drama puts back the human content into what is predominantly a materialistic curriculum."

The recorded reflection sessions also suggest that children in this study grew to recognize drama as a powerful learning medium—and language as a tool for learning and growth.—*J.C.*

CONTRIBUTIONS TO THE FIELD

This study contributes to our understanding of the impact of drama on language through its findings: mainly that drama encourages *expressive* and *interactional* language, as opposed to *informational* language, which, according to the author, dominates regular classroom life. The study's typology of language is one we do not see in other drama studies, although the scheme makes intuitive sense and seems valuable. This study is also the only one included in this Compendium that identified drama as a catalyst for discussions of moral values.—*J.C.*

COMMENTARY

This powerful study explores what happens when children engage in dramatization regularly over one full school year. Two hundred eighty students in nine different schools participated. As an experiment in drama and language, the program benefited from the participation of drama and speech specialists who worked with the classroom teachers to plan the drama activities.

One feature of the design might be seen as a weakness or strength. Dramatic activities were improvisational; they involved no writing or script and in some places involved the teacher in role, in other places not. This lack of standardization seems at first unorthodox, but in fact plays well to the goals of the research. The author wished to capture the language of improvisational drama across the many forms it might take; and she orchestrated enough settings to assure a considerable variety of dramatic situations.

The emergence of moral value discussions in follow-up discussions of the improvisational drama activities, unique to this study among those included in the Compendium, may be related to the fact that the subjects of this study were fifth- and sixth-graders. A majority of drama and learning studies involve younger primary school children who may be less likely to engage in moral debates of any complexity.

While this study exposes the tendencies of children to engage in discussion about human interaction and moral values during post-improvisation discussions, it does not in fact measure learning in these domains. But discussion and reflection in all likelihood represent a start on learning as well as a potentially powerful opportunity for learning.—*J.C.*

CONTRIBUTIONS TO THE FIELD

The significance of this study is its discovery that drama can be taught in two distinct modes, experiential, which focuses on attempting to live through some aspect of an experience, and presentational, which focuses on communicating something to an audience outside the classroom. By identifying these two discrete approaches, the study points to the need for further research into benefits or implications of each approach.—*C.G.-P.*

COMMENTARY

The study suggests that drama can positively contribute to children's language development. In particular, drama can impact students who have primarily been exposed to informational (lower-order thinking skills) language focused on transmitting facts and information. Drama can influence language development by using expressive language to provide students with opportunities to speculate, imagine, predict, reason, and evaluate their own learning (higher-order thinking skills).—*C.G.-P.*

"Drama provides opportunities for children to use language for a wider variety of purposes than otherwise typically occurs in classrooms."

STUDY NAME: **The Effects of Role Playing on Written Persuasion: An Age and Channel Comparison of Fourth and Eighth Graders**
AUTHOR: Betty Jane Wagner
PUBLISHED: Unpublished Doctoral Dissertation, October 1986, English Department, University of Illinois at Chicago

Research Questions

What are the effects of role-playing on subsequent persuasive writing among fourth- and eighth-graders?

What specific elements of role-playing are reflected in subsequent persuasive writing?

How does role-play persuasive language compare to written persuasive language?
(This is the "channel" comparison referenced in the title).

METHODS

The study involved 84 fourth-graders and 70 eighth-graders in a middle-class, suburban public school district, randomized into three groups. One group at each grade level engaged in role-playing as guided by a facilitator, a second group received instruction in persuasive writing, and the third group received no specific instruction. The researcher facilitated the role-play sessions and also provided the writing groups their persuasive writing instruction.

The researcher had the role-play groups (one at grade four and one at grade eight) enact three different situations in which they were trying to persuade the school principal to: (1) have a regular school party; (2) let students decide all of what they would study; and (3) make a change in the school cafeteria. The students in the role-play groups paired up and took turns as persuader and listener over 35 minutes for each of the three issues. All pairs in the grade-level experimental group role-played at the same time, and each pair's conversation was audiotaped. After a role-play, each student wrote a letter intended to persuade the real school principal about the issue the group had enacted. In parallel fashion, the students in the two instruction groups received 35 minutes of *instruction* in persuasive writing before each of the three writing exercises. All six intervention and writing episodes across the two grade levels took place over a span of five weeks. Data for the study came from the written letters and also from tape recordings of the student role-playing activities. A third group received no instruction.—J.C.

RESULTS

The core finding of this work is that role-playing in partners is more effective than a lecture with examples when it comes to impacting persuasive letter writing. Finer but interesting points in the results differed at the two grade levels. For fourth-graders, role-playing is significantly more effective than either instruction or no treatment at all. For eighth-graders, role-playing is more effective than no treatment in inspiring persuasive writing. Role-playing also scores higher than direct instruction for eighth-graders, but the difference is not statistically significant. Fourth-graders who received direct instruction in this experiment actually performed worse than the students who received no instruction.

When comparing the role-playing sessions with student writing, both eighth- and especially fourth-graders produced more persuasive assertions orally than in written form. And in an interesting twist, fourth-graders remember and use their role-playing partners' persuasive assertions in their written letters more than twice as often as their own persuasive assertions made during role-playing.—J.C.

CONTRIBUTIONS TO THE FIELD

This study provides evidence of the value of role-playing as a pre-writing activity. In addition to the finding itself, this study contributes through its focus on writing skills as an outcome of dramatic activity, a topic little touched in this Compendium.

The effect of role-playing on persuasive writing (as opposed to that of direct instruction or no treatment) is found to be stronger for fourth-graders than for eighth-graders (where the effect is nonetheless positive). This conclusion fits a larger pattern of results in the Compendium, where the effects of dramatic enactment are greater for younger subjects just about wherever age is tested as a factor.

And another result teased out by Wagner's work might stir some interest in yet another little-researched subject within drama and education—namely, the impacts of listening to fellow role-players in a dramatic situation. After students tried to be persuasive to an assigned role-playing partner, they tended to use their partner's arguments in subsequent writing more frequently than their own arguments.—J.C.

COMMENTARY

This study presents important findings regarding the value of role-playing as a pre-writing activity in the classroom and suggests that in addition to addressing the qualities of good writing directly, a teacher should take advantage of verbal role-playing activities in building writing skills.

This study lays the groundwork for further work on the relationship between oral and written skills. The study looks at the impact of role-playing on a specific type of writing only. Further research could examine whether extended training in role-playing could help students to build writing skills that are retained and transferable to other types of writing not the subject of this research.

The observation that role-playing in this study had more impact on the observer (the receiver of a persuasive statement during role-play) than on the direct actor (the student making a persuasive statement during role-play) signals an under-researched issue in this Compendium. Most of the studies we discuss concern the effects of dramatic action (particularly role-playing of one sort or another) directly on the actor. Wagner is interested in such main effects, to be sure, but the observation of effects on listeners evokes a relatively untapped but potentially vast area of formal inquiry by educational or developmental researchers. This is the impact of dramatization or theatrical presentation on audiences.—*J.C.*

CONTRIBUTIONS TO THE FIELD

The methods used by the author might be adapted by arts researchers attempting to do careful studies of the effects of arts instruction or arts skills on student performance in another subject area, even the one chosen by the author— persuasive writing. There is benefit in reading how other fields develop studies, how controls are established across complex variables, and how student products might be coded and analyzed. Studies in arts education would benefit from the same kind of care that this author takes. However, the actual conduct of this research and its results are not directly related to the arts, though in the operational definition of the author, "role-playing" is the same thing as "drama."—*T.B.*

COMMENTARY

Role-playing is a tool derived from interpersonal communication practice and is closer to "simulation" than dramatic art. The author describes those aspects of role-playing that are closest to art—pretense, lack of verisimilitude—as detracting variables in the students' efforts to create persuasive written communications, and her effort is to remove them by making the simulation as realistic as possible. At the same time, "persuasive writing," as it is used by the author, is closer to rhetorical and political writing than to writing as art. The author, in fact, contrasts it with "expressive" writing.—*T.B.*

"This study provides evidence of the value of role-playing as a pre-writing activity."

drama

53

STUDY NAME: "You Can't Be Grandma; You're a Boy": Events Within the Thematic Fantasy Play
Context that Contribute to Story Comprehension
AUTHORS: Peter A. Williamson and Steven B. Silvern
PUBLISHED: Early Childhood Research Quarterly, 1992, 7: 75-93

Research Question

What behaviors within fantasy play activities (playing out roles and scenes in a story) contribute to the development of story comprehension skills among kindergarten children?

METHODS

This study enlisted 120 randomly chosen children in six kindergarten classrooms, stratified for gender balance. As part of the selection process, children were randomly assigned to 30 groups of four. Thus each classroom provided five groups for the study. Each group heard, discussed, and re-enacted two familiar tales on days 1 and 2, and an unfamiliar tale on day 3. The children were videotaped during their dramatizations so that the researchers could categorize and analyze children's behaviors during re-enactment. The first two re-enactments were done to help build reliable measures of children's actions within fantasy play—such as "metaplay"—which could prove important to the research.

The third day's activities constituted one experimental test. After this day's story re-enactment, the children were tested for three achievements: recall of that day's story content using a criterion-referenced test; story recall, using storytelling; and story sequencing, using a picture arranging task. The storytelling assessment instrument also provided a measure of oral language competence of the subjects. (Recall that one aim of the analysis was understanding the influences of factors *within* dramatic enactment on story comprehension; thus all subjects used dramatic enactment on day 3).

Another comparison condition was established on the fourth day, when the children were read an unfamiliar story that they did not subsequently re-enact. They were tested using the same measures as applied on the third day. In addition, six days following the final story dramatizations, the children were tested again for story recall, story sequencing, and the use of productive language—both for their enacted story (day 3) and for their "heard" story (day 4). (A small bias favoring recall of the "heard" story seemed present in this design, since its recall was measured after five instead of six days). The analysis used data from these measures to assess if types of play within story enactment contributed to sustained recall, first regarding the enacted story and second, to recall of the "heard" story. The researchers focused particularly on instances of children's stepping out of role to ask questions or to direct other players. They refer to this as "metaplay," which generally indicates active concern about the progress of the re-enactment fueled by higher-order thinking about what's going on. The analysis also observed additional characteristics of behavior during the fantasy play sessions (such as the use of nonverbal skills and social problem-solving).

The authors used regression analyses to test for significant contributions of within-dramatization factors to story comprehension skills. This is an important feature of the study, because regression allows for assessment of the independent contributions of different factors to specific outcomes. The study explored differentiating aspects of child behavior during dramatization that might contribute relatively more or less to story comprehension. The authors included measures of productive (oral) language ability obtained when children re-told stories. These measures provided indicators of existing verbal ability differences among the subjects and thus comprise an important control variable.—*J.C.*

RESULTS

This study shows that acts of directing by young players (or metaplay) during re-enactment and productive language capacity of children make substantial independent contributions to story comprehension independent of differences in verbal ability. This result holds for both the immediate-recall tasks and for the delayed-recall tasks. In comparison, play or dramatization itself (in contrast to the no-dramatization condition of day 4) contributed relatively little to story comprehension. Children's play direction behavior contributed four times the predictive power for reading comprehension of enactment versus no enactment. It thus appears that the meta-behaviors of stepping out of role, thinking about, and questioning or attempting to direct players are associated with higher levels of story understanding.

Through controlling for verbal ability, the authors observe that metaplay is not simply evidence of verbal achievement—in addition to their dispositions to "direct," children in metaplay show more social skills and social problem-solving ability than children not engaging in metaplay.—*J.C.*

CONTRIBUTIONS TO THE FIELD

This study makes a strong contribution to the understanding of how engagement in dramatic activities can improve story comprehension for kindergartners. The study specifi-

cally examines fantasy play and finds that "metaplay," a key element of fantasy play, seems to have an especially strong and positive impact on children's story comprehension. "Metaplay," as suggested by the study's title, refers to instances where children go beyond simply acting out a fantasy play and step out of a role to act as the play's director or to raise questions about the play. This study finds that the effect of metaplay is stronger than the act of dramatization versus no dramatization.—J.C.

COMMENTARY

This study serves to accentuate a component of Jennifer Ross Goodman's 1990 study of fantasy play and literacy development (also summarized in this Compendium). Both studies present very rigorous designs, among the strongest reported in the drama research summarized in this Compendium. Both look within dramatic play to find specific elements that influence verbal-related skills, rather than using dramatic play as a whole as a lone predictor of child development. More specifically, this study finds that stepping out of role to offer verbal or nonverbal direction associates with increased understanding and sustained recall. Another important observation in this study is that effects on story recall were measured while controlling for the subjects' general oral language skills. This is one of few studies in drama using multiple regression analysis to provide controls within its analytical framework.

One implication of this study extends across the literature generally investigating classroom drama and reading comprehension. This is that drama-involved groups usually outperform non-drama groups. An open question remains based on this study: to what degree is the advantage assigned to drama groups carried by their members who engage in meta-cognitive activities (such as stepping out of role to "work on" a dramatic production)? This study provides a suggestion that drama alone versus no drama is not a large contributor to developmental advances; gains go to the more thoughtful and critical members of the cast.—J.C.

CONTRIBUTIONS TO THE FIELD

Building on a rich research tradition that shows that thematic-fantasy play improves comprehension as well as other cognitive abilities, this study breaks new ground. For the first time we have evidence that it is metaplay (or directing peers in the acting out of the story) that is critical in comprehension. Williamson and Silvern wisely conclude that it may well be the better comprehension that accounts for the metaplay rather than the other way around, but because the two go together, metaplay needs to be fostered and valued in early childhood programs.—B.J.W.

COMMENTARY

The findings of this study make a good case for giving children ample opportunities to design for themselves ways to act out stories they hear. As they direct their peers, they will be demonstrating or improving their comprehension of the stories in a way that is natural and enjoyable for them. Children who act out a story together without teacher tuition take charge of their own learning, and find the interpersonal and cognitive challenges engaging.

In light of the current pressures on preschool and kindergarten teachers to teach children to read at younger and younger ages, these findings provide an antidote to the pervasive and misguided emphasis on teacher-directed drill on lower-level skills of reading in preschool and kindergarten. Such an emphasis may result in better scores on standardized decoding tests, but in the long run the children may well be victims of the so-called third-grade slump in reading comprehension that characterizes far too many children. Children who engage in thematic-fantasy play in relation to stories, including those that represent their own ethnic or cultural heritage, are learning to pay attention to what matters most in reading—comprehension.

This study also has implications for children's writing skills. Much of recent research on the acquisition of writing skill has focused on the role of peer interactions and role-playing. Children who write with engagement and energy are usually talking with their peers and shaping their stories to entertain them (similar behaviors to those exhibited during fantasy play), and children who have opportunities to act out the stories they write (as they do through thematic-fantasy play) increase their enthusiasm for writing. Writing demands other qualities that are similar to those required for thematic-fantasy play, for example, constant shifting from high-level decisions to low-level mechanical concerns. In writing, children must "shift" between decisions regarding the overall gist of what a piece of writing is about to lower-level concerns such as spelling, or, in the case of very young children, even the formation of the letters themselves. In thematic-fantasy play, children must shift from high-level decisions as to who could play the grandmother back to the low-level miming of picking a flower.

Williamson and Silvern were appropriately cautious in their interpretation of their study and have suggested ways further studies can be designed to explore causality between metaplay, comprehension, and IQ. It would be appropriate to embed this study in Vygotsky's concept of a zone of proximal development (ZPD). He implies that what Williamson and Silvern call thematic-fantasy play provides a ZPD because of the process of symbolization. To effectively use symbols, a person must be able not only to know that this object is a purse, but for his or her purposes now it is Little Red Riding Hood's basket. In other words it is both the thing itself and what it symbolizes. The child who can explicate this distinction is in a ZPD where objects can be assigned an arbitrary function, just as a reader eventually has to learn to assign a particular squiggle on a page to a speech sound. Children who comprehend stories have to know simultaneously that their caregiver who is reading the harsh "All the better to eat you with, my Dear" is not about to devour them, but, rather, is choosing to play the role as a wolf in order to heighten the pleasure of the story. Expressive oral reading has this in common with thematic-fantasy play. A child can remain a trustworthy friend to his peers and also become a big bad wolf in a drama.—B.J.W.

"...stepping out of role, thinking about, and questioning or attempting to direct players are associated with higher levels of story understanding."

STUDY NAME: **The Flight of Reading: Shifts in Instruction, Orchestration, and Attitudes through Classroom Theatre**

AUTHOR: Shelby A. Wolf

PUBLISHED: Reading Research Quarterly, 1998, 33(4): 382-415

Research Questions

Are children's reading comprehension, expressive fluency, and attitudes toward reading affected by a year of periodic dramatic coaching based on texts?

What happens when an academically diverse classroom of 8- and 9-year-olds makes a transition from a traditional "round-robin" reading program to one involving the creation of and performing in a classroom theater where children are encouraged to consider and enlist multiple forms of expression?

METHODS

The subjects of this study are 17 children labeled "at risk" in a remedial third- and fourth-grade classroom. The class included children reading below grade level and children with special needs who until recent policy changes would have most likely been schooled in special education classrooms. Eleven of the 17 children had been retained at some point in their short school careers. The children experienced traditional round-robin reading instruction up to the time of the study. During the one year over which this study took place, the teacher and students transformed their reading program from one that used "traditional" instruction to one in which they worked mainly through classroom theater activities, under the guidance of a visiting expert (not the researcher). The theater instructor worked with the class once a week from mid- December through April. The class was exposed to multicultural trade books, dramatic expression based on these books, and literary discussion. Instead of traditional cycles of reading, hearing others read, minimal discussing, and reading some more, students began to approach their texts through interpretation aimed at performing narratives and excerpts from their readings. The researcher used participant observation, audio recording, and video recording to discern various qualities of classroom life during reading instruction. Particular attention was given to language and action that characterize (1) instructional practice, (2) children's approaches to reading, (3) children's attitudes about reading, and (4) the degree to which children create meaning from text.—J.C.

RESULTS

By the start of the year, the children in this classroom had experienced enough signals that they were special to realize that their specialness was not necessarily a good thing. They had received a variety of "injuries" due to poor reading, labeling, and lack of success in most school activities. The teacher's remediating approach to reading instruction served to further narrow children's opinions of reading and themselves as readers and only increased their dependency on their teacher for anything having to do with reading, including picking up a book. Through classroom theater, however, new reading resources became available to these children, especially peer discussions in which they could argue and negotiate meanings of texts. Amidst the challenge to dramatize, "…children called on background knowledge, blending their understandings into others (sic). They became decision-makers and experts as they interpreted the words and did not simply turn the pages…. Through increased opportunities for practice, the children not only got inside the text but improved their accuracy and momentum." Children expanded their understandings and explored alternative expressions; they began to see themselves as actors, as *expressers*, and for the first time, the author concludes, as *readers.*—J.C.

CONTRIBUTIONS TO THE FIELD

This study offers the field an example of a thoughtful, patient, and long-term inquiry into the life of a classroom over an entire school year. Instead of the more familiar use of treatment and control groups and a one-week research experiment to discern effects, the author in this case participates and observes in a classroom twice per week. A special quality of the resulting report is the very explicit account of how the author grapples with making valid sense of the voluminous notes and hundreds of hours of taped classroom language generated in the study. The sense-making is ably informed by the works of world-leading ethnographers, including Fred Erickson.

The results of this study should also be considered contributions to what we know about drama's roles in academic and social development. The classroom theater transformed students. At first they believed reading was a matter of just decoding story after story. When using classroom theater as a routine in their reading instruction, students took great interest in stories and displayed heightened inclinations to read for meaning and increased interest in the expression and movement involved in stories.—J.C.

COMMENTARY

This study demonstrates the value of what the author calls a "design experiment," one in which the evolution of events in a real classroom engaged in a new instructional model led to the sort of insights we might call "professional knowledge" as much as "research knowledge." However the products of such work might be characterized, the sense the author makes of this experiment should interest researchers, theater specialists, and teachers alike. The value of this work results from the tenacity and perspicacious orientation of the author to "see" what takes place before, during, and after the 10 weeks of in-class drama coaching by an expert. There is rich detail in the reporting, much reproduction of children's dialogue, and a very convincing argument that one can learn valuable things by watching classroom events.

At its center, this study has parallels with Seidel's evaluation of Shakespeare & Company's education program. In that study adolescents taking time and patience to unpack the complexity and richness of the language in a play come to see themselves as a different sort of learner—deeper and more accomplished. An analogous shift in self-perception and sense of achievement visited the much younger academically challenged children in this study.—J.C.

CONTRIBUTIONS TO THE FIELD

This is a very interesting study, richly detailed and embedded in an appropriate theoretical framework of social constructivism. Because of its focus on changes in decoding and comprehension, this study contributes to research in both educational drama and reading pedagogy. The study specifically contributes to the expanding body of research on the effects of improvisational drama and readers' theater strategies on reading in significant ways. It would have been appropriate for Wolf to acknowledge this body of research (for example, the Whirlwind drama study summarized in this Compendium).—B.J.W.

COMMENTARY

The major part of the study focuses on the teacher's reading strategies and the students' responses to them, and beams a spotlight on the contrast the children sensed in their characterizations of *reading* vs. *acting*. The children's understanding of *acting* encompassed expressive intonation in oral reading, an ability every good reading teacher has as a goal. Because Wolf chose to do an in-depth qualitative "design experiment," she was able to capture a thick description of what was going on in the children's understandings and attitudes; her method of inquiry served her well.

The teacher Wolf chose to study was one who believed in and was dedicated to the now widely discredited (as Wolf admits) "round-robin" reading for remedial readers. This teaching method created an extremely sharp contrast between what the children deemed *reading*, and the reader response and interpretation that the theater teacher introduced. Admittedly, the views of the teacher Wolf studied may be more characteristic of teachers of remedial students than teachers of other students, and, if so, this is a sad commentary on the status of reading instruction in remedial settings. What is needed from future research are studies that compare good psycholinguistically sound reading instruction with theater strategies (unlike this one, which is compromised because it seems to contrast *bad* reading instruction with *good* theater techniques). Such a focus might tease out a distinction between reading and theater instruction that are both aimed at some of the same goals, such as fluency, expressive oral interpretation, connecting new with prior knowledge, insight into character values and motives, and reader response. The contrast would probably not be as stark as was found in this study, but such research might show just what it is that theater can do that other instruction *that aims at the same understanding by the students* does not do. It is not clear in this study whether the reading teacher ever wholeheartedly embraced goals beyond accurate decoding despite her obvious enthusiasm for the theater project and her increase in wait time before supplying words. By the end of the year, her major goal narrowed to preparation for the test battery. Hence, the metaphor of flying, but only for a short time, was apt.

Educational policy-makers can use this study to show the value of classroom theater in facilitating an understanding and interpretation of literature that is deep and long lasting. Wolf's findings provide a persuasive warrant for the advocacy of more classroom theater and financial support for training programs and positions in schools for theater experts.—B.J.W.

"Educational policy-makers can use this study to show the value of classroom theater in facilitating an understanding and interpretation of literature that is deep and long lasting."

57

Essay:
Research on Drama and Theater in Education

James S. Catterall

Dramatizing makes it possible to isolate an event or to compare one event with another, to look at events that have happened to other people in other places and times perhaps, or to look at one's own experience after the event, within the safety of knowing that just at this moment it is not really happening. We can, however, feel that it is happening because drama uses the same rules we find in life. People exist in their environment, living a moment at a time and making those decisions which seem reasonable in the light of their present knowledge about the current state of affairs....So drama can be a kind of playing at or practice of living, tuning up those areas of feeling-capacity and expression-capacity as well as social-capacity. Poets do this in their poetry, painters in their painting, writers in their books, and filmmakers in their films.

Dorothy Heathcote, 1975 [1]

Introduction

About 40 years ago, a current surfaced in professional education writing and instructional practice reflecting a new legitimacy of drama and theater in the education of children. We may persist in debating what we want our children to know and be able to do; but when all is said and done, education is at least about preparation for effective living. In this context, and reflected in the writings of the world's pre-eminent classroom drama expert sampled above, we can readily see why some teachers would include dramatic activities in their instructional repertoires. Dramatic conventions offer a safe harbor for trying out the situations of life; for experimenting with expression and communication; and for deepening human understanding—developments devoutly to be desired, all.

Thinking and writing about drama in education in the middle of the 20th century did not involve much professional social inquiry—or research. Rather the deep experiences and up-close observations of teachers and coaches in the schools as well as the trainers of teachers engendered a broad consensus that drama *can teach*. Professional discourse began with such an assumption, and the concerns and divisions among the leading educationists focused not so much on the "whys" of drama in the curriculum but on the "hows." This conversation radiated at its brightest from the United Kingdom, where drama became widely used in the elementary schools as well as a course in the preparation of teachers.[2]

The presence of drama in American schools rests on informal traditions and is dictated largely by individual teacher preferences for engaging the medium. The range is wide—from U.S. teachers making pilgrimages to study with Dorothy Heathcote, to the lone teacher spontaneously organizing a role-playing exercise at the pop of an inspiration, and to entire teaching staffs in schools working in substantial partnerships with local theater companies. The common ingredient is that teachers use drama in their classrooms when they believe it accomplishes something.

The purpose of this Compendium is to report on the nature and extent of our knowledge about that "accomplished something." The lens we have chosen is the lens of scholarly research. This is not because we believe that the only things we can claim to truly "know" come to us through the efforts of formal research. Rather, we seek to check the "knowledge" of experience and intuition with that of more formal processes that examine the effects on human development of drama and theater in educational settings.

Definitions of Drama

Drama and theater in education are carried out in many formats, with many purposes, and in the guise of wide-ranging terminology. A unifying characteristic is the adoption of character roles of one sort or another by learners. Many studies included in the Compendium involve portraying a character from children's literature; some roles emerge from pure fantasy at the prompting of a teacher or coach. Most studies involve groups of children enacting scenarios or complete stories, sometimes with advance planning and sometimes not. These characterizations begin to hint at the general focus across the studies we chose for inclusion—research on drama in education concentrates mainly on young elementary- and kindergarten-age children, an observation to which we return when discussing specific research results.

"Dramatic conventions offer a safe harbor for trying out the situations of life; for experimenting with expression and communication; and for deepening human understanding…"

Research studies do not exhibit much in the way of a standardized vocabulary when they come to identifying dramatic activities. The studies included in the Compendium are no exception and display a diverse array of terms:

1 Dorothy Heathcote, *Drama and learning*. Chapter in Liz Johnson and Cecily O'Neill (Eds.) Dorothy Heathcote, Collected Writings on Education and Drama. Cheltenham, England: Stanley Thornes (Publishers) Ltd. Page 90. (1984). This essay was originally published in 1975.

Classroom drama. This term refers to the use of drama in the school class-room. Such activity is typically directed by the classroom teacher or by students themselves and sometimes engages the assistance or direction of a drama specialist, sometimes the researcher.

Creative drama. This term refers primarily to improvisational activities in which the participants invent fictional situations and characters of their own choosing, with or without specific guidance or context-setting by teachers or coaches. "Creative" refers to the inventiveness children bring to the dramatic act, orchestrated or spontaneous. A word of caution: improvising may smack of chaos in the canons of cognitive research. But as a process of invention and expression, improvisation proves of great interest to scholars of language development and reading, and with good reason, on the basis of what we report here.

Fantasy play. "Fantasy play" situations involve very young children (e.g., 5-year-olds) who tend to bring a great deal of inventiveness to the portrayal of even the most tried and true children's stories and characters.

Thematic fantasy play. "Thematic fantasy play" is dramatization guided by a theme or themes.

Is this art?

Given the description of the "field" offered and implied just above, it may be worth pausing before going forward to visit and dispense with this awesome question. As the details of the Compendium's studies in drama unfold, it is reasonable to ask what the fantasy role-playing of a 5-year-old or the classroom enactment of "Rumpelstiltskin" has to do with "art." We face the same issue raised by both Terry Baker and Karen Bradley in their overviews of studies in the visual arts and dance for this Compendium. Baker, for example, asks what elements of educational activity are to be considered an instance of the visual arts. We too faced challenges in deciding what to include as a study in the dramatic or theater arts.

We found no explicit conception of drama as an *art form* in the research studies we surveyed or in the studies we summarize here. And we found no empirical research into the academic and social effects of what was termed or even might be called the *theater arts* of any sort. This means that a great many things potentially relevant to a discussion of the academic and social effects of drama and theater do not enter the present conversation, especially things having to do with formal theatrical production and performance. Our focus necessarily became foundational. We indicated above that role-playing was the common ingredient of the studies we included in the Compendium. This flowed from our main criterion in selecting studies for the drama section: we chose studies where individuals adopt "roles" for one reason or another—characters other than themselves. The characters may be fictional or real, present time or historical, planned or improvised. The rationale for our main selection was that role-playing lies at the heart of the dramatic form, however infantile its execution and regardless of where baby steps might lead from an artistic point of view.

What did we find?

Here we turn to several characterizations of the studies we include in the Compendium. We first describe the targets and designs of the studies. Then we describe the main findings of the research.

Who is studied? Among our drama studies, there is a large concentration of research focused on young children. More than half of the drama studies included in the Compendium involve children between preschool and fourth grade as subjects, and a third of the studies focus on children in first grade and earlier. Only three studies involve middle schoolers, and three involved high school students.

Study designs. Nearly half of our studies are true experiments, which use random assignment of subjects to experimental and control groups. Most others construct comparison groups in rigorous ways. None depend solely on pre- and post-measures, although these are included among the data collection activities of some studies.

Studies in drama and learning, like many studies published in developmental psychology, tend to be of short duration. About a third of our studies were conducted over a matter of days. About half involved experiments or interventions lasting a few weeks or less. Three of our studies lasted a full school year, and one spanned two school years. This distribution reflects the field of experimental research in child development. Long studies are expensive, extended classroom studies may tax the patience of regular teachers, and children leave their initial schools and in doing so deplete experimental and control groups. And the academic context of the work of researchers again constrains the field: researchers publish more frequently when their projects occupy shorter periods of time. This is generally unfortunate, because there is good reason to value investigations of long-term

"Research shows consistent positive associations between dramatic enactment and reading comprehension, oral story understanding, and written story understanding."

2 In the presence of such convictions, we might ask why *elementary* schools and not all schools? The oeuvre of scholarly writing about classroom drama concerns young children. We see scarce reference to the use of classroom drama in secondary school classrooms, perhaps because disciplinary specialist teachers see little place for drama in their instructional repertoires. While drama's detachment from high school physics might be expected, its potential use in studies of literature and history seems evident on the basis of research with young children, if not self-evident. A tradition of *theatre in education* (TIE) much involved with secondary schools in the UK is the subject of much writing but has produced no empirical research that we could find.

programs because of their potentially deeper impacts and longer-lasting effects.

Focus on narrative understanding. The Compendium's studies point to scholarly interest in a rather narrow cluster of academic domains in which drama shows consistent positive impacts. Although the dramatic or role-playing activities and the designs of experiments vary considerably, the effects gauged in a strong majority of our studies lie in the area of narrative understanding. Research shows consistent positive associations between dramatic enactment and reading comprehension, oral story understanding, and written story understanding. Research on the youngest subjects, 5-year-olds, kindergartners, and first-graders attends almost exclusively to story understanding. Having enacted a story (as opposed to having the story read to them in many designs), children are better able to retell the story, to recall more details, and to put the story's elements in the correct sequence. Studies of older children show impacts of drama on reading skills, persuasive writing ability, narrative writing skills, and children's self- conceptions as learners and readers.

The younger the better? Several studies teased out an important phenomenon within the range of impacts of drama on young children. In the four studies testing for effects across age groups, the impacts of role-playing were consistently stronger for the younger or youngest participants. Effects for kindergartners and first-graders exceeded effects on second- and third-graders; and in one study (Wagner), effects of enacting stories on writing for fourth-graders were larger than effects for eighth-graders.

This observation might help to explain the concentration on young children as subjects in published drama studies. If dramatic enactment has its most profound effects on younger children, this is where studies will find effects and attain publication. And this will reinforce a focus on younger children by other scholars who tend to build on each other's work rather than push into unestablished territory.

Why such concentration on reading and language? We might expect studies of drama to be drawn to reading and story domains because dramatic activity has substantial traffic with the spoken and written word, and dramatic acts almost by definition involve "narrative" or story—"movement in time," as Heathcote likes to say. But more is probably involved. Reading and language development (along with mathematics) are the coin of the realm in the educational research community. Because they are considered most central, academic journals and book editors no doubt favor research in reading and verbal expression—and of course researchers must publish in these outlets. Another influence lies on the technical side of the education research business: reading and language development benefit from established instrumentation for measuring results.

"Straying" into research on social developments such as empathy and tolerance or self-conception as examples of touted benefits of engaging in drama generally requires the invention of custom measures, observations requiring judgments and inferences on the part of researchers, or the much-criticized use of self-reports. As a group, these measures are "softer" than test scores, and scholars using them must go to extra lengths to demonstrate the validity of their measures—as some Compendium authors manage to do. In our studies, inquiries into social development are often supplements to studies of reading and language.

Social development. Drama is typically a social, interpersonal event. But research has given comparatively little attention to potential social developments. Among our studies there are some exceptions: de la Cruz finds enhanced social development among special education children including generally courteous behavior, ignoring distractions, and acceptable use of free time. Fink's extensive study suggests that drama activities for kindergartners lead to development of what he calls "social perspectivism,"—the ability to comprehend the various social relations inherent in a situation involving a cluster of individuals. In another study (one of only three high school studies we include), Horn explores self-confidence and self-image among at-risk secondary students who became engaged in playwriting. And Schaffner shows evidence of lasting attention to moral dilemmas as a result of drama.

Another of our studies should be considered especially strong with respect to its reach into the complex worlds of academic, emotional, and social development. This is Seidel's assessment of the programs of Shakespeare & Company carried out between 1996 and 1998. This work is strong because it investigated a high-quality and extended program and because of its intensive methods of documenting the program's functioning and impacts. This study shows that Shakespeare's plays can be particularly effective because of their lifelike complexity. The complexity of issues and emotions in the plays promotes, "word-by-word, emotion-by-emotion, thought-by-thought investigation of meaning," at least when teachers and learners choose to devote time to such an approach and to these ends. The step-by-step approach of Shakespeare & Company invites those who study Shakespeare to go deeply into their own experience, which is linked directly to all types of learning.

Seidel's study documents the impacts of Shakespeare & Company's summer teacher training and fall student productions not only on the understanding and interpretation of Shakespeare's plays but also on acting and stage direction skills. The study illustrates a whole approach to teaching and learning that has implications across a wide spectrum of educational situations.

Unpacking drama

Research in drama, like research in most types of interventions, often simply compares drama-involved groups to non-involved groups. We see this in many studies included here. Our studies also show that qualities within or accompanying dramatic activity are important contributors to the effectiveness of role-playing. One such factor comprises various acts of getting out of role to direct, suggest, and/or discuss aspects of what is transpiring during a dramatic portrayal. Directing and suggesting during rehearsal or performance are indicative of meta-cognitive activities and are evidence of engagement and concentrated thought. Whatever effects a study measures are usually more pronounced for children expressing active concern for how things are going. Another productive activity surrounding dramatic enactment shown in one study (Schaffner) is the value of formal reflection by participants after a dramatic enactment. In the case of this study, de-briefing and discussion drew children into explorations of interpersonal relations and moral values in what they had just performed.

> "Heathcote's list implies an attractive agenda for research on drama in education because it delves into promising outcomes that have never been put to formal tests."

Podlozny's meta-analytic review also identified studies in which the influence of elements within the classroom influenced results for participants. Her analyses indicate that using a structured plot contributes to story understanding, reading achievement, and writing achievement. She found leadership, in contrast to the few studies included here, to have influence in some domains and not in others. She found leadership to impact oral and written measures of story understanding, but not to affect general reading and writing achievement. Interestingly, the meta-analysis indicates that dramatic activities using a mix of structured and non-structured plots produce the largest effects on oral language development. We conclude generally that awareness and promotion of specific child behaviors within drama, such as critical thought, questioning, opportunities for direction, and formal reflection, may be important to consider when designing dramatic enactment programs.

Transfer

Transfer refers to learning in one situation and context that produces capabilities and dispositions or inclinations producing effective performance in a different situation and context. Transfer is a central question explored across this Compendium, not just in the drama section. Does learning in art engender skills or dispositions, which in turn enhance academic or social development? We approach the larger questions regarding the transfer embedded across the entire Compendium in a separate essay within this volume.

Four of our studies show some evidence of transfer from drama activities. DuPont found that comprehension of text promoted in drama contributes to comprehension of text generally. Fink found that using imaginative play in facilitated experimental conditions associates with generally higher imaginative play subsequently. Horn finds that the writing involved in a drama experiment with struggling high schoolers cultivated general habits of mind during the year the class spent conceiving, writing, and producing a play. The disposition cultivated in this case was the general habit of seeking additional resources in order to write more effectively (specifically, using school and public libraries; turning to peers). This habit of mind is in short supply across student populations from grade 1 through graduate school, by all known assessments.

What is overlooked in available drama studies?

Since the discussion above indicates that the studies included in this Compendium tend to a relatively narrow focus and cluster at the early elementary level, it should occur to readers that a great deal of territory within drama and education remains unexplored. One obvious void is the lack of attention to older students. Researchers have aimed few experiments or inquiries at the higher grades, as noted above, probably due to such influences as the educational psychology community's bias toward basic and early developments of children and the relative prevalence of classroom drama in the elementary classroom. And teachers may be much less inclined in middle school and high school to involve drama or dramatic play in their academic teaching repertoires because of their concentrations on academic specialties regarded as having little to do with play.[3]

An unquestionable omission in the body of work on drama presented here is substantive attention to many potential outcomes beyond reading and language development. The foremost candidates among these would seem to be any learning that results from the interpersonal and intra-personal qualities of assuming characters and interacting to perform narrative scenes. Theater professionals have long concentrated on the importance of character study in order to perform genuinely on stage or in film. Learning about characters with worldviews, beliefs, and assumptions different from one's own would be expected to lead to skills or traits valuable generally such as increased empathy and understanding of others' views—a student's personal character affected by studying dramatic characters.

3 It is worth observing that professional scientists, mathematicians, and even historians typically characterize an important component of their work as play—the structured but unfettered exploration of ideas. This is not a typical quality of secondary school approaches to learning and instruction, where the curriculum embraces the results of historical play—breakthroughs, inventions, molecular structures, persons, and dates—rather than on creating ideas.

A scan of our studies produces practically no references to theater. The entire world of theater in education—visiting troupes specializing in thematic production and discourse, school theater societies and productions, the annual school musical, the local children's theater company—benefits from no empirical research that managed to work its way into our files. We know very little on the basis of research about the effects of dramatic presentations to audiences generally, or about impacts on either the performers or the audiences in the case of school productions.[4] Explanations are suggested above, including the fact that the older age groups involved in theater do not fall into the sights of reading development researchers. But surely elements of oral language development are involved in theater performance, as may be psychological developments of performing regularly on stage (such as self-confidence and esteem).

Conclusion

We could close this essay with a familiar refrain, "We'll have to leave such untested questions up to future research." And because we did not find these questions addressed in the vast literature considered for the Compendium, they do point to promising subjects of future inquiry. We can do added service to the topic by returning to the world that began this essay—the realm of professional knowledge. And once again to Dorothy Heathcote, whose compelling claims for drama comprise a tantalizing menu for future research.

Heathcote articulated what amounts to an inventory of "guarantees"—what she believes will happen when teachers use drama thoughtfully and effectively in their classrooms. The promised effects of drama she has culled from a lifetime of role-playing and observing teachers and students using drama touch on most subjects within the academic and social agendas of our schools. These "guarantees" are:

1. Making abstract concepts concrete.
2. Teaching a narrow fact so that it is fully learned—placed in a context for added meaning.
3. Introducing artifacts so that children are curious about them and experience them at a significant level—an important quality of any learning.
4. Inducing students to reflect on experience and see what they have in common with other people.
5. Opening doors to curriculum areas students might fear to venture into, including science, mathematics, and literature.
6. Giving students freedom coupled with responsibility.
7. Clarifying values.
8. Developing tolerance for a variety of personalities and ideas.
9. Showing students how they can stay with something they don't like, perhaps geometry or Tennyson's poetry, to a point of accomplishment.
10. Increasing students' vocabularies and helping students develop a finer control of rhetoric through interactions with others.
11. Bringing classes into situations that will increase their social health.
12. Helping students discover that they know more than they thought they knew.
13. Leading students to the real world more clearly in light of what they have learned in an imagined one.
14. Helping students capture more of what is implicit in any experience. That is, dramatization encourages probing into the meanings of terms, the use of words in the context of action, the nature of human relationships and individual motivations—and more generally encourages reflection on experiences and what one is learning from them.

This list of promises reflects the drama professional speaking to educators and to learners. In reading through its elements, we can say that the drama studies in this Compendium have made a sortie or two into the hearts of these claims with profit to show for the effort. It also appears, on the face of things, that this inventory would receive widespread acceptance as a set of developmental goals. In addition to the aims it suggests for our children, Heathcote's list implies an attractive agenda for research on drama in education because it delves into promising outcomes that have never been put to formal tests. Succeeding in even a small part of this agenda would amply expand the state of research-based knowledge about drama in education on hand today.

4   When we say we know little or nothing on the basis of research, we need to be clear. These issues are not addressed in the studies selected for the Compendium. This does not imply that these questions have never been asked by researchers or that efforts of researchers have never shed a ray of light on them. We may have excluded studies relevant to theatrical production based on our criteria of design and validity; and we may simply have missed deserving studies in our search.

multi-arts

STUDY NAME: **Using Art Processes to Enhance Academic Self-Regulation**
AUTHORS: Susan M. Baum and Steven V. Owen
PUBLISHED: Paper Presented at ArtsConnection National Symposium on Learning and the Arts:
New Strategies for Promoting Student Success, New York, February 22, 1997

Research Questions

Do artistically talented students use more self-regulation strategies (such as paying attention and persevering) when they are in classes that integrate the arts with academics than when they are in traditional classes?

Do they learn more academic content in arts-integrated lessons?

Do they show gains on standardized academic tests as a result of learning in arts-integrated classes?

METHODS

Fourth-, fifth-, and sixth-grade students from New York City classrooms participated in an observational study. The students were talented in music, theater, or dance and were participating in a talent development program in their particular art form provided by ArtsConnection. The students were also in classrooms in which the arts were integrated into the regular curriculum, and in which the teachers were involved with ArtsConnection staff development.

Students were observed as they were taught the same academic content in two different formats—a traditional format without the arts, and one in which the arts were integrated. Observers documented the use of the following self-regulatory skills: paying attention, persevering, problem-solving, self-initiating, asking questions, taking risks, cooperating, using feedback, and being prepared. Students were also given a content-based quiz after each lesson.

Test scores in reading and mathematics were examined over a three-year period for a separate pool of students. Three groups of students were compared (no information was given about how many were in each group):

Young Talent Academic Group: Students participating in the Young Talent Program arts instruction and who were achieving on or above grade level in school. These students were presumably enrolled in classes that integrated the arts.

Young Talent at-Risk Group: Students participating in the Young Talent Program who were at risk academically, especially in reading. These students also participated in MAGIC, a program that also used the arts to support academic instruction in a manner similar to the arts-integrated classes.

Control Group: Students who were not participating in the Young Talent Programs in the arts, and who presumably were not enrolled in classes that integrated the arts with the curriculum.—*E.W.*

RESULTS

Self-regulation. Significantly more self-regulatory behaviors were seen in the lessons in which the arts were integrated into the curriculum than in lessons with straight academic instruction, as shown by correlated t tests, $p<.001$.

Content learning. Content learning in the arts-integrated vs. non-arts-integrated lessons in the same sample of students was examined via t tests. No significant differences were found for one lesson ($p = .26$). For the other lesson, students in the non-arts lesson did better than those in the arts-integrated lesson, a difference that almost reached significance ($p = .07$).

Reading scores at the outset of the study were highest for the Young Talent academic group and lowest for the Young Talent at-Risk group. While students in the control and Young Talent academic groups showed fairly steady performance over the three years, the Young Talent at-Risk students showed marked improvement in the third year (conclusions drawn from inspection of the graphs).

The extent of teacher training in arts-curriculum integration predicted reading scores for the at-risk students (with a correlation of .44).

Math scores were not enhanced by the arts program. But it should be noted that the arts in this program were integrated with the language-based curriculum, not with mathematics. At the beginning of the study, math scores were highest for the Young Talent academic group, and lowest for the Young Talent at-Risk group, as shown by an ANOVA main effect of Group, $p <.001$. All three groups gained in math over three years, as shown by a main effect of Time, $p<.001$. Neither of the two Young Talent groups, however, gained more than the control group.—*E.W.*

CONTRIBUTIONS TO THE FIELD

This study is notable as one of the first to look at whether students show more self-regulation in arts-integrated classes, and because it examines the effect of the arts on academically at-risk children.

The study found that artistically talented students engaged in more self-regulatory behaviors during classes in which the arts were integrated into the lesson. But they did not learn more in such lessons than in traditional ones.

When artistically talented but academically at-risk students were involved over the course of three years in arts training, learned in arts-integrated classrooms, and participated in an additional program that used the arts to support academic classes, they made greater gains in reading than did a control group. In math, their gains did not exceed those of the control group, though this is not surprising since the arts in the program were integrated with the lan-

critical links

guage-based curriculum, not with mathematics.—*E.W.*

COMMENTARY

It is not clear why the at-risk students showed significantly greater gains in reading (compared with the control group) than did the students who were not at risk. It may be significant that the arts programs received by the two groups of students were not identical. Future research should compare both types of children in identical arts programs. Another possibility is that the at-risk students showed more reading gains because they initially lacked self-regulatory skills and hence were more helped by the arts-integrated classrooms. This hypothesis could be tested.

We cannot conclude from this study that the improvement in reading by the at-risk students was a result of enhanced academic self-regulation. If this were the case, students should have showed gains (exceeding the control group) in mathematics as well.

Future research should investigate whether these findings generalize to students not selected for artistic talent.—*E.W.*

CONTRIBUTIONS TO THE FIELD

This study's contribution to arts education research is its attention to the potential of the arts to serve as intermediaries in the learning process. That is, the study suggests that the academic value of the arts may reside as much in the ancillary behaviors and attitudes they encourage as in their direct effect on content acquisition. In this case, artistically inclined students seemed to self-regulate (a global term that encompassed several attention-related behaviors) themselves more in arts-integrated lessons than in "traditional" lessons (i.e., those without the arts involved). The researchers explore why—or why not—such integration might influence content and skill acquisition in other disciplines.—*D.C.*

COMMENTARY

In order for this study, and others like it, to have a high degree of significance for schools, it would have to explore in more detail the differences among the arts programs the different groups of students in the study experienced. Such probing might explain better why the researchers saw the results they did and would offer readers a clearer understanding of the researchers' definition of arts integration. The term "arts integration program" is much too broad to serve as a variable for a study. Instead, it is a category under which a host of specific practices gather. For research on arts integration like this to have the potential of having significant implications for education, the various implemented forms of arts integration will have to be illuminated brightly.—*D.C.*

"Significantly more self-regulatory behaviors were seen in the lessons in which the arts were integrated into the curriculum than in lessons with straight academic instruction."

multi-arts

STUDY NAME: **Learning In and Through the Arts: The Question of Transfer**
AUTHORS: Judith M. Burton, Robert Horowitz, and Hal Abeles
PUBLISHED: Studies in Art Education, 2000, 41(3): 228-257

Research Questions

Do children in arts-rich schools show more creativity and higher academic self-concept than those in arts-poor schools?

Do arts-rich schools have different climates than arts-poor schools?

METHODS

Fourth-, fifth-, seventh-, and eighth-graders in 18 public schools were studied (2,406 students). These students attended a diverse group of schools ranging from ones in which the arts were integrated into the curriculum by classroom teachers to ones in which the arts were taught as separate subjects by specialists. Some schools were "arts rich" while others were "arts poor" as defined by "quantity of arts programming." Students were given a questionnaire about how many in-school arts and private arts lessons they had received. Students were given a figural creativity test (the Torrance), a self-concept test, and a questionnaire about their arts experiences (which led to a score for how much arts instruction each child had received in school, and a score for amount of arts lessons outside of school). Teachers were given three questionnaires: they were asked to rate their perceptions of students' imagination, risk-taking, expression, and cooperative learning; they were asked to rate their school climate in terms of affiliation, student support, professional interest, achievement orientation, formalization, centralization, innovativeness, and resource adequacy; and they were asked to rate how much they integrate the arts, collaborate with arts specialists, and use the arts as a tool to teach other subjects.—*E.W.*

RESULTS

66

Children in the top quartile of high arts exposure (both in and out of school), as determined by the student questionnaire, were compared with those in the lowest quartile of arts exposure. High arts children scored higher on the figural creativity test (no statistics reported). High arts children scored higher (from teacher ratings) on expression, risk-taking, creativity-imagination, and cooperative learning. A regression analysis showed a significant relation between (a) amount of arts instruction and teachers' efforts at arts integration and (b) teachers' perceptions of students' risk-taking. High arts children scored higher on several subscales measuring academic self-concept. Teachers and principals in schools with strong arts programs believed that the presence of the arts led their teachers to be more innovative, to have increased awareness of different aspects of students' abilities, and to find school a more enjoyable place to work. Arts-rich schools scored higher (from teacher ratings) on affiliation, student support, professional interest, teacher innovativeness, and resource adequacy, and lower on achievement orientation, formalization, and centralization, suggesting that arts-rich schools are not top-down structures.

Qualitative measures (interviews, observations) in five schools were also conducted. Teachers in the arts-rich schools were more likely to speak of their students as able to express ideas and feelings, take risks, and to focus their perception. Drama teachers spoke of drama as leading to empathy and ability to collaborate.—*E.W.*

CONTRIBUTIONS TO THE FIELD

This study is a rich qualitative and quantitative study of the relationship between arts education and creative thinking, academic self-concept, and school climate. It found that students in arts-rich schools scored higher in creativity and several measures of academic self-concept than students in schools without that level of arts. Arts-rich schools also had more innovative teachers (as measured by teacher self-reports).—*E.W.*

COMMENTARY

This study is correlational in design and does not allow causal conclusions. It is possible that children in arts-rich schools scored higher on creativity and academic self-concept as a direct consequence of their experiences with the arts. However, since the arts-rich schools had more innovative teachers, it is equally possible that teacher innovation is the factor that led to greater creativity and academic self-concept.

Future research should investigate whether schools that grant the arts a central role attract better, more innovative teachers as a direct consequence of the new role for the arts. More study is needed on how arts in the schools can alter the school climate. Measures beyond self-report are needed, such as systematic objective observation of teaching in arts-rich vs. arts-poor schools by trained observers blind to the hypothesis.—*E.W.*

CONTRIBUTIONS TO THE FIELD

This study connects arts integration to two important stu-

> "Teachers and principals in schools with strong arts programs believed that the presence of the arts led their teachers to be more innovative..."

dent outcomes—creativity and self-concept—and one significant school outcome—school climate. Such research is important because it lends ammunition to the "value-added" justification for including the arts in the everyday curriculum.—D.C.

COMMENTARY

The study explores aspects of students' school performance that have logical connections to arts-related activities. In other words, the study identifies the arenas of academic and personal performance in which arts researchers should think about staking their claims (i.e., creativity and self-concept)—as opposed to defining such performance more narrowly in terms of standardized tests geared to specific disciplines.

While the study is correlational in design (among certain student and school variables), it has important implications for how arts-rich schools become so. It not only details what the participating sites did to integrate the arts but also offers an account of how the arts-rich schools managed to establish their approaches. Thus, the study situates arts-related practices in the schools' contexts, a feature that arts education research has to incorporate into study designs if the findings are going to have meaning for educators.—D.C.

"...students in arts-rich schools scored higher in creativity and several measures of academic self-concept than students in schools without that level of arts."

STUDY NAME: **Involvement in the Arts and Success in Secondary School**
AUTHOR: James S. Catterall
PUBLISHED: Americans for the Arts Monographs, 1998, 1 (9), Washington, D.C.

Research Questions

Do students in middle and high school who have high involvement in the arts perform better than those with low arts involvement on a variety of academic indicators? And if so, does this relationship hold up when the sample is restricted to students from the lowest SES quartile in the United States?

METHODS

Data from 25,000 students participating in the National Educational Longitudinal Study (NELS) of 1988 were examined for this study. Students in the NELS study were followed from eighth to tenth grade. Students were classified in terms of arts involvement both in and out of school. Arts involvement was measured by number of arts courses taken, number of out-of-school arts courses taken, and attendance at museums outside of school. Students in the highest quartile of arts involvement were compared with those in the lowest art-involvement quartile on a variety of academic measures. Academic measures for eighth graders were: grades in English; scores on composite standardized tests; dropping out of school by grade 10; boredom in school half or most of the time. Academic measures for 10th-graders were: composite standardized test scores; reading scores; scores on a test of history/geography/citizenship. Tenth-graders were also assessed in terms of community service involvement and television watching.

A sub-study was conducted on 6,500 students from the lowest SES quartile. The identical methods and measures were used.—*E.W.*

critical links

RESULTS

The relationship between arts involvement and academic achievement was positive in both eighth and 10th grades for the broader sample of 25,000 students cutting across all SES levels. High arts students earned better grades and performed better on standardized tests. High arts students also performed more community service, watched fewer hours of television, and reported less boredom in school.

When high vs. low arts-involved students from the lowest SES quartile were compared, the same findings emerged. High arts students again earned better grades and scores, were less likely to drop out of school, watched fewer hours of television, were less likely to report boredom in school, had a more positive self-concept, and were more involved in community service.—*E.W.*

CONTRIBUTIONS TO THE FIELD

This study demonstrated that students who are highly involved in the arts in middle and high school in the United States perform better on a variety of academic measures than do students who are minimally involved in the arts. This positive association for the general student population between arts involvement and academic achievement was found in a focused study of students from the lowest SES quartile in the United States.—*E.W.*

COMMENTARY

This study is important because it demonstrates that the correlation in the United States between choosing to study the arts and achieving well academically is not a function of SES. However, because this study is correlational in design, it does not allow us to conclude that arts involvement *caused* academic achievement to rise. It is equally possible that high academic students choose to involve themselves in the arts, perhaps because they come from families that value academic achievement as well as the arts.—*E.W.*

CONTRIBUTIONS TO THE FIELD

This study draws on data collected from more than 25,000 students contained in the 10-year database of the National Educational Longitudinal Survey (NELS). The author examines the relationships between students' arts participation and their achievement, attitudes, and behavior in secondary school. The analysis establishes a significant correlation between eighth- and 10th-grade students' arts activities and their grades, standardized test scores, staying in school, and being interested in school. This study lays the groundwork for a viable rationale for arts inclusion in the schools. Although the researcher is unable to demonstrate cause and effect, the research shows that an arts-rich learning environment is associated with a host of positive educational measures. The study (or more accurately put, the secondary analysis of the NELS data), therefore, connects the arts to academics and to other "value-added" outcomes.—*D.C.*

COMMENTARY

Studies that highlight the association between arts education and student achievement offer a direction for further study, and, thus, have considerable imaginative value for arts education researchers. However, further study is absolutely necessary in order for correlational designs to have substantive meaning for educators. In addition to being unable to tease out which way the effects flow—from arts involvement to achievement or achievement to arts involvement—the study is unable to illuminate the types of arts experiences students are having. More arts involvement is apparently desirable, according to the study, but almost certainly the richness and texture of this involvement matter, as do the characteristics of the programs in which the students participate. Empirically unpacking the nature of the involvement and the programs will make it possible for the primary findings to have actual implications for enhancing the role of the arts in education.

This study is additionally important because it mines the available database for a variety of measures of academic performance, from content and skill acquisition to general attitudes. Despite the fact that American educational policy is consumed with test scores, the arts may have more logical and actual connections to other aspects of students' academic and everyday lives. To exclude the latter from consideration and focus only on test scores in research would be to force the arts to justify their presence in schools by reaching goals they are potentially ill suited to accomplish.—*D.C.*

"High arts students...earned better grades and scores, were less likely to drop out of school, watched fewer hours of television, were less likely to report boredom in school, had a more positive self-concept, and were more involved in community service."

69

multi-arts

STUDY NAME: Involvement in the Arts and Human Development: Extending an Analysis of General
Associations and Introducing the Special Cases of Intensive Involvement in Music and
in Theatre Arts
AUTHORS: James S. Catterall, Richard Chapleau, and John Iwanaga
PUBLISHED: Unpublished Manuscript, The Imagination Project, Graduate School of Education and
Information Studies, University of California at Los Angeles, April 1999

Research Questions

Do high school seniors who have been highly involved in the arts at least since eighth grade perform better academically than students who have not been involved in the arts? And what academic achievement patterns are associated with intensive involvement in theater and in music?

METHODS

Students were classified in terms of how involved they were in the arts. Arts involvement was measured by number of arts courses taken, number of out-of-school arts courses taken, and attendance at museums outside of school. High arts-involved students were ones who had been involved in the arts since the eighth grade. The top quartile of students in terms of arts involvement (n=3720) was compared with the lowest quartile (n=3720) on a variety of academic tests.—E.W.

RESULTS

As in the earlier finding by Catterall (1998) with eighth- and tenth-graders, the students with high arts involvement scored higher on standardized test scores than those with low arts involvement. More specifically, 57.4 percent of high arts-involved students scored in the top two quartiles of standardized tests, compared to only 39.3 percent of low arts-involved students; 56.5 percent of high arts students scored in the top two quartiles in reading, compared to 37.7 percent of low arts students; and 54.6 percent of the high arts students scored in the top two quartiles of history/geography/citizenship tests, compared to 39.7 percent of low arts students. This same relationship was upheld when the lowest SES quartile of students was examined, though the difference was smaller in magnitude. Specifically, 30.9 percent of low-SES high arts students scored in the top two quartiles of standardized tests, compared to only 23.4 percent of low-SES low arts students; 32.9 percent of low-SES high arts students scored in the top two quartiles in reading, compared to 23.6 percent of low arts students; and 30.7 percent of the low-SES high arts students scored in the top two quartiles of history/geography/citizenship tests, compared to 30.4 percent of low-SES low arts students.

Students who report consistent high levels of involvement in instrumental music over the middle and high school years were also performing better in math at grade 12. Specifically, 48 percent of high-SES students in orchestra or band performed at the highest levels in math, compared to 38.6 percent of high-SES students not involved in music. Even more striking was the group difference for the low-SES students: 33.1 percent of low-SES students in orchestra or band performed at the highest levels in math, compared to only 15.5 percent of low-SES students who were not involved in music.

Students who report sustained involvement in theater performed better in reading (about 48 percent of drama students scored high in reading, compared to 30 percent of students not involved in drama). Low-SES students in theater also showed greater gains in self-concept than did low-SES students not in theater (as measured by questions about how much they value themselves, their abilities, and their achievements). The differences between the groups were small, however (about 53 percent vs. 48 percent, as indicated by the authors' charts), and the authors caution that the differences would not be considered significant. Finally, low-SES students in theater responded more tolerantly to two questions about racism than did low-SES students not involved in theater, suggesting that students involved in drama have higher levels of empathy and tolerance than do those not involved in drama. The self-concept and empathy/tolerance comparisons were carried out only on the low-SES quartile.—E.W.

CONTRIBUTIONS TO THE FIELD

This study extends the 1998 study also by James Catterall examining the relationship between arts involvement and academic achievement among 10th-graders who had been involved in the arts since at least eighth grade. The findings show that in the United States, high school seniors who have been highly involved in the arts since middle school do better academically than those who have not been involved in the arts. In addition, those involved in music do better in math than those not involved in music; and those involved in drama do better on verbal and social measures than do those not involved in drama. This study is impor-

tant because it demonstrates that the correlation in the United States between choosing to study the arts and achieving well academically is not a function of SES.—E.W.

COMMENTARY

This study, like the 1998 study by Catterall (this volume) is correlational in design. Thus we cannot conclude that it is arts study that causes academic achievement, nor that music study leads to math achievement, nor that drama study leads to verbal and social improvement. We cannot know whether students with particular academic and social profiles gravitate to the arts, or whether the experience in the arts molds the academic and social profiles that these students exhibit.—*E.W.*

CONTRIBUTIONS TO THE FIELD

This study found that those students who are most involved in arts experiences also perform better in standardized measures of academic performance, achieve higher grades, and are most engaged in school. The comparative performance of high-arts-involved students increased from eighth- to 12th-grade, supporting the view that effects build over time. Significantly, the relationship between arts involvement and academic performance was found to be robust for students from low-socio-economic (SES) backgrounds. Further analysis found relationships between involvement with music and math proficiency for low-SES students. Relationships were also found (for low-SES children) between drama involvement and various academic and social outcomes, including development of reading proficiency, self-concept, motivation, empathy, and tolerance. These findings are consistent with other studies examining general cognitive and social effects from arts learning, and suggest areas for further study.—*R.H.*

COMMENTARY

The authors demonstrate that children from high-SES families are much more likely than low-SES children to be consistently involved in arts activities or instruction. Economically disadvantaged students often do not have the same opportunities to become engaged in the arts. But, as this study shows, those low-SES children who *do* participate in the arts also perform better, academically and socially. Therefore, from a policy perspective, it may be beside the point whether arts instruction is the fundamental *cause* of increased performance, or instead is one of the *conditions* of superior schools. Either way, economically disadvantaged youngsters should have the same opportunities as others to partake in the benefits that the arts can bring, through either improved academic performance or improved schooling. From a research perspective, these findings indicate a direction for further, more focused study on relationships between specific artistic domains, and academic and social outcomes.—*R.H.*

"Significantly, the relationship between arts involvement and academic performance was found to be robust for students from low-socio-economic (SES) backgrounds."

71

multi-arts

STUDY NAME: **Chicago Arts Partnerships in Education (CAPE): Evaluation Summary**
AUTHORS: James S. Catterall and Lynn Waldorf
PUBLISHED: In E. Fiske (Ed.), Champions of Change: The Impact of the Arts on Learning. The Arts Education Partnership and The President's Committee on the Arts and the Humanities, Washington, D.C., 1999

Research Question

Do low-SES urban public school students in schools that integrate arts and academics (through partnerships with teachers and artists) perform better on standardized tests than do students who are in schools that do not integrate arts with academics?

METHODS

This study examined the effect on test scores of the Chicago Arts Partnerships in Education (CAPE). CAPE schools brought artists and teachers into partnerships so that they could develop curricular units in which an art form was integrated with an academic subject. Fifty-four percent of the teachers reported having developed one arts-academic integrated unit, while 24 percent reported having created four to five such units. Units typically lasted four to six weeks. Typically it was a visual art form integrated into a reading or social studies unit. The reading and mathematics test scores for CAPE schools were compared to scores from other Chicago public schools at grades 3, 6, 8, 9, 10, and 11.—E.W.

RESULTS

In none of the comparisons made between CAPE and control schools did the control schools perform better than the CAPE schools.
Math: In the K-8 grades, 40 comparisons were made between CAPE and control school math scores. Of these, 16 comparisons showed CAPE schools increasing their lead over control schools. At the high school level, 8 out of 12 comparisons showed CAPE schools increasing their lead.

Reading: In the K-8 grades, 40 comparisons were made between CAPE and control school reading scores. Of these, 25 showed CAPE schools increasing their lead over control schools. At the high school level, 7 out of 12 comparisons showed CAPE schools increasing their lead.

The differences between CAPE and comparison students were statistically significant in elementary school, especially by sixth grade. No differences were found at the eighth-grade level. While the differences still favored the CAPE students at the high school level, these differences were not statistically significant.—E.W.

CONTRIBUTIONS TO THE FIELD

This study demonstrated that the low-SES children in arts-integrated schools perform better than those in comparison schools in terms of test scores. The difference was statistically significant at the elementary level, but not at the high school level.—E.W.

COMMENTARY

This study reports an interesting but difficult-to-interpret finding. We cannot know whether the relative advantage of the students in the arts-integrated (CAPE) schools is due to the role of the arts in their schools or whether it is due to the energizing effect of any new kind of program (the Hawthorne effect). Future research should compare CAPE students to students in another kind of new and exciting program that does not involve the arts.

"...low-SES children in arts-integrated schools perform better than those in comparison schools in terms of test scores."

This kind of comparison would allow us to determine whether academic performance rises because of the energizing effects of a new program that teachers believe in, or whether their performance rises only as a function of the arts.—E.W.

CONTRIBUTIONS TO THE FIELD

The study establishes an association between low-income students' academic achievement and their attending schools that have arts integration activities. In doing so, it compared student performance in schools that had established partnerships with local artists and arts agencies with those that had not created such connections to the arts community.—D.C.

COMMENTARY

Studies such as this are unable to demonstrate cause and effect and, thus, must be regarded as more suggestive than conclusive. Nevertheless, the study makes two equally important intellectual contributions: its suggestion that artist and teacher partnerships can have a positive effect on student achievement and its attention to what these partnerships look like and how the role of the arts evolves in participating schools. With respect to the former, the use of comparison sites adds an element of rigor to the study, but without knowing extensive details about what these comparison schools were like it is impossible to determine whether the two groups of schools were organizationally and educationally similar other than in terms of arts integration. Regarding the form the arts partnerships took, the authors demonstrate clearly (1) that there are a variety of ways of enacting partnerships, (2) that some of these ways may be more effective than others, and (3) that school context, organizational arrangements, and leadership all play a role in sustaining and expanding the partnerships over time. This is the kind of research that bridges the gap between educational justifications for integrating the arts into everyday school instruction and how to actually afford the arts such a meaningful role in schools.

Additionally, the study addresses other "student outcomes" that the arts might influence, such as workplace and life skills. The study argues that there appears to be a stronger connection between incorporating the arts into schools and student benefits in these two arenas than solely in content acquisition in certain core subjects.—D.C.

STUDY NAME: **The Role of the Fine and Performing Arts in High School Dropout Prevention**
AUTHORS: N. Barry, J. Taylor, & K. Walls
PUBLISHED: Center for Music Research, Florida State University, Tallahassee, FL, 1990

Research Question

Is involvement in the arts associated with lowered high school dropout rates?

METHODS

Forty students at risk for high school dropout were surveyed (including both students currently in high school and some who have graduated but were once thought to be at risk). Students were asked why they had decided to stay in school. In addition, 11 at-risk students were observed in arts classes as well as academic classes for their degree of attention and engagement.—*E.W.*

RESULTS

Of the 22 students who responded that they had seriously considered dropping out of school, six (27 percent) said that they stayed on because they liked the arts or music, and three (14 percent) said they stayed because they wanted to go on in an arts field. Thus, nine out of 22 (41 percent) said that something about the arts kept them in school. Thirty-six of the students were asked directly whether participation in an arts course affected their decision to remain in school. Of these, 30 out of 36 (83 percent) said yes. When asked how the arts course influenced them, seven (23 percent) cited job opportunities.

Field observations of 11 at-risk students revealed that in arts classes, these students were "on task" 84 percent of the time, as compared with only 73 percent of the time in non-arts classes. Thus, it appears that academically at-risk students are somewhat more often engaged in arts classes than in academic classes. Whether such engagement is what led students not to drop out cannot be determined from this study.—*E.W.*

CONTRIBUTIONS TO THE FIELD

This study investigates an important potential social outcome of arts education—decreasing school dropout.—*E.W.*

COMMENTARY

A small group of students at risk for high school dropout who remained in school often cited the arts as a reason for their decision not to drop out.

This study did not actually measure dropout rates, but rather asked students who did not drop out about their reasons for remaining. Future research should compare dropout rates for two groups of equally at-risk students, ones who do participate in the arts and ones who do not. Ideally these students should be "assigned" randomly to arts or non-arts. Without random assignment, the research remains subject to the self-selection hypothesis: perhaps students who are motivated enough to choose to take the arts and who then become engaged in these classes are also those who are motivated enough to remain in school.

Future research might compare arts vs. sports to determine whether for some students, engagement in the arts keeps them in school, while for others, engagement in sports is what motivates them to stay.—*E.W.*

CONTRIBUTIONS TO THE FIELD

The Arts and High School Dropout Prevention project was designed to investigate arts teachers' claims that students identified as at risk of dropping out of school attend and perform well in their classes. Employing a qualitative approach, the study also reveals some of the aspects of effective arts classes that support increased engagement, motivation, and learning. While limited by sampling issues, as noted by the authors, this study makes a contribution to our understanding of how to document and describe the processes and outcomes of arts education.—*J.W.-D.*

COMMENTARY

High school arts teachers often anecdotally describe the positive effects of arts education as a strategy for engaging and motivating their "at-risk" students. These teachers assert that students identified as potential "dropouts" participate in positive ways in their art classrooms and develop artistic skills and expression when they are struggling in other classes. Arts teachers also claim that the attendance records of at-risk students in their classes are good, in comparison with some other classes. Given national concern with persistent high school dropout rates, early identification of students at risk of dropping out and effective strategies for keeping them engaged are of critical interest. Research identifying the key characteristics of effective arts teaching and supportive arts learning environments may provide strategies and resource recommendations that will generalize to other contexts. The study described in this report, conducted by members of the Arts and High School

Dropout Prevention project at the Center for Music Research at Florida State University, was funded by the Florida Department of Education in an effort to systematically document the relationship between participation in the arts and students identified as "at risk" of dropping out of high school.

The at-risk students participating in this study attribute their motivation to stay in school to their arts experiences. The authors report a number of factors related to the arts that positively affected the motivation of these students, including the development of and/or opportunity to exercise keen interest in the arts, a context that promotes the constructive acceptance of criticism, a positive and supportive social environment where it is safe to take risks, meaningful opportunities to achieve artistic and creative satisfaction, and the development of self-discipline. Observations of these students in both their arts and non-arts classes revealed the strategies and motivational techniques the arts teachers of these students used, including hands-on involvement to promote on-task behavior, individualized instruction coupled with positive reinforcement, recognition for creative accomplishment, genuine and personal interest in the students, maintaining high standards and expectations, and a quality arts program with adequate offerings, supplies, equipment, and staff.

While the design of this study has limitations with respect to sampling, it provides evidence that qualitative data, in this case open-ended survey responses, provide compelling and rich descriptions of the social processes of arts classrooms and the effects of quality arts experiences for students—which in turn may illuminate those characteristics of these contexts that are central to student engagement, motivation, and learning. The authors recommend that future research attend to the sampling issues of a very limited sample size and participant self-selection.—*J.W.-D.*

"This study investigates an important potential social outcome of arts education—decreasing school dropout."

75

multi-arts

STUDY NAME: **Arts Education in Secondary Schools: Effects and Effectiveness**
AUTHORS: John Harland, Kay Kinder, Pippa Lord, Alison Stott, Ian Schagen, Jo Haynes, with Linda Cusworth, Richard White, and Riana Paola
PUBLISHED: National Foundation for Educational Research (NFER), The Mere, Upton Park, Slough, Berkshire SL1 2DQ, UK, October 2000

Research Question

Does involvement in the arts in secondary school boost general academic performance?

METHODS

This was primarily a qualitative study based on student self-report, but it also included a quantitative examination of the relationship between arts concentration in secondary school and performance on national exams. The study had four major components:

Case studies of five secondary schools in the United Kingdom with strong arts reputations were carried out through annual interviews with two cohorts of students (79 each year) who were doing well in arts courses, interviews with arts teachers and school officials, and observations of arts classes. The focus of the interviews was on what students perceived the effects of arts education to be.

Performance on the United Kingdom's national academic exams (GCSE) was reviewed for 27,607 students from 152 schools in the 11th year of secondary school, particularly looking at the amount and type of each student's arts study.

Questionnaires were administered to 2,269 11th year students in 22 schools to relate exam performance, prior attainment scores, and key stage 3 national test results.

Interviews of a small group of school administrators were conducted to probe their views of the impact of the arts on school culture.—E.W.

RESULTS

Case study results showed that students performing well in at least one art form reported a wide range of positive effects from arts education. While the most common effect reported was direct learning of skills in the art form, students also reported that arts classes resulted in enjoyment, relief of tension, learning about social and cultural issues, development of creativity and thinking skills, enriched expressive skills, self confidence, and personal and social development. Thus, students clearly perceived that the arts facilitate their personal and social development.

Responses differed by art form. Students reported that dance increased body awareness, visual art led to expressive skill, drama enhanced empathy, and music promoted active listening. The authors conclude that to achieve the full effect of the arts, students need exposure to each of the individual art forms. Learning gains from exposure to one art form are not the same as gains from exposure to another art form, and the arts should not be treated as "one" unified discipline.

Results from the larger sample found no evidence that the arts boost general academic performance as measured by performance on the national exams taken at age 16. For instance, when social class and prior attainment were controlled, there was no relationship between performance on the English or mathematics exams, on the one hand, and taking two years of visual art, drama, or music, on the other hand.

School administrators reported that the arts affect the school culture by encouraging a positive, cohesive atmosphere. They also acknowledged that school improvement depends on many factors besides the arts.

The authors conclude that the arts should have equal status with all other subjects, and also that the different art forms should have equal status in the curriculum.—E.W.

CONTRIBUTIONS TO THE FIELD

This is a large-scale and well-designed study conducted in the United Kingdom. The qualitative self-report component of this study demonstrated that secondary school students who are doing well in the arts and attending schools strong in arts believe that the arts contribute to their personal and social development. School administrators believe that the arts have a positive effect on school culture.

However, the quantitative component of this study demonstrated that after controlling for social class and prior achievement, no relationship existed between studying the arts in secondary school and performance on national exams. Thus there is a disconnect between what students and administrators believe and what the tests show. Future study should examine whether the positive effects attributed to the arts by students and administrators are illusory, or whether they in fact exist but are simply not captured by the national exams.—E.W.

COMMENTARY

This study reveals an interesting contrast between the administrators' perceptions that the arts facilitate academic achievement and the finding of no relationship between arts study and exam performance. This result directly contradicts the

U.S. findings that students with more arts courses score higher on the SAT. This discrepancy can be understood if we recognize that both results are correlational, not causal. Perhaps in the United States academically strong students are advised to study the arts, while in the United Kingdom, academically strong students are not encouraged to study the arts.

The primary outcomes reported by arts-strong students were social ones. Future research should examine social outcomes using objective measures to determine whether students' self-reports of social benefits are borne out in empirical measures of social outcomes.—*E.W.*

CONTRIBUTIONS TO THE FIELD

Conducted in the United Kingdom, this ambitious, large-scale, mixed-methods study addresses the central question of whether or not arts education positively affects the general academic performance of secondary students. The researchers also attempt to identify the critical factors and processes that may promote such effects and use these factors as the basis for policy recommendations to promote best practices in arts education. Commissioned by the United Kingdom's National Foundation for Educational Research (NFER) and funded by a range of corporate, arts-related, and governmental organizations, this work was part of a national effort to balance advocacy of the arts with a rigorous examination of "the effects and effectiveness of arts education." This is an executive summary of the much larger comprehensive report generated by the research team.

Implemented over several years, this research was conducted in two phases—a set of school-level case studies and an analysis of national test data. The findings from the case studies conducted in five exemplary secondary schools provide evidence that, in general, the arts do promote a range of positive learning and social outcomes for students. Positive outcomes for schools, employers, and local communities are also described. In the case study schools, selected for their robust arts programs, students, teachers, administrators, and members of the larger school community share a strong belief that the arts make a significant contribution to students' personal and social development, provide opportunities for learning that generalizes to other contexts and content areas, and have a positive effect on school culture. However, when compared to these qualitative results the analysis of test results appears contradictory. Drawn from a larger, more representative sample of schools, the test data reveal no significant relationship between involvement in arts study and improved exam performance. These statistical results also appear to contradict findings from research conducted in the United States that reveal a strong relationship between involvement in arts study and high SAT scores. According to the authors, intervening factors such as the quality of arts teaching or differences in cultural patterns of participation may help explain these discrepancies.—*J.W.-D.*

COMMENTARY

A real strength of this research is its design—employing both qualitative and quantitative methods allows contrasting results to emerge and points to the need to reconsid-

er the results of purely correlational studies. The qualitative results provide a meaningful context for the more limited findings generated by the quantitative analysis. The positive personal and social effects and the kinds of arts skills and knowledge described by participants in the qualitative component of this research are echoed in numerous other studies and point to the need to develop appropriate means of capturing these outcomes and affording them the status in school that society affords them once students are out of school.—*J.W.-D.*

> "…students performing well in at least one art form reported a wide range of positive effects from arts education."

STUDY NAME: **Living the Arts Through Language and Learning: A Report on Community-Based Youth Organizations**

AUTHOR: Shirley Brice Heath

PUBLISHED: Americans for the Arts Monographs, Washington, DC, November 1998: 2, 7.

Research Question

Do low-SES, at-risk students who are intensively involved in the arts through after-school organizations perform better in school than those who are not so involved?

METHODS

Heath studied adolescents involved in 120 non-school organizations of three types: arts organizations, athletics organizations that also had a strong academic bent, and community service organizations. Forty-eight of the organizations were arts-based. Of these, 32 were primarily drama-based but also involved work in other arts to support drama productions—e.g., music, dance, writing scripts, and scene painting. The remaining 16 organizations focused on visual or musical arts. All of the arts organizations involved students in working toward a public performance or exhibition for the community. All of the organizations had a strong community service orientation.

Students were observed over an 11-year period (1987-1998) as they participated in their after-school site. The students came from at-risk homes and schools. In comparison to students surveyed in the National Educational Longitudinal Sample (NELS) in 1990, the arts-involved students came from schools with double the potential for violence. They came from families with twice as much divorce and recent unemployment. And their families were five times more likely than those in the NELS sample to have been recently on welfare.

The students were involved in an after-school arts organization for at least three hours a day three times a week for one full year. Thus, these students made an exceptional commitment of time. All students participated in these organizations voluntarily. Their activities included not only work in their chosen art form but also indirect academic training. For instance, writing and reading were often involved (for example, scripts and gallery catalogues were read and written); math was involved (they calculated travel costs); oral verbal skills were involved (they were involved in verbal critique sessions and learned a technical vocabulary related to their art form); and critical thinking was involved (in their frequent critique sessions, students were asked to think and reason about their work in a quite systematic way). Finally, social skills also were involved, as students sometimes served as receptionists or travel coordinators for their organizations.

One hundred forty-three students in these after-school arts organizations were given a series of questions that also were administered to the NELS sample of 17,000 10th-graders in 1990. The NELS sample served as the control group.—*E.W.*

RESULTS

Students involved in the arts organizations stood out from the NELS control group in a variety of ways. They were:

- two times more likely to win an award for academic achievement
- four times more likely to win schoolwide attention for academic achievement
- four times more likely to participate in a math or science fair
- three times more likely to win an award for school attendance
- over four times more likely to win an award for an essay or poem
- nearly twice as likely to read for pleasure
- over three times more likely to be elected to a class office in school
- over four times more likely to engage in community service
- eight times more likely to win a community service award

The arts-involved students also had higher than average educational aspirations. For instance, in the NELS sample, 62 percent said they would go to college, but in the arts group, 83 percent viewed themselves as college-bound.

The arts-involved students came from families that valued education and that held high aspirations for their children. A higher percentage of parents of the arts-involved students wanted their children to get a higher education as compared with the parents in the NELS sample. And more parents of the arts-involved students often attended school events.

Heath hypothesizes that several key factors in the arts organizations promoted academic success. For example:

- **Achievement ethic.** All the arts organizations had high expectations that were non-negotiable. And all students were made to feel responsible for the final performance or exhibition.
- **School-related activities.** Students participated in a wide range of activities that involved activities connected to school-type work, such as reading (scripts, dance notations, newspapers, brochure, and reviews), calculating costs, and both planning and organizing.
- **Peer critique.** All students participated in continual peer critique and thus were always challenged. In addition, critique is likely to promote fluency with language.
- **Conditional reasoning.** Discussion often took a hypothetical stance (what if we tried this, have you thought of that?).
- **Risk-taking.** The arts organizations value risk-taking and divergent thinking.—*E.W.*

CONTRIBUTIONS TO THE FIELD

This study adds to the body of correlational research showing that students who become engaged in the arts and learn a rather broad range of skills and dispositions through that engagement tend to be students who are academic achievers, before and/or after that engagement. This study strongly extends that body of work to students from lower socio-economic backgrounds and those in more troubled environments.—*E.W.*

COMMENTARY

Because this study is correlational in design, we cannot conclude anything about causality. It is possible that involvement in after-school arts actually fostered the development of cognitive skills and these in turn led to higher academic achievement. If so, this may have occurred because of many verbal activities called for in the after-school arts programs as well as the high achievement ethic in these programs. It is equally possible that the kinds of students willing to engage in nine hours a week of after-school arts are high-energy, motivated students who also do well in academic areas. It is also possible that these students were motivated before joining an arts organization but developed even stronger skills through the arts that increased their academic performance. Only a study with an experimental design could help us choose among these alternatives.—*E.W.*

CONTRIBUTIONS TO THE FIELD

This study makes major contributions to our understanding both of the impact of arts learning experiences on ways of thinking and using language and on young people's habits of participation in other learning contexts, and how to conduct arts research that can adequately capture these kinds of results.—*J.W.-D.*

COMMENTARY

For several decades, much attention has been focused on identifying strategies for improving the academic achievement and encouraging the social and cognitive development of those youth who are typically identified as "at risk" by schools and society. Much of this research has focused on school as the primary environment where the kinds of experiences that foster such learning occur. In a departure from this tradition, these researchers turn their attention instead to non-school environments and nonacademic programs in a 10-year longitudinal national study of low-income students participating in community-based arts programs. In addition to providing evidence that quality community arts programs provide an environment where the goals of improved academic achievement and social and cognitive development are effectively addressed for students in low-income communities, this ethnographic study documents the specific kinds of experiences and the related learning that occurs. They particularly looked at arts learning that carries over into other learning contexts and

arts learning related to language development.

The larger study represented in this summary makes a significant contribution to our understandings of how best to document and describe arts learning that is not captured by limited standardized measures of general academic achievement. If children are to be capable of more than is described by current achievement tests, researchers such as Heath and her associates and others must continue to add to this body of work.—*J.W.-D.*

"This study makes major contributions to our understanding both of the impact of arts learning experiences on ways of thinking and using language and on young people's habits of participation in other learning contexts…"

multi-arts

STUDY NAME: **Do Extracurricular Activities Protect Against Early School Dropout?**
AUTHORS: Joseph L. Mahoney and Robert B. Cairns
PUBLISHED: Developmental Psychology, 1997, 33, 2, 241-253

Research Question

Are students who are involved in extracurricular arts activities less likely to drop out of middle or high school than those who are not involved in the arts?

METHODS

Three hundred ninety-two students (206 girls, 186 boys), recruited in the early 1980s, were followed from seventh to 12th grade and were interviewed annually about extracurricular activities. Students were classified as having had any vs. no involvement in fine arts, athletics, or vocational extracurricular activity. Students were also monitored for early school dropout, defined as failure to complete 11th grade.—E.W.

RESULTS

Sixteen percent (27 girls, 34 boys) were early school dropouts. Students who dropped out of school had participated in significantly fewer extracurricular activities at all grades, including several years prior to dropout. At the middle school level, it was only athletic participation that differentiated dropouts from non-dropouts: those who did not drop out had been significantly more involved in athletics than those who did drop out. Fine arts participation was not related to dropout, nor were vocational activities. At the high school level, there was a near significant effect (p = .08) showing that those who dropped out were more likely to have had *no* involvement in extracurricular arts (27 percent) than to have had arts involvement (7 percent). An even more significant difference was found for those involved in athletics vs. not involved (p<.01), and for those involved in vocational training vs. not so involved (p =.01).—E.W.

CONTRIBUTIONS TO THE FIELD

This study is consistent with the 1998 study by James Catterall (this volume) showing that students who participate in the arts perform better on a host of academic indicators. In this case, the indicator is staying in school.—*E.W.*

COMMENTARY

The authors wisely conclude that school dropout is associated with multiple properties of the individual and the social context, and that it is unlikely that a single cause is involved. They also note that these correlational results provide only weak evidence for causation. We cannot determine whether participation in extracurricular activities protects against dropout, or whether students who are less likely to drop out to begin with choose to involve themselves in such activities. However, it may well be that participation in extracurricular activities helps protect against school dropout for some students. These activities are not limited to the arts but include sports and vocational training as well. Future research should investigate why students choose to study the arts outside of school.—*E.W.*

"...participation in extracurricular activities may provide at-risk students with opportunities to develop positive connections to school and to more conventional social networks..."

CONTRIBUTIONS TO THE FIELD

This study points to positive effects of extracurricular activities on lowering dropout rates for boys and girls, particularly for students with early participation. The greatest impact was observed among those who were at the highest risk for dropout—for those students who had been identified as competent or highly competent during middle school, involvement in extracurricular activities was only modestly related to early school dropout. The authors speculate that participation in extracurricular activities may provide at-risk students with opportunities to develop positive connections to school and to more conventional social networks, and to promote their individual interests, achievements, and goals. The reduction in school dropout for at-risk students was even greater during early high school, a significant trend as it occurs at the point where students reach the age of 16, when school is no longer mandatory, and overall dropout rates typically climb.

An examination of the findings related to involvement in particular activity domains reveals that while in middle school, only participation in athletics was positively associated with a reduced dropout rate. At the secondary level, participation in athletics, vocational training, and fine arts were associated with a reduced rate of dropout.

The study offers guidance to the field by suggesting that future research explore what it is that motivates students to join extracurricular activities and to maintain their participation and what impact participation in school extracurricular activities may have when students leave or complete their formal schooling.—*J.W.-D.*

COMMENTARY

While the authors identify weaknesses in this study related to the limitations of a purely correlational design and an examination of individual factors in isolation of the complex context of social experience, their work raises important equity issues related to access to and participation in activities that may promote school success as defined by high school completion. Given the findings, it is unfortunate that extracurricular participation rates were consistently lower for at-risk students—those students who may very well benefit the most from such involvement.

In order for this study, and others like it, to have a high degree of significance for schools, it would have to explore in more detail the characteristics of the individual extracurricular programs the students experienced. For example, the term "fine arts programs" is much too broad to offer guidance to schools attempting to build effective extracurricular arts programming.

Another suggestion implicit in the study is to better understand why arts have dropout-reducing effects in high school but not in middle schools where athletics have the major connection. Could the arts strengthen their effects on middle schoolers? And is it the case, as the authors ask, that the effect is stronger in high school due to an expanded and more diverse menu of activities? Increasing the diversity of activities offered at the middle school may create a platform for strengthening the engagement of at-risk students.—*J.W.-D.*

81

multi-arts

STUDY NAME: **Does Studying the Arts Engender Creative Thinking? Evidence for Near but Not Far Transfer**

AUTHORS: Erik Moga, Kristin Burger, Lois Hetland, and Ellen Winner

PUBLISHED: Journal of Aesthetic Education, Fall 2000 34 (3-4): 91-104

Research Question

What is the evidence that learning in the arts leads to creative thinking skills?

METHODS

A comprehensive search was conducted for studies investigating connections between arts study and creative thinking. An initial collection of over 2,700 studies was reduced to a set of eight studies based upon stringent selection criteria. To be included, the studies had to: (1) empirically assess the relationship between arts study and outcome measures based upon creative or higher-order thinking, (2) include the visual arts, and (3) have a control or comparison group that did not study the arts. A total of 10 effect sizes were derived from the pool of eight studies.

The researchers performed three meta-analyses on the selected research. The first meta-analysis examined four of the studies that were based on a correlational design. The second meta-analysis synthesized three effect sizes derived from the experimental studies that used verbal creativity scores as an outcome measure. The third meta-analysis combined three effect sizes from the experimental studies using figural (drawing) creativity measures.—R.H.

RESULTS

The meta-analysis of the correlational studies demonstrated a reliable association between study of the arts and performance on standardized creativity tests. Students who study the arts are also more likely to score higher on measures of creative thinking. Effect sizes in the correlational group ranged from $r = .09$ to $.43$ with a mean effect size of $r = .27$. Stouffer's Z and a t test of the mean Zr were both significant ($Z = 8.91$, $p < .0001$ and $t = 3.75$, $p = .03$).

The meta-analysis of the three effect sizes derived from the experimental studies with verbal creativity outcomes produced a mean effect size of $r = .05$. However, this was not found to be significant (Stouffer's $Z = .35$, $p = .64$ and t test of the mean $Zr = .81$, $p = .50$). Therefore, this meta-analysis did not provide evidence of a causal effect of arts study on verbal creativity. This may be due to the short duration of the studies. One study exposed students to the arts for only four days, while the others were four months long.

The meta-analysis of the experimental studies with figural creativity outcomes provided some evidence of a causal relationship between arts study and creative thinking. Effect sizes ranged from $r = .12$ to $.30$ with a mean effect size of $r = .19$. This effect was significant according to Stouffer's $Z = 3.57$, $p = .0002$ but the t test of the mean Zr only approached significance (3.19, $p = .09$).—R.H.

CONTRIBUTIONS TO THE FIELD

Through a meta-analysis of available correlational research, the authors found a significant association between arts study (that includes visual arts) and standardized measures of creative thinking. A meta-analysis of quasi-experimental studies found positive effects on creativity scores based on interpretations of subjects' drawings, although tests of statistical significance produced mixed results. The authors conclude that this indicates "some evidence (although equivocal)" of a causal effect of the arts on figural creativity scores. A meta-analysis of arts study and verbal creativity scores found no evidence of a causal effect. This may be due to the selection of a very small group of studies for analysis that met the filtering requirements of the authors' chosen meta-analytic process, or the short duration of the selected studies.—R.H.

COMMENTARY

This study highlights the limitations of this approach to synthesizing research when applied to a very small set of studies that employ different outcome measures, subject populations, and research designs. Researchers interested in pursuing the promising links between the arts and creative thinking will find the gathered studies a useful starting point for developing appropriate designs. Researchers will also likely determine that approaches other than meta-analysis are most suitable at this time for unraveling these links.

The authors point out that their findings may be limited by the creativity measures used in the analyzed studies. Future researchers should develop new measures and designs to further explore links between the arts and creative thinking. In their discussion, the authors suggest several alternative approaches that researchers should consider, such as more qualitative creativity measures better suited for capturing the kinds of creative thinking that are engendered by the arts. Or researchers could employ open-ended problem-finding activities, based upon the work of Getzels and Czikszentmihalyi.

The authors also point out that their conclusions "are strongly limited by the dearth of experimental studies found." However, they go on to draw a conclusion not readily apparent from their data. The researchers believe they have evidence of near transfer, but not far transfer, because results are stronger on the figural (drawing) creativity test than the verbal creativity test and the students all had some instruction in visual art. Although their interpretation of transfer is one possible explanation for this phenomenon, other explanations are possible. The paucity of available studies and the variability, and possibly validity, of the outcome measures must be considered in the interpretation, as well. This might be a minor point for debate, if the authors hadn't chosen as part of their title "Evidence for Near but Not Far Transfer," thus giving their conjectures the weight of well-validated findings.

It would have been valuable if the researchers had been able to pursue additional analyses of subject populations, research conditions, and outcome measures in the collected studies, as was done in other meta-analyses reviewed in this Compendium. This kind of examination could aid the design of future inquiry while providing practitioners with information to guide program development.—R.H.

CONTRIBUTIONS TO THE FIELD

The value of this work is its careful and comprehensive review of the entire research field (including published and unpublished work), uncovering 2,713 studies that investigated the effects of visual art on creativity.

The research used a widely accepted technique, meta-analysis, allowing the authors to assess the aggregate contribution of multiple studies that employed a range of creativity tests, as well as varied statistical techniques.

The most important contribution, beyond the fact that this is the first systematic review across all the research on this topic, is simply that only a small number of studies met the researchers' standards for acceptable scientific rigor. The clear message is that the field needs more research.

Another important contribution is the finding that there is a modest relationship between visual art instruction and creativity, but that it is difficult to sustain the connection when creativity is expressed in non-art forms (i.e., through verbal conceptual modes). As the authors note, in addition to more studies we need better ways to measure creativity.—B.W.

COMMENTARY

The researchers found only four correlational studies meeting their strict standards of acceptable research that investigated the relationship between visual art instruction and creativity and four experimental studies. The former group of four studies included a total sample of only 1,513 students while the latter group of four studies involved only 758 students. So, in almost 50 years of research only 2,271 students have been exposed to carefully designed treatments on the learning effects of visual art. Such a sample is not much larger than a single comprehensive high school. One obvious response is to decry the lack of carefully designed research in this field. It is also not unreasonable to argue that such a small sample hardly qualifies for such sophisticated quantitative analysis.

The more appropriate point is, perhaps, that the med-

ical/agricultural model upon which these standards for meta-analysis are derived is not necessarily the best one from which to understand the complex endeavor of education or more specifically visual art education. The varied contexts in which instruction is delivered, even from classroom to classroom in the same building, make it difficult to meaningfully transfer successes in controlled experimental settings to messy classrooms.

While it is important to understand the value that visual art can add to students' creativity, it is just as important (if not more so) to know the hows and whys behind visual art contributing to creativity, as well as the organizational and instructional conditions that allow visual art to help students become more successful students. Thus, the 2,713 studies should also be mined to learn what the many qualitative studies could add to these important questions.—B.W.

"Researchers interested in pursuing the promising links between the arts and creative thinking will find the gathered studies a useful starting point for developing appropriate designs."

multi-arts

STUDY NAME: **The Arts and Education Reform: Lessons from a Four-Year Evaluation of the A+ Schools Program, 1995-1999. (Executive Summary of the series of seven Policy Reports Summarizing the Four-Year Pilot of A+ Schools in North Carolina)**
AUTHOR: Nelson, C. A.
PUBLISHED: Thomas S. Kenan Institute for the Arts, 2001, Winston-Salem, NC

Research Questions

The A+ program evaluation addresses four key questions arising from its comprehensive school reform strategy and its belief that the arts are fundamental to how teachers teach and how students learn. The questions are:
* What is A+ and how have schools implemented it?
* What is different for A+ schools, communities, teachers, and students after four years?
* What evidence is there that these effects have been institutionalized?
* What lessons does the A+ experience hold for effective school reform generally?

METHODS

The Executive Summary reports on the methods used by the research team. These include "varied and multi-focused" data collection methods: profile surveys of all A+ schools, parent surveys, student surveys, partner surveys, interviews and focus groups; focused case studies in 10 schools, abbreviated studies of all A+ schools, test scores; school-based data from case studies schools (meeting observations, observation of classroom instruction and performances, guided tours of neighborhoods and communities, shadowing of classroom and arts teachers, document collection of meeting agendas, curriculum materials, planning webs, newspaper articles, budgets, newsletters, school improvement plans, and documentation of research findings and feedback meetings), interviews with program supporters and state policy-makers, and observations of regional meetings and training sessions.

Members of the evaluation team synthesized these data in a series of seven thematic policy reports. The reports deal with Context, History, Creativity, Resilience, Wise Practices, Effects, and Identity. A selection of those reports will be described in the accompanying sections of this review.—*T.B.*

RESULTS

The results of this elaborate project are numerous. As a synthesis of the findings, one might say that this school reform project demonstrates that the arts do contribute to the general school curriculum, to learning for all students, to school and professional culture, to educational and instructional practices, and to the schools' neighborhoods and communities. It is important that these contributions extend beyond what most arts in education programs promise to educators.—*T.B.*

CONTRIBUTIONS TO THE FIELD

It is difficult to overestimate the contribution that the A+ report makes to the fields of school reform and arts in education. The project framed its participation in the debate about the role of the arts in education reform by concentrating on a broader discussion of communities, role groups, school culture or identity, and professional cultures.

The report presents a program evaluation that uses innovative research practices that can be used in other innovative school programs. Many researchers identify the need to develop methods that are appropriate to the contexts of individual programs, but most then settle for the traditional methods of testing and surveys. The sociological and ethnographic methods used for this research allow flexible analysis and are particularly appropriate because each site presents a unique set of instructional, social, and policy variables that would be missed by a single methodology.

The research effort employed a large number of researchers, but the report, as exemplified in the Executive Summary, is finely edited so that the researchers seem to write with one voice. The Executive Summary contributes as a stand-alone summary report to the field.—*T.B.*

COMMENTARY

The A+ program described in this report was a four-year pilot program in 25 North Carolina schools, spread across the state. It is not an arts-in-education program; it is a school reform program that searches for ways that the arts can contribute to comprehensive school change. Although there are partnerships with cultural agencies, and teaching artists employed, the major parts of arts instruction are provided by certified classroom and arts teachers.

The A+ program works from the top down through the Kenan Institute for the Arts and the various agencies of the state of North Carolina. It also works from the bottom up through the parents, teachers, principals, and local community officials related to each participating school. The program features a set of networks that have role-group, regional, and grade-level identities and that meet for summer professional development sessions requiring participation by the entire school community.

The Kenan Institute staff was warned early in the program that the schools would not stay with the project, and many obstacles developed along the way, including an almost devastating new state standards mandate that the report indicates almost brought several participating sites to a halt in their efforts. However, at the end of the pilot project, as a result of flexible program development support that allowed schools to reconfigure their activities to account for and accommodate new standards and testing requirements, only two schools had dropped out. They were replaced by others and by additional schools that wanted to join. In addition, other states have asked Kenan to work with them to replicate the program.

It would seem to an outside observer that the magnitude and complexity of the program would prohibit replication, but such seems not to be the case, as other states such as Mississippi and Oklahoma have begun the process of replicating the project. The report details school-based planning and development activities and the processes by which local conditions and needs shape the adaptation that must be comforting to other school personnel considering replication. It is not clear, however, how the very significant contribution of an intermediate and funding agency such as the Kenan Institute can be replicated in other states.

The most serious questions raised by this report, for this reviewer, derive from the unevenness of the treatment of the arts in the sites. Admittedly the program does not present itself as an arts program. Yet, one would hope that, in the future, the field will be enriched as comprehensive reform efforts such as A+ find ways to reduce the unevenness of arts programming at their replication sites and more fully document ways that strengthening the arts also strengthens the schools.

Accompanying this overall summary are reviews of a sample of the policy reports included in the full A+ report. Individual researchers wrote these, though they were commonly edited, and they reflect some of the unevenness in the report. The research team was very large, especially by arts education evaluation standards. An effort as methodologically complex as this could only be done by a large and diversely skilled staff over an extended period. Though not every program will be able to afford such elaborate support, it is very important to have such models.—T.B.

CONTRIBUTIONS TO THE FIELD

The Executive Summary of the A+ Report provides a review of the comprehensive evaluation of the A+ project and schools. Though every report in the set of A+ evaluation reports makes a significant contribution to the research literature, this summary provides the "take-home message." The "Overview of Key Findings" chart found early in the summary succinctly summarizes findings on the purity of the implementation; the effects of the project on students, teachers, schools, and communities; evidences of the longevity of reform-based changes; and findings that inform the general literature on school reform. The accompanying narrative further defines and describes each finding. The focus of the summary is restricted to (1) commonalities and emerging themes from a study of very diverse reform implementations, and (2) positive outcomes of the reform initiatives. The result of these restrictions is more of an advocacy document than a research report, thus limiting the contribution of the summary to the research literature when taken as

a stand-alone document. Nonetheless, the scientific findings of the evaluation generally paint a positive picture of effective reform, so the summary is a nice addition to the full set of reports when these are read together.—M.S.

COMMENTARY

The A+ evaluation report has many implications for policy and practice. This summary describes the breadth of the positive educational effects of arts-based reform. Educational policy-makers and practitioners who are considering arts-based reform may be enticed by these outcomes, but they would be well-advised to read the entire set of evaluation reports to gain a more complete perspective of the time, effort, and resources that are involved in creating and sustaining reform initiatives. (Section IV of the summary does hint at the demands of sustained reform). Some fundamental characteristics of the successful implementations that emerge from the separate reports include (1) strong administration and faculty commitment to the reform efforts, (2) creative bottom-up development of a strategic plan that emphasizes the local development process instead of external plans and products, (3) a willingness to revise and adapt, and (4) external facilitation and resources that support local efforts. Note also that even the best arts-based reform efforts do not always provide outcomes that are viewed as "successful" by state accountability legislation. Thus, there is still an imperative for educators to advocate for broader expectations and revised definitions of success.—M.S.

"It is difficult to overestimate the contribution that the A+ report makes to the fields of school reform and arts in education."

STUDY NAME: **Placing A+ in a National Context: A Comparison to Promising Practices for Comprehensive School Reform. (Report #1 in a series of seven Policy Reports Summarizing the Four-Year Pilot of A+ Schools in North Carolina)**
AUTHORS: Amee Adkins and Monica McKinney
PUBLISHED: Thomas S. Kenan Institute for the Arts, 2001, Winston-Salem, NC

Research Question

How does the A+ model of comprehensive school reform compare with national standards for school reform as defined by Shields and Knapp (1997)?[1]

METHODS

(Please see the description of study methods included in the review of the A+ Executive Summary).

RESULTS

The policy paper reports that A+ places high on Shields and Knapp's scale of six national dimensions of effective reform practice:

1. Balanced scope,
2. Clear focus on teaching and learning,
3. A long-term time frame,
4. A locus of authority that encourages school-level initiative but embraces support from the top,
5. Opportunities and support for collaborative engagement, and
6. Ongoing professional development directed at instructional change.

The model is judged, by the A+ researchers, to be a promising practice for comprehensive school reform. In the end, however, the researchers emphasize that a single national model does not account for all the variables found in day-to-day school activities and that the work must be operationalized to fit the situation.—*T.B.*

CONTRIBUTIONS TO THE FIELD

By placing the A+ program in the larger context of Shields and Knapp's national standards and practice and by substantiating its place through multifaceted documentation methods, the researchers have moved the program onto the larger playing field of educational change. Because they have taken a wider or broader set of definitions of performance—beyond tests and student grades—to include engagement, expression, and attitudes, they have helped reframe the discussion. To the limited extent that the report documents that arts contribute to the program's overall success, the arts are thereby moved into this larger national discussion, as well. For the field, this movement may be seen as a beginning or rudimentary set of steps, but placed in the context of such a large and long-running reform effort, we might legitimately expect more dramatic movement at the A+ replication sites.—*T.B.*

COMMENTARY

It is not possible to do justice to the richness of the A+ report in a review of this type. The report provides an excellent basis for much more elaborate symposia, workshops, and professional development activities that explore its rich details.

The inclusion of seven strategic school reform elements, including the arts, in A+'s effort to improve the delivery of North Carolina's standard course of study greatly enriches the discussions, vocabulary, and practical tool kit of arts-in-education practitioners. Of these strategies, two-way integration of the arts, more thematic integrated curriculum, increased teacher collaboration, and enhanced partnerships with parents and the community go noticeably beyond the practices of most other arts-in-education initiatives.

The researchers point out that there are elements of the A+ program that go beyond the national standards set by Shields and Knapp. Their national focus on "school-based" reform, for example, is less complex than the A+ work with statewide networks and cultural resources from local communities. The national standards establish a scale for such items as "Experience" and "Collaborative Engagement." Other effective school reform projects place in the middle of the range of scores for these features. The A+ program falls close to the extreme high end of the "Experience" scale. Their experience with complexity led the A+ staff not to abandon their wider scope but to find ways of "grounding it" in their focus on instruction. On the "Collaborative Engagement" scale, A+ falls in the middle, since not all A+ communities have rich external resources with whom to partner. In many of the A+ schools, collaboration was between school personnel and others in the education community.

Changes in classroom instructional practices influenced the students' art performances, according to the researchers. The A+ concept of "informance" was devel-

1 P. Shields and M. Knapp. (1997) "The Promise and Limits of School-based Reform: A National Snapshot." Phi Delta Kappan. 79(4) 288-294.

oped to describe instruction requiring student performance in the arts that was shaped by the academic content of the lessons. The educative character of the performances also helped staff use them for assessments of student learning.—*T.B.*

CONTRIBUTIONS TO THE FIELD

This report illustrates an approach to evaluating school reform that goes beyond the assessment of student outcomes. Though the ultimate goal of such reform is to positively influence student learning, traditional assessments fall short of measuring the breadth of the educational experience. By placing the A+ project on a multidimensional scale of characteristics associated with successful school reform efforts, the evaluators are able to identify the A+ model as a comprehensive mode of reform. In so doing, they shift the emphasis away from school attempts to increase either the frequency or the status of the arts, placing it instead on a picture of how school focus on developing an arts-integrated curriculum can serve as a catalyst for developing broader and richer educational experiences that supplant traditional views of learning in any area, arts or otherwise. This is instructive both for evaluators who seek methods for capturing the evidence of in-depth school change and for school personnel who are considering the scope and potential mediums for initiating such change.—*M.S.*

COMMENTARY

This study has numerous implications for both policy and practice. An overriding theme is that the arts can promote positive school change, but this is most completely accomplished through addressing multiple dimensions of the school. This requires endorsement and subsequent participation by both teachers and administrators. The change is not easy to achieve. In fact, the A+ model suggests that schools be required to invent their methods of change because it is the process of developing and implementing these methods that evokes a change of school culture. External resources exist to support, rather than prescribe, the methods. There are specific policy implications for the six dimensions of scope: focus on teaching and learning, time frame, locus of authority, collaborative engagement, and professional development opportunities. The A+ schools teach much about effectively addressing these dimensions, and some about what does not work in this process. The scope of arts-based reform should be comprehensive enough to challenge the practices of both arts and content area teachers, though it must retain focus on specific goals (arts-infused teaching and learning, in the case of the A+ schools). The focus on teaching and learning is inherent in arts integration, infusion, or immersion, though the A+ model suggests benefits from an extended theoretical framework (exemplified by the focus on multiple intelligences). Like other reform efforts, planning must be for sustained and enduring change, even in the face of challenges (such as the state accountability initiatives focusing on traditional learning that challenged the A+ schools). It is especially important in arts-based school reform that

the locus of authority includes both school-driven development and administrative support at multiple levels. Success of arts education initiatives also depends on multiple collaborative endeavors (e.g., collaboration of arts and classroom teachers, school and community partners, parents and teachers). Substantive change also demands extensive professional development opportunities that focus on encouraging and supporting change (e.g., the summer institutes of the A+ project).—*M.S.*

"This report illustrates an approach to evaluating school reform that goes beyond the assessment of student outcomes."

STUDY NAME: **The A+ Schools Program: School, Community, Teacher, and Student Effects. (Report #6 in a series of seven Policy Reports Summarizing the Four-Year Pilot of A+ Schools in North Carolina)**
AUTHORS: Dick Corbett, Monica McKenney, George Noblit, and Bruce Wilson
PUBLISHED: Thomas S. Kenan Institute for the Arts, 2001, Winston-Salem, NC

Research Question

What effects does the A+ schools program have on schools, communities, teachers, and students?

METHODS

(Please see the description of study methods included in the review of the A+ Executive Summary).

RESULTS

Five effects are described—from across the entire set of survey responses and collected data—as those that most prominently characterize what it means to be an A+ school. They are:

1. The A+ program legitimized the arts as worthy subjects and tools for promoting learning in all students.
2. A+ pushed schools to build new connections between teachers, across schools, and between schools and their communities.
3. A+ schools provided evidence of enhanced organizational capacity to leverage internal structures and manage external environments.
4. In A+ schools arts integration became a central organizing principle that contributed to a coherent arts-based identity.
5. A+ schools provided enriched academic learning environments and opportunities for students.—*T.B.*

88

critical links

CONTRIBUTIONS TO THE FIELD

By identifying a set of five effects that hold up across the A+ report's wealth of documentation information and performance data, the researchers add richness to the information base available to those engaged in both school reform and arts education program development.

By identifying adaptation to obstacles, changing contexts, and political factors as a creative process in school reform, the program contributes to the establishment of situational program evaluation, adding important and specific variables to the research agenda. As the researchers say, there is not one program here "…but rather a collection of A+ 'programs.'"—*T.B.*

COMMENTARY

Treating each of the effects separately in the analysis, the researchers pinpoint specific evidence of impact and then argue that, in spite of the varied situational elements among the schools, these effects can be generalized across the schools and can apply to future school reform efforts. But the finding is weakened by being asserted more than documented. Yet, it seems that there are plenty of examples of evidence relevant to the argument for generalization, even with the variations that occur at each school. It

"The A+ program legitimized the arts as worthy subjects and tools for promoting learning in all students."

may be that there is such a wealth of evidence available that the researchers were unable to manage it all for this report. For example, in the section on institutionalizing the reform effort, they report, "All the schools offered more arts to students than they had at the beginning of the reform." Also, the elements most cited as successfully implemented by the teachers indicate a base for generalization across school reform efforts. The importance of these facts, however, is not stated in relationship to the varied contexts that might have interfered with the implementation.

The report also points out that in-school collaborations were strengthened and expanded in most cases, but external partnerships with colleges, community resources, and businesses were not. The report points to a range of causes, including, for example, the relative absence of such resources in rural communities. The challenge of marshalling external resources in a consistent way for statewide reform efforts has to be confronted by all who would attempt them. The fact that A+ turned more to internal school community relationships—cross-discipline teaching, restructured class scheduling—as solutions speaks to the difficulty of finding solutions in reconfiguring external resources.

Attendance, attitude, and academic performance data (they performed as well as but not better than non-A+ schools in the state) document the impact of the program on students. The data indicate that the effects were equitably distributed across all the students. These results deserve greater emphasis in the field and in the report than they receive, and the topic could well deserve being revisited by the researchers providing more detail and identifying related factors.—*T.B.*

CONTRIBUTIONS TO THE FIELD

A pragmatic view of any educational program maintains that the worth of the program is evaluated based on the program's effects on the target learners. This position is certainly that of policy-makers who demand accountability in exchange for resources. This report (one of a series of reports on the A+ program) describes the effects of the A+ program not only on students but also on teachers, the school, and the community. The report might thus be seen as the heart of the A+ series of reports. As they have done in other reports in the series, and consistent with the goals of A+, the evaluators go beyond a reliance on existing measures of school success in documenting the effects of the program. Multiple sources of observational, perceptual, and achievement data are used to document the five major effects. Together these make the strong case that the A+ program (1) legitimized the role of arts classes and the role of the arts in other aspects of the curriculum, (2) built new connections through increased planning between the faculties within and across schools, (3) promoted changes in organizational capacity that enabled schools to adopt new modes of instruction and promote these efforts within the community, (4) provided a sense of identity at a local level as well as a sense of community in a statewide network, and (5) established increased arts opportunities and enriched learning environments across school curricula.—*M.S.*

COMMENTARY

Taken in sum, the effects described in this report show that the A+ project schools clearly addressed their educational goals and realized the benefits of giving the arts a higher status in the learning process. Whether the true value of the project's initiatives will be accepted and lead to changes in public policy is uncertain. On the one hand, the goals of the North Carolina high-stakes accountability system do not fully recognize the value of expanding educational goals beyond achievement in a few selected subjects. On the other, the A+ initiative was designated as a valid reform effort at both the state and federal levels and the state added A+ funding to the budget. Advocacy efforts should stress that this study documented cultural, ecological, and instructional improvement in areas that are not typically assessed, without compromising those areas that are. Indeed, even those subjects that are the focus of state accountability efforts may be benefiting. As the faculties in the A+ schools understand, additional and alternative assessment tools will be needed before the full impact of broad "whole child" educational reforms are regularly documented.—*M.S.*

multi-arts

STUDY NAME: **The Arts in the Basic Curriculum Project: Looking at the Past and Preparing for the Future**
AUTHOR: Michael Seaman
PUBLISHED: Unpublished Evaluation Report, College of Education, University of South Carolina, Columbia, S.C., 1999

Research Question

Did the Arts in the Basic Curriculum (ABC) project affect test scores in non-arts subjects?

METHODS

The Arts in the Basic Curriculum project (ABC) began in 1987 in South Carolina. This program was founded on the belief that the arts are important in themselves and also that they increase student learning potential, complement learning in other disciplines, and establish a foundation for success in school and lifelong learning. The program includes art specialists (artists in residence) and the development of state arts standards. This evaluation study sought to describe in depth the ABC schools.

Interviews of principals, arts and classroom teachers, and students were conducted in the ABC schools, and observations were made. Interviews and observations were used to describe the program in depth. Standardized test scores were collected in order to compare changes in scores over years in ABC schools vs. matched schools not involved in the program. We report here only on the examination of non-arts outcomes (test scores).—*E.W.*

RESULTS

While no statistical comparisons were carried out, graphs showed clearly that the scores were comparable across ABC and non-participating schools. The researchers conclude that the comparability of test scores shows that the increased time spent on art at the ABC schools did *not* lead to lower test scores.—*E.W.*

CONTRIBUTIONS TO THE FIELD

This study demonstrates that when students spend additional time in arts programs their performance in other school subjects does *not* decline. The study found also that teachers and administrators rate the ABC program very positively. There was strong support for arts education in the ABC schools.—*E.W.*

COMMENTARY

While the ABC program was founded in the belief that the arts would enhance learning in other areas of the curriculum, this evaluation presents no evidence for this hypothesis. The ABC program neither enhanced nor lowered standardized test scores. It is important to note that the researchers appear to have begun not with the hypothesis that the arts would enhance test scores, but with the opposite hypothesis—that the arts might lower test scores because students in arts-rich schools would spend less time on academic subjects. That this did not occur is itself important to educators striving to include the arts for their own sake but having to defend them against worries their inclusion in students' schedules may compromise student performance on academic subjects.—*E.W.*

CONTRIBUTIONS TO THE FIELD

This evaluation addresses one of the common ways arts education is expanded in states—a state grants program—enabling a fuller understanding of how such programs may be helpful in increasing the emphasis on the arts in schools and districts and how such efforts may develop a wider network to support arts education across a state. Those who have or wish to have similar programs can learn about the organization and operations of the program as well as its effects on schools and the state arts education community. The evaluation also enables a better understanding of how schools and districts that have strong arts programs are different from other schools and districts. The recommendations also suggest trade-offs in such approaches and issues that may need to be anticipated in implementing a similar grants program.—*G.N.*

COMMENTARY

This evaluation documents and assesses the organization and operations of a statewide arts education grants program that had important effects on the availability and quality of arts education available in project sites, and thus in the state. It also assesses the most significant achievement of the project to be the establishment of a statewide network of artists, arts educators, school administrators, classroom teachers, arts administrators, and others. This network was largely developed through a series of professional development forums and workshops. The ABC project also shifted the conceptions of arts education from performance and products to regarding dance, drama, visual art, and music as academic disciplines, in part by creating an arts curriculum guide for the state. Investigations of the school sites and matching non-project schools revealed that ABC schools had more time devoted to teaching the arts and more arts integration. Those ABC schools that were arts immersion (required courses in all four arts) had more collaboration between teachers, better student behavior, and more parent involvement. This meant that the school ecology and climate were altered by the arts programs in arts immersion schools.

While there was an expressed concern that increased time for the arts could detract from student achievement in core subjects, test data revealed no decrease in achievement in arts immersion schools compared with matched non-ABC schools. This was true despite the fact that tests were seen as less important in school policy of arts immersed schools. The study concluded that the grant program itself creates a sense of ownership for program improvements and increases morale.

Schools with the strongest arts programs had administrative support, adequate and additional funding, more professionally involved teachers, parent support, district support, and support of community arts organizations. The ABC project also had school district projects, not just school sites. Such grants resulted in increased breadth of programming and the development of district-wide curricula. District sites had more arts education coordination.—G.N.

"While there was an expressed concern that increased time for the arts could detract from student achievement in core subjects, test data revealed no decrease in achievement in arts immersion schools compared with matched non-ABC schools."

91

multi-arts

STUDY NAME: **Mute Those Claims: No Evidence (Yet) for a Causal Link between Arts Study and Academic Achievement**

AUTHORS: Ellen Winner and Monica Cooper

PUBLISHED: Journal of Aesthetic Education, Fall 2000, 34 (3-4): 11-75

Research Questions

Is there a correlation between arts study and academic achievement?

Does academic achievement improve when students are exposed to the arts?

METHODS

A comprehensive literature search was conducted for studies investigating the relationship between arts study and academic achievement. Selection criteria reduced the number of studies harvested to 31. Studies were selected if they met each of four criteria: (1) considered the arts in general, as opposed to learning within specific arts disciplines; (2) had comparison or control groups; (3) had an outcome based upon academic achievement; and (4) had sufficient data presented to compute an effect size. The studies were then categorized into correlational and experimental groups.

Three meta-analyses were performed on the correlational group. The first meta-analysis considered five studies where academic outcomes were presented as composite or summed math and verbal scores. The second meta-analysis investigated the relationship between the arts and verbal skills, while the third investigated the arts and math. Two meta-analyses were performed on the experimental group, one investigating math outcomes and the other, verbal outcomes.—R.H.

RESULTS

The three correlational meta-analyses found significant associations between arts study and academic outcomes. Effect sizes in the composite academic (verbal and math) meta-analysis ranged from $r = .04$ to $r = .08$ with a mean of $r = .05$. Stouffer's Z and a t test of the mean Zr were both significant ($Z = 50.89$, $p < .001$ and $t = 5.97$, $p = .004$). The arts and verbal meta-analysis found effect sizes ranging from $r = .14$ to $.25$, with a mean of $r = .19$ (Stouffer's $Z = 333.43$, $p < .001$ and t test of the mean $Zr = 16.52$, $p = .0001$). The arts and math analysis contained studies with effect sizes ranging from $r = .00$ to $r = .17$ with a mean effect size of $r = .10$ (weighted $r = .11$). These effects were also found to be significant ($Z = 189.73$, $p < .0001$ and $t = 6.936$, $p < .0001$).

Twenty-four effect sizes were derived from the experimental studies for the meta-analysis of the effect of arts on verbal performance. The effect sizes ranged from $r = -.25$ to $r = .66$. The mean un-weighted effect size was $r = .07$ (weighted $r = .01$). Although the Stouffer's Z test was significant ($Z = 3,82$, $p < .0001$), the t test of the mean Zr was not ($t = 1.66$, $p = .11$). Similar results were obtained from the arts and math meta-analysis. Effect sizes ranged from $r = -.14$ to $r = .34$ (mean $r = .06$, weighted mean $= r = .02$). The Stouffer's Z test was significant ($Z = 3.10$, $p = .001$), while the t test of the mean Zr was not ($t = 1.63$, $p = .13$).—R.H.

CONTRIBUTIONS TO THE FIELD

The study demonstrates an approach to synthesizing sets of experimental and correlational research studies. The authors applied this meta-analytic approach to studies investigating the relationship between arts learning and academic achievement. The findings confirmed an association between arts study and academic achievement but did not establish a significant causal link from the arts to academics.—R.H.

COMMENTARY

Although the authors refer to a "climate of rising claims" about the effects of the arts, it is doubtful that we claim more for the arts than in times past. The arts have long been thought to have unusual and extraordinary powers, from Plato's belief that music influenced moral development to beliefs that the arts promote mystical, supernatural, or religious experiences, motivate group identity (including patriotism), and so on. It's not surprising that now many believe that the special experience of artistic learning promotes improved thinking skills and school performance, qualities now held in higher esteem than these past extra-artistic outcomes.

If anything, we expect less from the arts today (if one accepts that cuts in arts programs over the past 30 years reflect public expectations). But we seem to expect more from certain methods of social science research, particularly that the richness and complexity of the artistic experience will be sufficiently captured to employ a sound experimental design when investigating transfer of learning from the arts. That belief underlies the present study. The authors found significant correlations between multi-arts experiences and a synthesized set of outcome measures. However, they describe mixed results from tests of statistical significance in their meta-analysis of experimental studies, and thereby state that there is not yet enough evidence to claim that the arts have a causal effect on academic achievement (although the mean effect sizes were positive).

They conclude that more research is needed. But one must wonder if the time and effort would have been better spent considering the best approach to reviewing the literature, and ultimately reflecting on the benefits and limitations of the particular approach they took. The meta-analysis procedure employed here requires a pool of experimental studies that validly measure the transfer process in question, in terms of treatment, process, and outcomes, while at the same time controlling for extraneous variables. The inconclusive findings in the causal analysis illuminate the need for better measures, particularly in appropriate outcomes. As one of the authors points out, "…researchers have focused too narrowly on test scores and grades as outcomes. Researchers need to begin to look at transfer outcomes that, while more relevant, are certainly going to be more difficult to measure." (Winner and Hetland, "The Arts in Education: Evaluating the Evidence for a Causal Link," *Journal of Aesthetic Education*, 34(3-4), p. 6)

The lesson learned here may not be that we should mute claims of manifold effects of learning in and through the arts. Instead, researchers should continue to try and understand the artistic experience and its various outcomes in ways beyond experimental means. There is room for a multiplicity of approaches, and there is a need for researchers to synthesize findings in innovative ways.—*R.H.*

CONTRIBUTIONS TO THE FIELD

The value of this work is its careful and comprehensive review of the entire research field (including published and unpublished work), uncovering 1,135 studies that investigated the effects of the arts on academic achievement.

The research used a widely accepted technique, meta-analysis, allowing the authors to assess the aggregate contribution of multiple studies that employed a range of student achievement tests as well as varied statistical techniques. The meta-analysis was supplemented with a more traditional review of 27 studies that lacked appropriate control groups or enough statistical evidence to calculate an effect size and 17 studies that investigated motivational outcomes rather than achievement outcomes.

Of the 1,135 studies originally identified, 66 studies (actually 31 studies with multiple outcomes, thus more than doubling the sample) met the authors' criteria for inclusion in the meta-analysis. The summary of these studies provides compelling but cautionary evidence for the correlational relationship between study of the arts and academic achievement. However, with the more stringent test of experimentally designed studies (where causal relationships can be more clearly delineated), the association between arts instruction and enhanced achievement almost disappears.

The biggest contribution of this work is that it should promote more creative thought about the relationship between arts instruction and academic achievement (What are the important intermediate links? How does culture play into the contribution of the arts to academic achievement—the dependent variable defined by this study?), as well as how we conceive of achievement (How can we push the definition beyond narrowly defined test scores into attributes more highly valued by the world? Most employers for example, value staff that can problem-solve, reason clearly, work well with others, communicate clearly in public settings, etc.).—*B.W.*

COMMENTARY

By the canons of a research tradition steeped in the value of carefully controlled experiments, it is certainly appropriate to call for a muting of the claims for the connection between the arts and student achievement. But educational research is no longer dominated by this one view of acceptable research. Consequently, any muting must also await a careful review of findings from alternative conceptions of acceptable science.

Furthermore, an important limitation of meta-analysis is its reliance almost entirely on standardizing the strength of outcomes (i.e., carefully measuring what students learn) without also taking equal care to describe the process by which an intervention (in this case, the arts) may have contributed to this learning. So, for example, with the more than three million high school students who were involved in the correlational analysis we know that some of them had extensive arts instruction (defined as four years) but we know nothing about the quality of that instruction. In the experimental studies with a total sample of more than 30,000 elementary school students we know very little about the nature or duration of the arts intervention. Until we have more qualitative research to complement this quantitative focus, we will never be able to unravel the mystery of how or under what conditions the arts may contribute to learning.

This research ends on an important note by calling attention to the limitations of holding arts accountable for the same outcomes of learning as mathematics and language arts. The arts, the authors point out, contribute unique and often difficult-to-measure learning outcomes. Yet, the authors are guilty of what they ask other researchers and policy-makers not to do: all of their data draw only upon studies that investigate the relationship between arts instruction and student achievement on the more readily quantified indicators of verbal and math skills. Why were there not any reviews of studies that looked at other outcomes?—*B.W.*

"…researchers have focused too narrowly on test scores and grades as outcomes. Researchers need to begin to look at transfer outcomes that, while more relevant, are certainly going to be more difficult to measure."

93

multi-arts

STUDY NAME: **Why the Arts Matter in Education Or Just What Do Children Learn When They Create An Opera?**

AUTHOR: Dennie Palmer Wolf

PUBLISHED: In E. Fiske (Ed.), Champions of Change: The Impact of the Arts on Learning. The Arts Education Partnership and the President's Committee on the Arts and the Humanities, Washington, D.C., 1999: 92-98

Research Questions

When elementary school students form a company to write and produce an original opera, what kinds of learning take place? For example, do students become more persistent workers and do they become better at solving problems in groups?

METHODS

This is a qualitative, multi-year evaluation of a program called Creating Original Opera (COO), a program in which elementary students form a company to write and produce an original opera. The study investigated the claim made by teachers in the program that "the opera makes students work harder and smarter" and that when working on opera, students work together over long periods to solve problems. Through observations of classes and student work, the researcher noted the kinds of collaborative learning occurring while students were creating an opera. The researcher compared the collaborative learning process when children were making opera vs. when they were engaged in an open-ended math problem or when they were making an oral presentation on American Indian leaders in social studies.—E.W.

RESULTS

The ways in which children worked together when creating opera differed from how they worked together in non-opera settings. In opera settings, students were likely to participate, they were more likely to connect what they said to previous comments, they were more likely to make constructive critiques of others, they were more likely to revise their own earlier ideas, and they were more likely to link their comments to a theme that had been raised by the group. In addition, these cohesive collaborative behaviors increased in frequency over time. Thus, what students learn from creating operas is how to participate actively and collaboratively, how to take turns, and how to ask questions. They become able to listen to others and take off from what others propose. The researcher suggests that the next step would be to ask whether opera work has given students an enhanced ability to interpret texts that have multiple layers of meaning.—E.W.

CONTRIBUTIONS TO THE FIELD

This study documents the sustained collaboration in solving problems that goes on among children when they work together to create an opera.—E.W.

COMMENTARY

This is a rich, qualitative study showing that when children work together to create an opera, they engage in collaborative problem-solving over time. This observation therefore provides us with a testable hypothesis that the kind of collaborative problem-solving used in opera might transfer to academic subjects and lead to greater learning in these areas.—E.W.

CONTRIBUTIONS TO THE FIELD

This article highlights the methodology and the research employed to investigate the impact of a unique arts education initiative. The results of the study, significant in and of themselves, are used to illustrate the power of the qualitative approach and to illuminate a path for future research.—J.W.-D.

COMMENTARY

Accepting the broad premise that the arts do matter in education, Dennie Palmer Wolf conducted a multi-year qualitative evaluation study of Creating Original Opera (COO) designed to begin answering questions related to the specific effects of arts education experiences. This article provides rich descriptions of the ways in which children engage in the learning process while participating in COO, an arts education program in which elementary school students form companies in their classrooms to write and produce original operas. Wolf's work provides further documentation that the arts can indeed matter in children's learning by describing the process by which children participating in COO classrooms engaged in learning and the outcome of that process—increased collaborative problem-solving. Further, the capacity to make meaning and convey it to the work of others promoted by these arts experiences is, according to the author, "robust enough to transfer." This research also offers some insight into the conditions that may make transfer more likely—classrooms where teachers create opportunities for authentic and collaborative experiences.

A major contribution of this study is its methodology. The qualitative design provides a model for other researchers attempting to answer central questions about the nature of the effects of arts education programs and how it is that these effects occur. Looking closely at student/teacher interactions and student work over several years provides a more useful understanding of these effects than correlational analyses of test scores, attendance records, and other quantitative data sets. This study goes beyond identification of gross effects to paint a picture of the lived experiences wherein such effects are created—clarity about the effects and clarity about the experiences that promote the effects are equally important. Future research needs to focus even more clearly on what is learned and why such learning occurs in arts education contexts.—*J.W.-D.*

STUDY NAME: **SAT Scores of Students Who Study the Arts: What We Can and Cannot Conclude about the Association**

AUTHORS: Kathryn Vaughn and Ellen Winner

PUBLISHED: The Journal of Aesthetic Education, Fall 2000, 34(3-4):77-89

Research Questions

What is the relationship between SAT scores and the number of years of arts study? Which SAT test is more strongly associated with studying the arts: the verbal or the math? Are the relationships stronger for different arts disciplines?

METHODS

Students taking the SAT were asked to voluntarily respond to a questionnaire indicating the number of years of arts classes they took or planned to take. These responses were compared to verbal, math, and composite SAT scores. A meta-analysis of the data investigated differences in effect sizes between math SAT and arts, and verbal SAT and arts. Additional analysis investigated the relative relationships of the different arts classes with SAT performance.—*R.H.*

RESULTS

- Students who take arts classes have higher math, verbal, and composite SAT scores than students who take no arts classes.
- SAT scores increase linearly with the addition of more years of arts classes, that is, the more years of arts classes, the higher the SAT scores.
- The strongest relationship with SAT scores was found with students who take four or more years of arts classes.
- The authors report "effect sizes for math scores are consistently smaller than those for verbal scores."
- Acting classes had the strongest correlation with verbal SAT scores. Acting classes and music history, theory, or appreciation had the strongest relationship with math SAT scores. However, all classifications of arts classes were found to have significant relationships with both verbal and math SAT scores.—*R.H.*

CONTRIBUTIONS TO THE FIELD

This study confirms the oft-cited relationship between arts study and SAT scores. Significant relationships were found between all of the arts disciplines and both math and verbal SATs. The article serves as a forum for the authors to remind readers that the correlation between participation in high school arts programs and SAT scores is not sufficient in itself to claim that arts study leads to improvement in academic performance. More research is needed to interpret the relationship.—*R.H.*

COMMENTARY

The study highlights the need for more focused investigations to understand the relationships between arts and academic performance. Additional studies should examine specific relationships, such as those between acting and verbal ability. It is reasonable to assume that some acting classes teach similar skills and concepts as those found in English classes. These skills and concepts may transfer across disciplines, or they may represent two related wings of the same overarching discipline.

A limitation of the SAT studies is that we know very little about the characteristics or quality of the high school arts programs. Which kinds of drama programs, for instance, are most likely to correlate with SAT performance? Most studies tend to simply count the amount of time spent in

arts classes and compare this with a performance measure. Studies such as this will become more useful in the future when they measure the quality or characteristics of an arts program or, preferably, learning of arts themselves.

Although the authors repeatedly urge caution when making causal claims for the arts, the consistent positive correlations across all of the studies cannot easily be ignored. Evidently, higher-performing students have access to arts classes, and participate in them, as well. At the very least, even denying a causal relationship, this indicates a demand for arts classes from highly motivated students. Availability of arts classes is a characteristic of high-performing schools. As the authors point out, many independent schools have retained their arts programs, as have affluent suburban school districts. Inner-city schools, often with lower-performing students, have not fared as well in retaining their arts programs, thereby denying their students a complete education.—*R.H.*

CONTRIBUTIONS TO THE FIELD

The value of this research is in the large sample (more than 10 million American high schoolers), the methodology used to assess the consistency of findings across time (meta-analysis), and the nature of the variables being assessed (i.e., the correlation between arts courses taken in high school and performance on the SAT).

The findings are remarkably consistent, given the equivocality of most social science research. Increased years of enrollment in arts courses are positively correlated with higher SAT verbal and math scores. It is difficult to challenge the strength of this relationship, given the careful documentation in this research. The problem, though (as the authors make abundantly clear), is that correlation does not mean causation. It is not sound science to rush to the conclusion that the best way to enhance SAT performance would be to increase arts offerings. But this research provides an important springboard for future research that should address the question of whether the positive association between arts enrollment and SAT performance will hold up to the scrutiny of additional variables.—*B.W.*

COMMENTARY

An important contribution of research is that it helps refine or redirect the questions that need to be asked in the future. What questions need to be asked to test whether the positive association between arts class enrollment and SAT performance is a causal one? An obvious place to start is to look at the quality of the educational experience of students who fell in the category of having four or more arts classes in their high school careers since they are in the category that performed much better on the SAT than other students. They represent only 14 percent of the total sample. Are their opportunities to study advanced core subject courses (e.g., math, science, English) different from other students'? Are family or school resources for these students different? Furthermore, what role does the quality of an arts experience (as opposed to just the quantity) add to the relationship? These and other questions are made more intriguing and relevant to future researchers because of the strong findings in this research.—*B.W.*

"Although the authors repeatedly urge caution when making causal claims for the arts, the consistent positive correlations across all of the studies cannot easily be ignored."

Essay:
Promising Signs of Positive Effects: Lessons from the Multi-Arts Studies

Rob Horowitz and Jaci Webb-Dempsey

The selection of multi-arts studies collected in this Compendium is diverse, in terms of both the arts learning experiences they describe and the particularities of the research they report. These selections explore learning in multiple art forms and in contexts that range from whole-school and school district renewal efforts to community-based arts programs to arts integration efforts in individual elementary school classrooms. This body of work includes studies that look closely at what happens in a small sample of classrooms, as well as studies conducted on a national level. They include a range of approaches from correlational to ethnographic. Some were designed as basic research on the impact of the arts on children's learning or school change, while others are evaluations of particular programs.

While each study includes particular variables related to their specific context, as a collective they fundamentally share a focus on: (1) describing the processes, contexts, and environments that promote or support arts learning, and (2) documenting the impact of arts learning on other kinds of learning (however those "other kinds" of learning may be defined or measured). It is these central questions about process and context, outcomes, and transfer that are critical to the identification and refinement of a research agenda that will establish the future role of the arts in education.

Three Critical Issues

Certainly, the attempt to understand the effect of multiple-arts experiences on children's learning is a daunting task. Researchers have taken up this challenge in various ways, with designs ranging from meta-analyses of quantitative studies through ethnographic approaches. Several of these approaches are represented in this collection. While researchers may and should debate the merits of particular lines of inquiry, other issues fundamental to both arts learning and arts research loom. First, what is the nature of the arts learning experience, and if we can sufficiently understand it, how are we to capture or measure it? Second, are the learning disciplines of art, music, dance, and drama similar enough to each other to merit being grouped together as "arts education," or are we better off dissecting each discipline separately? And finally, what kinds of outcomes should we expect as a result of arts learning, or, put another way, how do the arts contribute to human development?

Let's put aside the first two questions for the moment, and turn to the third. (Debating the nature of arts learning is an eternal challenge!) Researchers investigating outcomes of arts learning often make a fundamental choice: are they to focus on specific academic skills, such as those reflected in standardized measures of reading or math, or do they look towards broader, more general capacities of the mind, self-perceptions, and social relationships?

The collection of work presented here offers progress in both areas, the specific and the general. Catterall's research provides significant evidence of a link between arts participation and improved academic performance, as measured by test scores in specific academic subjects. As researchers continue to discuss the causal implications of this work, they should note the remarkable similarity of findings across this set of studies—by researchers working independently—within general cognitive, personal, and social domains of learning. For instance, Catterall, Harland, and the Teachers College group all found that drama experiences develop a sense of empathy for others. Harland's findings on creativity, expressive skills, and self-confidence are remarkably consistent with the Teachers College (TC) findings, as well as Catterall's work. Positive risk-taking, as an outcome of arts experiences, emerged independently in the work of Heath, Baum, and TC. The self-regulatory behaviors described by Baum are similarly described in other studies, but by other names. (Baum's definitions of "paying attention," "self-initiating" behaviors, and "persevering" have natural counterparts in TC's "focused perception," "task persistence," and "ownership of learning.") The SCANS workforce skills cited by Catterall in his CAPE evaluation also reflect similar cognitive and social capacities worthy of continued investigation, such as motivation, decision-making, creative thinking, and speaking skills.

Therefore, this research indicates collective progress in the search for identifying outcomes of arts education beyond skills within the arts disciplines themselves. General capacities of the mind, social competencies, and personal dispositions developed through arts learning may have wide application in a variety of academic and life experiences. There are ample opportunities here for researchers to build upon this work. Researchers, and those who fund them, should consider that the habits of mind and personal dispositions explored in this collection are

> "The positive cognitive, personal, and social outcomes emerging from this collected research represent capacities central to the goals society typically articulates for public education..."

closer to the "true" work of the arts educator than those basic competency skills measured by standardized reading and math tests. There is evidence here, for instance, of drama experiences supporting the development of self-confidence, positive risk-taking, and empathy for others—valuable and desirable outcomes, but unlikely to be measured in a pencil-and-paper exam.

"There are positive findings collected here with implications for curriculum, professional development, partnership, and learning. Administrators and policy-makers can be secure in supporting strong arts programs based upon the evidence presented here."

Whatever the merits of high-stakes testing for improving basic verbal and math skills, there can be little doubt that results from these tests have been misapplied to other educational concerns,[1] a prominent example being the use of student test results as a proxy for teacher quality. This misapplication has led to school environments where "what gets tested gets taught," a subsequent narrowing of curriculum, and a limiting of the quality of learning opportunities for young people.[2] Innovative arts programs are sometimes thought to be at risk unless they demonstrate their value within the standards-and-accountability calculus. It is doubtful, though, that researchers will be able to successfully employ high-stakes testing results as credible outcomes of arts programs except in those instances where program activities are clearly intended to achieve results that can appropriately be measured by such tests. Even then the limitations of traditional standardized testing would prohibit the documentation of critical and broadly transferable arts outcomes. The positive cognitive, personal, and social outcomes emerging from this collected research represent capacities central to the goals society typically articulates for public education—productive social membership, critical and higher-order thinking, and commitment to the skills for lifelong learning.

Despite the promising findings on outcomes presented here, more progress is needed to address the first two issues we identified at the outset of this essay. As a field, we still can't identify, define, and measure the collective multiple or integrated arts learning experience very well. Because of this, most arts transfer studies measure participation in arts classes as a surrogate for assessing arts learning, but then measure learning outcomes directly, be they creativity, self-concept, or math performance. Transfer studies in arts education will always be somewhat insufficient until we can more effectively measure arts learning. The quality of arts programs should be considered, as well. We can't predict a transfer outcome unless we are first confident that there is a properly defined causal event: in this case, arts learning.

Researchers should also continue to develop better and more creative research designs, considering the complexity and richness of the arts experience in schools. Is the answer to be found in better-controlled experimental studies, as some have suggested?[3] Perhaps not yet, at least until we can better define the arts learning process. Systematic, well-designed qualitative studies can help us understand what the arts learning experience is for children, and what characteristics of that experience are likely to travel across domains of learning. Such research can also help us develop appropriate forms of measurement—assessments that reflect the rich nature of arts learning experiences and the complexities of arts learning outcomes. In the future, researchers can develop and validate measures based upon solid qualitative work.

Describing Processes and Environments

Clearly, qualitative research is needed to build rich, meaningful descriptions of the processes and environments that promote arts learning. Exploring the processes of arts learning means looking at both arts teaching and learning, simultaneously and separately, as both method and means. Effective teaching processes identified in this body of research include "hands-on involvement to promote on-task behavior," "individualized instruction coupled with positive reinforcement," "recognition for creative accomplishment," "genuine and personal interest in students," and "maintaining and communicating high standards and expectations," all of which are characteristics of quality teaching regardless of the discipline being taught. Characteristics of more constructivist and learner-centered approaches to teaching are also present in descriptions of arts learning contexts. The relevancy of activities, respectful climate, and opportunities for learners to take responsibility that are cited in a number of these studies as providing a context for learner risk-taking and increased motivation and engagement are indicative of these approaches.

These studies, examined collectively, suggest that these desirable processes and teaching characteristics are inherent to dynamic, multiple-arts teaching environments. Although these qualities may be desirable in other academic contexts, their frequency across this set of studies is striking. Multiple and integrated arts learning environments may inherently provide teachers with varied opportunities to develop and exercise the positive strategies outlined in these evaluation and research studies. There is need for additional research to better delineate the characteristics of multiple and integrated arts programs that can lead to a broader impact on learning and schools. Likewise, researchers need to be on guard when designing inquiries that compare arts programs with

multi-arts

1   Wasserman, S. Quantum theory, the uncertainty principle and the alchemy of standardized testing. *Phi Delta Kappan*, (September 2001), 28-40.

2   Eisner, E. W. What does it mean to say a school is doing well? *Phi Delta Kappan*, (January 2001), 367-372.

3   Eisner, E. W. (1998). Does experience in the arts boost academic achievement? *Art Education*, 51 (1), 7-15. Winner, E., Hetland, L. (2000). The arts in education: evaluating the evidence for a causal link. *The Journal of Aesthetic Education*, 34 (3-4), 3-10.

desirable pedagogical approaches to programs devoid of both the arts and good teaching. Otherwise, we will merely demonstrate the value of sound teaching practice, and not the arts.

Characteristics of effective arts learning environments, as reported in the larger-scale evaluations such as the NFER study conducted in Great Britain, include standards and expectations that focus on the value of the arts, accessible and adequate offerings in all art forms, and sufficient resources to support quality arts experiences, such as supplies, equipment, and, most important, qualified teachers. Again, these kinds of characteristics are generic to effective learning environments, regardless of the core focus of the curriculum. Seaman's *The Arts in the Basic Curriculum Project: Looking to the Past and Preparing for the Future* provides insight into how schools and school districts that have viable arts programs differ from other schools and districts. In these evaluations, similarities in environmental factors emerge—including a shared understanding of, and commitment to, the importance of the arts across the larger school community, administrative support, adequate materials and space, adequate and additional funding, district support, parent support, and networking among educators and members of the arts community. These factors reflect differences in school culture and climate. Studies that systematically describe the change process as schools adopt an arts focus, integrate the arts across the curriculum, make the arts accessible to all students, invite the arts community into the educational process, and make quality arts teaching a valued activity can contribute to the broader national conversation about school renewal.

Documenting Impact and Transfer

The multi-arts selections include studies designed and implemented as evaluations of arts education initiatives, studies that explore arts involvement as a mediating factor in the lives and learning of "at-risk" youth, and studies designed to investigate the relationship between arts involvement and general academic achievement, both broadly and narrowly defined. There are positive findings collected here with implications for curriculum, professional development, partnership, and learning. Administrators and policy-makers can be secure in supporting strong arts programs based upon the evidence presented here.

Researchers, however, should be less secure in resting on their laurels. Questions remain, indicating the need for much work ahead. For example, as researchers we must take the issues of *quality* and *quantity* of arts programs head-on. How "good" (or effective) are the programs we are evaluating or researching? How "good" is "good enough" for us to track teaching and learning from one domain to another?

In the same vein, how much arts is enough arts? Is there a tipping point, below which an arts program will have little extrinsic effects, but beyond which these programs have significant impact on children, teachers, and schools? Administrators and policy-makers would welcome our answers to these questions. As researchers we need better answers in order to design better studies.

We also should pursue more precise identification, definition, and measurement in three areas: (1) arts learning; (2) outcomes of arts learning, including cognitive and social competencies, and personal dispositions; and (3) characteristics of the contexts, processes, and environments of arts teaching and learning. But assuming we can improve measurement in these areas, what then? We need to develop better models for understanding how learning within artistic domains interacts with learning in other disciplines. Are we to think of the relationship of arts and other learning as parallel, symbiotic, interactive, or multi-layered? It is overly simplistic to assume that learning in one complex domain (such as the arts) can be sufficiently isolated within a school context and then be shown to affect other subjects in a linear fashion without regard to the context of schools, families, culture, and the nature of the learning process itself. The directionality of transfer effects must be explored, as we try and understand how learning in one discipline influences learning in others.

Issues of equity also should be addressed. Future research should examine the paths by which young people come to "live and learn" in the arts—and how some are systematically excluded. How is access to the arts mediated by race and class, both in terms of school and community offerings and in terms of who self-selects to participate? Work done in this area looking at youth categorized as "at risk" points to arts learning experiences as a powerful factor for influencing personal, social, and intellectual development. Research should be focused on the identification of the barriers to access, while more clearly articulating the process of how the arts might intervene on behalf of learning.

In closing, this selection of multi-arts studies provides direction for building quality arts learning experiences and for the design of future research efforts aimed at documenting the unique impact of arts learning—both learning that enhances the artistic endeavor and learning that transfers to other disciplines and other contexts. The challenge is to follow through and use what this work tells us to garner support from funding agents, policy-makers, educators, and the public for the design and implementation of quality arts programs and a relevant research agenda.

music

STUDY NAME: **Effects of an Integrated Reading and Music Instructional Approach on Fifth-Grade Students' Reading Achievement, Reading Attitude, Music Achievement, and Music Attitude**

AUTHOR: Laura Jean Andrews

PUBLISHED: Unpublished Doctoral Dissertation, 1997, University of North Carolina, Greensboro, N.C.

Research Questions

What are the effects of an integrated reading and music curriculum on fifth-graders' reading achievement, reading attitude, music achievement, and music attitude?

Do gender and/or music backgrounds influence the effects of an integrated reading and music instructional approach on fifth-graders' reading and music attitudes and achievement?

METHODS

Two intact classes of fifth-grade students, balanced for gender (11 females, 18 males in each class) from one North Carolina school participated in the study. A strength of the study is that criteria for subject selection (a "sampling frame") are stated. Thus, the study used a sample selected to represent a specified population, and not a convenience sample.

The integrated class (n = 29) received 20 minutes of integrated reading and music instruction delivered by the researcher at the end of two regular reading classes a week for 11 weeks. The control class (n = 29) received no integrated instruction during reading class time. Both classes had regular reading classes (50 minutes x 5 classes per week), and both classes attended a general music class led by the researcher (30 minutes x 2 classes per week). Subjects were pre- and post-tested. The music integration program, designed collaboratively by the researcher and the classroom teacher, focused on specific higher-order thinking skills such as comparing and contrasting, understanding text organization, and identifying musical forms. Children were engaged in these challenges through reading, discussing, singing, listening, performing, and creating. In addition, instruction linked reading and music to social, cultural, and historical contexts. For example, during a unit focusing on American Indians, integrated instruction involved listening to and discussing music of the Navajo and Zuni tribes, listening to and reading about the American Indian flute, and chanting rhythmic patterns using vocabulary words like "roadrunners" and "caravans."

Four measures were employed. The *Music Attitudes Profile* (assesses attitudes toward learning about music by having students indicate whether they agree or disagree with statements such as "I like what we learn in music class" and "I am afraid of not doing well in music class" using a 5-point Likert scale); the *Elementary Reading Attitude Survey* (assesses reading attitudes by having students indicate how they feel about various reading activities by circling one of four cartoon drawings representing different emotional states); the *Silver Burdett Music Competency Tests*, *Book 5* (uses multiple-choice question format to assess basic music skills such as discriminating differences in musical style and recognizing relationships between musical sounds and notation); and the *Vocabulary and Reading Comprehension* subtests of the *Iowa Tests of Basic Skills* (assesses reading skill using items that emphasize word analysis, vocabulary, and reading comprehension). Subjects were issued identification numbers to assure anonymity. Reliabilities were checked for all measures and found to be acceptable. The reliability of the music achievement test (SBMCT) was quite low (r = .50), but no other standardized test was available. In addition, the researcher administered the *Music Background Questionnaire* to all children prior to treatment to evaluate children's previous music training and music environment at home.

A 2 x 2 x 2 (instructional approach, gender, music background) multivariate analysis of variance (MANOVA) was used for analysis. All independent variables and potential interactions were also examined through univariate analyses of subjects' post-treatment reading and music achievement and attitude scores.—*L.H.*

RESULTS

With significance set at *p* < .05, both the integrated and non-integrated classes improved significantly from pre- to post-test in reading and music achievement, with no significant differences between groups. Attitude scores did differ by group. Music attitude increased from pre- to post-test for the integrated class (*p* = .001) and decreased for the non-integrated class (*p* = .026). For the second research question about gender and background, girls demonstrated better attitudes toward reading than boys in both experimental and control groups, and boys had greater music achievement. No significant effects were related to music background.—*L.H.*

CONTRIBUTIONS TO THE FIELD

This study assessed the effects on achievement and attitude in both reading and music that resulted from integrating music into a reading program. Testing both types of outcomes honors the value of music learning and gives music (or any art form) full partnership in the integrated course of study.

The study found that music and reading attitudes improved when music was integrated into reading instruction. However, achievement in reading and music were not affected.—*L.H.*

COMMENTARY

This study suggests that improved attitudes do not ensure

better achievement. As important as it is to engage students' positive attitudes in their classroom learning (and music apparently had that effect), integrated arts curricula should also advance learning of both the art (in this case, music) and the target discipline (in this case, reading).

Because the experimental (music integrated) and control (music not integrated) groups were similar in level of achievement, these results do not support a conclusion that integrating a music module into reading instruction improves achievement in reading or music. Results do suggest that fifth-grade students' attitudes toward music and reading are positively affected by an integrated reading and music curriculum. However, the researcher cautions that a "Hawthorne effect" (higher scores for students in the music integrated group resulting from their perception of special treatment and increased exposure to the researcher) may have influenced the results of the present study. Similarly, "resentful demoralization" for the control group may account for lower scores on post-testing (resulting from feeling excluded from special treatment).

The researcher suggests that future studies might obtain significant results for achievement if a longer treatment period were used. Future research should also investigate the relationship between attitude and achievement. Attention to identifying the specific elements of the curriculum responsible for observed differences would further understanding of the effects of integrating arts with instruction in other subjects.—L.H.

CONTRIBUTIONS TO THE FIELD

This study illustrates the problem of differentiating the effects of music instruction and music-integration classes on reading. That is, since the music instruction was identical for both the control and the experimental groups, the music-integrated reading experimental group differed only in the degree to which *explicit* connections were drawn between music, text setting, and lyrical content. Transcripts of the music lessons themselves (included as appendices to the study) suggest how "traditional" music lessons can contribute to language development through its integration with music.

Results from this study show that the reliance on relatively broad or superficial aspects of integration designed into this study—such as the association of music with literature or the presence of specific vocabulary in songs—as opposed to a specific focus on underlying concepts shared between music and linguistic processes (phrase/sentence structure, diction, etc.)—is more likely to affect attitudes *about* reading than ability in reading skill during an 11-week period of instruction.—L.S.

COMMENTARY

As the author cites from guidelines for integrated studies in North Carolina, "integrated instruction approaches use the language and methodology from more than one discipline and focus on unifying themes, issues, problems, concepts, and experiences shared between the disciplines."

That the results of this study do not strongly support the

relationship between reading skill and music is not surprising given the relative superficiality of the integration approaches taken, the length of time of the experimental effect, and the confounding effect of applying general music lessons to both control and experimental groups.

The lesson transcripts included in this study provide a glimpse of some teaching methods that may be counterproductive to the aims of integrated learning. These lessons rely on a small range of reinforced musical skills, the method of teaching inquiry is dominated by posing only "right or wrong" questions, and the lessons are filled with positive attitude statements rather than modeling the kind of deep inquiry needed to sustain interest in and impact of integrated learning.

Research cited in this study Compendium (Lowe 1995) shows, for example, how vocal song rehearsal combined with close examination of the text yields better results in language reading achievement. The author may have gotten better results by strengthening the integrated lessons in ways that draw on deeper connections between music and reading processes as suggested by the general guidelines issued from state boards of education and supported by earlier research.—L.S.

"...music and reading attitudes improved when music was integrated into reading instruction."

STUDY NAME: **The Effect of Early Music Training on Child Cognitive Development**
AUTHORS: Terry D. Bilhartz, Rick A. Bruhn, and Judith E. Olson
PUBLISHED: Journal of Applied Developmental Psychology, 2000, 20 (4): 615-636

Research Question

Does music training not involving the keyboard enhance spatial-temporal, mathematical, and verbal reasoning?

METHODS

Seventy-one 4- and 5-year-old preschoolers from both low- and high-income families participated. All children were pre-tested on six subtests of the Stanford Binet. There were two visual tests: Bead Memory (a visual memory test in which one must recall and reassemble sequences of beads of different colors and shapes) and Pattern Analysis (a visual test in which one must use blocks to reproduce patterns). There were two verbal tests: Vocabulary, and Memory for Sentences. And there was one math test: Quantitative.

Children were assigned to experimental and control groups by a combination of random assignment and block assignment by class. The 36 children in the experimental group received a 30-week music program (Kindermusik for the Young Child) consisting of 75 minutes of weekly instruction and home assignments including singing, instruments, exploring and notating rhythms, learning to read and write music, composing, and movement. The 35 children in the control group received no special instruction. After the 30 weeks, the same tests were given as post-tests. (Five children were unavailable for post-testing).—*E.W.*

RESULTS

The music group outperformed the control group on the Bead Memory test, but not on any of the other tests. However, this difference was significant only for middle- and higher-income children in both groups, $F(1,43)=6.29$, $p<.016$. Low-income children in the music group did not comply with the program (attendance, parental involvement, and completion of home assignments was low), and this may explain why these children did not outperform the control group on Bead Memory. Children in the music group who were most involved in the program (showed the highest compliance) improved on Pattern Analysis more than did the other music children ($p<.01$); however, there was no difference between the music and control groups on this test.—*E.W.*

CONTRIBUTIONS TO THE FIELD

This study adds to the body of research examining a possible link between music training and spatial thinking.

The study showed that preschoolers who get music training improve more than those who do not on a visual test in which one must recall and reassemble sequences of beads of different colors and shapes (Bead Memory test). Children with music training did not improve on another visual test (Pattern Analysis test), and also did not improve on verbal and mathematical tests.—*E.W.*

"This study provides additional evidence of a link between music training and spatial-temporal reasoning."

COMMENTARY

Future studies should advance clear hypotheses about which tests should be expected to improve as a result of music training, and a plausible explanation for these hypotheses should be developed. It would be helpful to provide a suggestion for why the kinds of visual-spatial skills used in the Bead Memory subtest were sensitive to music training, while those required by the Pattern Analysis subtest were not.—*E.W.*

CONTRIBUTIONS TO THE FIELD

This study provides additional evidence of a link between music training and spatial-temporal reasoning. Preschoolers who received instruction in singing, pitch recognition, notation, composition, and other music skills scored higher than a control group on the Bead Memory subtest of the Stanford-Binet Intelligence Scale. This subtest measures abstract reasoning abilities, including visual memory, imagery, and sequencing.

The study is notable because it employed a multifaceted approach to music instruction. Because most research in this area has been based upon keyboard training, the findings add support for a general causal connection between music and aspects of cognitive development.—*R.H.*

COMMENTARY

The study included design characteristics that should be of interest to future investigations. For one, the researchers measured achievement of music abilities and thereby were able to determine that the group that received music instruction had significantly improved rhythmic and pitch-matching skills. Thus, they can more easily attribute changes in cognitive skills to musical growth.

The researchers also strengthened their study by adding what they termed "compliance variables." They observed variance in the level of participation in the treatment group, and thus sought to measure the degree to which children and their parents complied with the music program's requirements. Compliance variables included parent attendance, children attendance, and completion of out-of-class assignments. In their analysis, they examined the relationship between patterns of participation and outcomes on the Stanford-Binet scale. This enabled the researchers to provide a more detailed analysis than if they had simply compared overall results from the treatment and control groups.—R.H.

STUDY NAME: **Can Music Be Used to Teach Reading?**
AUTHOR: Ron Butzlaff
PUBLISHED: The Journal of Aesthetic Education, Fall 2000, 34 (3): 167-178

Research Questions

Is there a relationship between music instruction and performance in reading? Does music instruction lead to enhanced reading ability?

METHODS

A meta-analysis was performed on a set of research studies that met three criteria: they used a standardized measure of reading performance, the reading test followed music instruction (a precondition for establishing a causal relationship), and sufficient statistical data were provided to estimate an effect size. These criteria yielded 30 studies. Twenty-four of these were defined as correlational because the studies did not provide pre-test reading data and students were not randomly assigned. Six studies were defined as experimental, with randomly assigned music and control groups, and both pre- and post-reading tests.

The largest studies by far in the correlational-study group were conducted by the College Board, with sample sizes over 500,000. These 10 studies, from 1988 to 1998, showed associations between verbal SAT scores and participation in one or more high school music performance classes. The SAT studies reported positive correlations ranging from .16 to .22. The other studies considered scores on other measures, such as the Stanford Achievement Test, and classes in instrumental music, Suzuki violin, and other music classes taught by either classroom teachers or music specialists. The reported ages of the other students range from first to fifth grades. The specific instructional content of these classes—as well as their duration, intensity, or quality—is unspecified, at least in the meta-analysis article.

The six experimental studies included sample sizes ranging from 12 to 46. The author does not report their ages. None of the studies used the same reading test as a dependent variable. The music treatment across the six studies is described differently, as well, and includes music therapy, singing songs, and note reading on a keyboard instrument. The effect size (r) varies from -.34, for the music therapy program, to .64 for an instrumental music program. The researcher set the effect sizes for two of the studies to .00 (p = .50) because they reported no significant difference or gain between the control and experimental groups.—R.H.

RESULTS

The meta-analysis of the correlational studies demonstrated a strong and reliable association between music instruction and standardized measures of reading ability (r = .17). Stouffer's Z and a t test of the mean Zr were both significant (Z = 301.38, p < .0001 and t = 4.2, p < .001). The study confirms a consistent relationship between music in schools and reading ability across the 24 studies.

Analysis of the experimental group also yielded a positive effect size (r = .18, or .11 weighted according to sample size). The Stouffer's Z statistic was also consistent (Z = 2.38, p = .009), providing some evidence of a causal relationship between music and reading, at least based upon this small set of studies. However, based on other significance and reliability tests, the author concludes that there is not sufficient evidence here to support that claim (such as the t test of the mean Zr, t = 1.06, p = .34).—R.H.

CONTRIBUTIONS TO THE FIELD

Through a meta-analysis of other research, the study found a consistent correlation between reading ability and music instruction. Although the connection between in-school music programs and performance on the SAT verbal test has already been widely publicized, this study found similar results across a larger set of studies using other standardized reading tests. This helps to build confidence in the music-reading relationship and points the way to more focused research.—R.H.

COMMENTARY

The author states that there is a "strong and reliable association between the study of music and performance on standardized reading/verbal tests". A reliable causal link between music and reading was not found, however, although a positive mean effect size was still found within the experimental group. The inconclusive findings in the causal meta-analysis are not surprising if we examine the studies they were based upon. The studies contain widely divergent musical interventions, and each uses a different test of reading ability. It is unclear how consistent the music instruction is among the different studies. The only study with a negative effect size was based upon music therapy, while all of the others used some kind of musical instruction as an independent variable. Moreover, two of the studies did not provide specific data on effect sizes or reliability.

There are apparently too few studies to work with in the experimental group, showing a clear need for a larger base of research if we are to pursue this kind of meta-analytic approach. Other researchers could differentiate among the studies in other ways besides the correlational and experimental groupings. Researchers might consider, for instance, whether all of the correlational studies employ a similar design, or whether some of them might be reclassified into a quasi-experimental group, along with several of the experimental studies.

More reflection on the limitations and lessons learned from the meta-analyses would be helpful. Is this the best method available to synthesize available literature on the relationship between complex disciplines like music and reading? Where does the method fall short, and when is it best applied?

Future researchers should address a flaw inherent in most arts transfer studies. We know very little about the music *learning* experience, and tallying seat time in a class is a poor substitute for investigating the richness and complexity of musical development.—*R.H.*

CONTRIBUTIONS TO THE FIELD

This study provides four reasons why educators should be interested in looking into the potential benefits of teaching language in the context of music studies. The rationale stems from four ways to approach conditions for learning transfer that may exist between music and language: (1) music and written language employ highly differentiated symbol systems yet both involve analogous decoding and comprehension reading processes (such as reading from left to right, sequential ordering of content, etc.), (2) there are also interesting parallels in underlying concepts shared between music and language reading skills (such as sensitivity to phonological or tonal distinctions), (3) music reading involves the simultaneous incorporation (and reading) of written text with music, and (4) learning in the context of a highly motivated social context such as music ensembles may lead to "heightened academic responsibility and performance" that may enhance reading achievement.

Results from correlational studies in this meta-analysis are "highly significant" suggesting a strong relationship exists between music and reading. Experimental studies that randomized the selection of subjects and employed pre- and post-reading tests also provided statistically significant, if not as robust, positive results.—*L.S.*

COMMENTARY

While the author mutes the positive findings in this meta-analysis by referring to the less robust effects shown in the small number of experimental studies, nonetheless, the trends of the results are clear: measures of reading skill and music education share a strong positive association. This finding should encourage music and language educators alike to pursue the integration of these subjects into one another in ways that may serve as entry points for more public school students to discover underlying connections between their academic and arts pursuits.

While the magnitude of the positive effect sizes has increased in research studies over time, the author is suspicious that, more recently, experimenters have "set out to show that music had a positive impact on students' academic performance." Given the rationale for music's close association with language reading processes and the increasingly positive findings in correlations between music and S.A.T. scores in language reported in this study, another interpretation of these data is possible. That is, increasingly positive trends in recent research suggest instead that the enhancement of language achievement through forms of music education may be the result of more sophisticated, integrative teaching and learning in both the language and music classrooms.

Regardless of differences of interpretation of these data, the trends reported in this study support the need for both educators and researchers to look more closely and deeply into the integration of language and music reading processes in the context of both academic classrooms and rehearsal studios.

Researchers in the future would be well advised to design experiments that take into account measures of musical learning and skill while looking into the interactive (as well as one-way causality) methods for studying the effects of the integration (as well as the current long-distance transfer model) of music and language instruction.—*L.S.*

"…confirms a consistent relationship between music in schools and reading ability across the 24 studies."

STUDY NAME: **The Effects of Three Years of Piano Instruction on Children's Cognitive Development**
AUTHOR: Eugenia Costa-Giomi
PUBLISHED: Journal of Research in Music Education, 1999, 47 (3): 198-212

Research Question

What is the effect of three years of piano instruction on children's spatial, verbal, and quantitative skills?

METHODS

Forty-three fourth-grade children were given three years of private traditional piano instruction (30 minutes per week in years 1-2, 45 minutes per week in year 3) and were compared with 35 children in a control group. Children were pre-tested on measures of verbal, quantitative, and spatial ability, musical ability, and fine motor ability. There was no difference between the music and control group on any measure at pre-test. Children were post-tested after one, two, and three years of the program on the same spatial, quantitative, and verbal measures as used in the pre-test.—*E.W.*

RESULTS

An analysis of variance showed that after one and two years of treatment, children in the music group scored higher than those in the control group on the one spatial test given (from the Developing Cognitive Abilities Test) ($p = .05$). There were no significant differences between scores of the music and control groups on any of the quantitative or verbal subtests.

Following the third year of treatment, the music group was no longer ahead of the control group in spatial scores. This occurred because of a dramatic increase in control children's spatial scores. Comparison of group means over the course of the three-year period revealed that the experimental children's spatial scores steadily increased each year, while control children's spatial scores remained constant or showed very little improvement during the first two years, followed by rapid improvement during the third year.

A multiple regression analysis revealed that effort to learn piano (as measured by weekly practice time and number of lessons missed) explained 21 percent of the variance in spatial abilities of the experimental group following three years of treatment. This suggests that motivation to learn piano affected the extent of spatial gains.—*E.W.*

CONTRIBUTIONS TO THE FIELD

This study is the only *longitudinal* study of the effect of music instruction on non-musical cognitive skills.

After one and two years of piano, children scored higher than those in the control group on spatial but not verbal or quantitative measures. After three years, however, the control group had caught up in spatial scores and thus the music group was no longer ahead in spatial reasoning.—*E.W.*

COMMENTARY

It is not clear why the spatial gains of the music group did not last during the third year of piano instruction, and future research is needed to explore this issue.

It is possible that the music group stopped making spatial gains in the third year because not all of the students were attentive enough at learning the piano. This explanation is suggested by the finding that effort to learn piano accounted for about a fifth of the variance in spatial score at year three.

Costa-Giomi also suggests that the fact that children were entering puberty in the third year might have affected the results (due to hormonal influences on spatial ability). The study could be repeated with younger children to test this hypothesis.—*E.W.*

CONTRIBUTIONS TO THE FIELD

This study adds to our understanding of the effects of music training on spatial abilities. Unlike other research in this area, this is a longitudinal study that examined effects over a three-year period.

Children receiving weekly piano instruction scored higher than a control group on spatial measures for the first and second years of the study. This adds support to the findings of other researchers that music training has at least a temporary effect on spatial reasoning. In the third year of the study, the control and treatment groups had similar spatial scores. The author suggests that this may be due to differences in motivation and persistence of the piano students, or the effect of changes in hormonal levels on spatial task performance.—*R.H.*

COMMENTARY

This study makes an important contribution by adding to the body of work suggesting effects of keyboard training on spatial skills. The study is significant, in part, because it found effects within intact school groups instead of a laboratory setting. This kind of quasi-experimental approach may be necessary in a longitudinal study of this duration. Perhaps the length of the study led to the introduction of uncontrolled variables that influenced the results. This may explain the lack of effects beyond spatial reasoning and particularly the interesting phenomenon of the flat effects in the third year.

The records on practice times and lessons are helpful to the interpretation. In retrospect, it is clear that more data that add depth and substance to the music treatment would help explain the results, particularly the drop-off after three years. Future researchers designing similar studies should gather more comprehensive data on group characteristics and the nature of the musical experience. This could lead to a more nuanced interpretation, and connect the research conclusions to classroom practice.—*R.H.*

"The study is significant…because it found effects within intact school groups instead of a laboratory setting."

MUSIC

STUDY NAME: Enhanced Learning of Proportional Math Through Music Training and Spatial-Temporal Training
AUTHORS: Amy B. Graziano, Matthew Peterson, and Gordon L. Shaw
PUBLISHED: Neurological Research, 1999, 21: 139-152

Research Questions

Can understanding of fractions and ratios be enhanced by a training method consisting of a combination of a spatial-temporal math video game and piano keyboard training?

Does the addition of piano keyboard training make a difference in math outcomes?

METHODS

This study made use of a researcher-designed spatial-temporal math video game designed to train understanding of the spatial basis of fractions and ratios. The video game consisted of two stages. In the first stage, children manipulated images mentally. For example, they identified what given shapes would look like if they were turned upside down, and they were shown shapes and asked to imagine them folded in half. In the second stage, children worked on spatial presentations of fractions and proportions. For example, they were shown two shapes, one of which could be fitted twice into the area of the other. They were asked how many buckets of paint it would take to paint the larger shape if it took two buckets to paint the smaller one. All instructions were presented through computer animation and required no reading.

One hundred and thirty-six second-graders from an inner-city school participated. One group (n=26) received a combination of spatial-temporal math video game training (one hour twice a week for a total of 61 sessions) and piano keyboard training (over the course of the same time). Keyboard instruction consisted of learning to read music and play simple melodies. A second group (n=29) received the same amount of video game training but instead of piano got English-language training on a computer (reading, pronunciation, spelling, sentence structure). Both piano and English training were given three times a week for a total of 42 one-hour sessions. A third group (n=28) received no special training at all. There were three additional groups who received only the video game training, for three months, two months, and one month, respectively.

Children were pre- and post-tested with three tasks from the WISC-III: Object Assembly, Block Design, and Picture Arrangement. Children were also post-tested with the Spatial-Temporal Math Video Game Evaluation Program, which presented the same kinds of spatial problems used in the training.—*E.W.*

RESULTS

Spatial-Temporal Math Video Game Evaluation Program: The group that received a combination of video game and piano scored 15% higher than the group that received a combination of video game and English (p<.05). Both of these groups scored dramatically higher than those who received no video game training at all, demonstrating that the video game training enhanced performance on the kinds of skills it was designed to train. Those who received only the video game showed a positive association between length of training and score on the Evaluation Program.

WISC-III Tasks: Both groups were reported to show about the same level of improvement (approximately 1.5 points) on the Object Assembly, Block Design, and Picture Arrangement tasks.—*E.W.*

CONTRIBUTIONS TO THE FIELD

This study advances our understanding of the relationship between music, spatial reasoning, and spatial aspects of mathematics.

Children given a combination of piano keyboard lessons and experience with a video game designed to train spatial ability and spatially presented proportional math concepts scored higher on proportional math concepts than those who received the same video game training with English-language instruction instead of piano. Thus the combination of piano plus video game seemed to enhance learning of the concepts taught by the video game. Both groups, however, improved about the same amount on three tasks from the Wechsler Intelligence Scale for Children (WISC-III):

Object Assembly (a jigsaw puzzle task), Block Design (a task in which one must reproduce a 2-D design using 3-D colored blocks), and Picture Arrangement (a task in which one must order a series of pictures to tell a sensible story).—*E.W.*

COMMENTARY

Future research should examine whether combined piano and video game training enhances performance not only on spatially presented math problems similar to those actually used in the video game but also on traditionally presented math problems. Future research should also make sure to use the video game evaluation program not only at post-test but also at pre-test to be sure that abilities are matched prior to training.—*E.W.*

CONTRIBUTIONS TO THE FIELD

The study contributes to our understanding of the relationship between music instruction, spatial-temporal reasoning, and proportional math skills. Children who received keyboard instruction in combination with training in spatial reasoning and proportional math concepts (through exposure to a researcher-designed video game) scored significantly higher on measures of proportional math than children who either studied a combination of English and piano, or received no instruction.

These findings provide additional evidence of a link between music study and the development of spatial-reasoning skills. The findings also indicate that music study, combined with spatial-temporal training, enhances learning of some specific math skills.—*R.H.*

COMMENTARY

This study adds two new ingredients to the music-and-spatial-temporal-thinking stew. For one, instruction in spatial-temporal skills was directly provided, in addition to keyboard training, as part of the experimental treatment. It is reasonable to assume that this instruction would increase spatial-temporal scores, and it did. Perhaps more significant, the researchers determined that the combined music and spatial-temporal instruction led to enhanced performance on proportional math tasks. This helps to develop a more concrete chain of causality from music to math skills, at least when combined with training in spatial-temporal task performance. Further research is indicated to test various approaches to music instruction, such as those requiring movement, and their relationship with math skills.—*R.H.*

"This study advances our understanding of the relationship between music, spatial reasoning, and spatial aspects of mathematics."

MUSIC

III

STUDY NAME: **The Effects of Background Music on Studying**
AUTHOR: Susan Hallam
PUBLISHED: Unpublished Paper, School of Education, Oxford Brookes University, Wheatley Campus, Wheatley, Oxford, UK OX33 IHX

Research Question

Do children write better when listening to either calm or exciting music than when they write in silence?

METHODS

Fifty-four children from two mixed-grade (fifth- and sixth-grade) classrooms were divided into two experimental groups and one control group. All children were asked to write an exciting story and were given one hour. Children in one experimental group wrote while listening to calm music. Those in the second experimental group wrote while listening to exciting music. Those in the control group wrote in silence. Stories were scored in terms of whether the story had a beginning, middle, and end, flowed, held one's attention, was exciting, and had clear grammar. After writing, children in the music groups were also asked whether they were aware of the music, liked it, thought it helped them, and how it made them feel.—*E.W.*

RESULTS

Story scores did not differ for the silent and the calm music groups. But scores in the exciting music group were significantly lower than scores in the other two groups. The difference occurred because those in the exciting music group scored worse on criteria where higher-level thinking was involved (whether story had a climax; was exciting; held attention). On elements that were perhaps less challenging, there was no difference among groups (whether story had a beginning, middle, and end; level of detail; flow). Observations revealed that exciting music had a negative effect on behavior: children in this group were more likely to be off task and ask non-work related questions.

Despite the difference in scores, children in all groups were split 50/50 in terms of whether they thought that the music was helpful or distracting. Moreover, those in the exciting group were more likely to report liking the music (72 percent) than those in the calm group (22 percent).

These findings show that exciting music can interfere with school-related tasks, as might be expected. (However, this finding should be replicated so we can be sure that the children in the exciting condition were not less skilled to begin with). Contrary to expectation, calming music did not have a positive influence on performance. Self-report questionnaire results showed that children's perceptions of how music affects their work are often incorrect. Children believed that the music they liked was helpful, and music they did not like was distracting. Most children in the exciting group liked the music and half perceived it as helpful even though in fact it was hurtful.—*E.W.*

CONTRIBUTIONS TO THE FIELD

This study adds to the body of literature investigating the effect of background music on school tasks. The study showed that when background music is exciting, it interferes with creative writing, even though students like the music and do not perceive it as distracting. Calm music had no effect either positive or negative.—*E.W.*

"This study clearly illustrates the risks of employing background music listening activities into various forms of study without a conceptual framework for evaluating the context of its use..."

COMMENTARY

Future research should investigate which dimensions of music make music calm vs. exciting, and should investigate how calm and exciting music affects other tasks besides creative writing.—*E.W.*

CONTRIBUTIONS TO THE FIELD

This study clearly illustrates the risks of employing background music listening activities into various forms of study without a conceptual framework for evaluating the context of its use and intended impact on study tasks. The finding that various kinds of music can have a negative impact on creative writing or concentration should alert educators to the need for a deeper consideration of music as a possible tool or support for multi-tasking.

This study reviews elements of a broad conceptual framework for predicting the positive or negative effects of background music on cognitive tasks that includes (1) gauging the nature of the music, whether it is stimulating or relaxing, (2) the effects of music as determined by the characteristics of the individuals, their age, musical expertise, familiarity with the music, (3) the environment within which the studying is taking place, and (4) the characteristics of the studying task itself.—*L.S.*

COMMENTARY

This study is valuable for the care with which the related literature is reviewed and the range of factors that are investigated. This provides a developmental and cognitive scope that educators lack when they seek to apply background music as a positive influence on academic performance.

The investigation of metacognitive strategies opens up a new line of inquiry that may prove to be very useful when considering the role music plays in learning at different ages.—L.S.

"The investigation of metacognitive strategies opens up a new line of inquiry that may prove to be very useful when considering the role music plays in learning at different ages."

MUSIC

STUDY NAME: **Learning to Make Music Enhances Spatial Reasoning**
AUTHOR: Lois Hetland
PUBLISHED: The Journal of Aesthetic Education, Fall 2000, 34 (3-4): 179-238

Research Question

Does active instruction in music enhance preschool and elementary students' performance on spatial tasks?

METHODS

The researcher conducted a literature search for published and unpublished studies that examined the relationship between music and nonmusical cognitive outcomes. Fifteen studies were selected for meta-analysis according to these criteria: (1) they were reported in English, (2) participants were taught to make instrumental or vocal music, (3) they contained one or more control groups, (4) they contained outcome measures on mental rotation or spatial visualization, (5) sufficient statistics were provided to compute an effect size. Sample sizes ranged from 12 to 219 (mean N=78). Subjects ranged from ages 3 to 15. The musical treatments varied from four weeks to two years.

The researcher conducted a literature search for published and unpublished studies that examined the relationship between music and nonmusical cognitive outcomes. Three meta-analyses were performed on the studies. The first analysis tested the hypothesis that active music instruction enhances performance on spatial-temporal tasks. These tasks required either mental rotation or several steps for solving problems in two or three dimensions in the absence of a physical model. The outcome measure for spatial-temporal reasoning was most commonly the Object Assembly subtest of the WPPSI-R, although several other tests were used as well. Contrast analyses investigated subject variables (age and SES) and program variables (duration, lesson format, parental involvement, keyboard vs. non-keyboard, piano vs. xylophone, notation, movement, and composing or improvisation). Several other contrast analyses tested research design characteristics.

The second meta-analysis investigated the effect of music making on a measure of general intelligence, Raven's Standard Progressive Matrices. The third analysis examined studies that used spatial tests other than spatial-temporal reasoning measures. These included tests of spatial recognition, spatial memory, and spatial visualization.—*R.H.*

RESULTS

Consistent effects were found across the studies in the first meta-analysis. According to the author, "active music instruction lasting two years or less leads to dramatic improvements" in spatial-temporal reasoning. There was a mean effect size of r = .37 with a mean r = .39 weighted for sample size. Significance tests indicated that these results are very unlikely due to chance or error (Stouffer's Z = 8.74, p < .0001 and t of the mean Zr = 7.50, p < .0001). Contrast analysis indicated that individual lessons were more effective at increasing spatial-temporal reasoning scores than group lessons. Study of musical notation was also found to be more effective than music instruction without notation. However, effects remained robust with group lessons and instruction without notation. The other contrast analyses did not provide significant or practical results, indicating consistency across subject, program, and design characteristics.

The second meta-analysis found a small, but not significant, relationship between music making and Raven's Standard Progressive Matrices test (r = .08, weighted r = .03; Stouffer's Z = 1.32, p = .09; t of the mean Zr = 1.23, p = .29). The third meta-analysis demonstrated that effects of music making are not limited to spatial-reasoning performance, but may include other spatial tasks as well. However, few studies were found to include in this meta-analysis, and they employed different outcome measures. Nonetheless, according to the meta-analysis design as defined by the authors, a causal relationship was found between active music learning and spatial reasoning (r = .26, weighted r = .20; Stouffer's Z = 5.27, p < .0001; t of the mean Zr = 6.11, p = .0003).—*R.H.*

CONTRIBUTIONS TO THE FIELD

The study provides confirmatory evidence that music making leads to enhanced spatial reasoning skills. Through a meta-analysis of relevant studies, consistent causal effects were found on measures of spatial-temporal reasoning. Music making was also shown to cause enhanced performance on other spatial tasks besides spatial-temporal reasoning. However, the diversity of spatial measures and the small sample size (of studies) suggest that this second result is not easily interpreted and further study is needed to understand this promising finding.—*R.H.*

COMMENTARY

Because the results are consistent across the analyzed studies, there is little evidence presented that a particular approach to music instruction is more likely to lead to enhanced spatial skills. The exception is learning traditional music notation, which apparently leads to stronger effects. However, results are sufficiently robust with or without notation as part of music instruction. The author points out that the different approaches to music instruction in the analyzed studies are representative of many of the national standards in music education. Therefore, music educators need not fear that the findings presented here will distort instruction in favor of a particular music pedagogy found to increase spatial skills. Program administrators or music teachers should not use these results to alter their instruction in favor of an approach believed to be more effective in promoting spatial thinking. On the other hand, advocates and policymakers can use these results to support strong music education programs without concern that they are only looking toward "secondary" but non-musical outcomes.

Nonetheless, researchers should maintain an interest in differentiating among various approaches to music making and their effects on thinking skills. The contrast analyses in this study indicate an approach to teasing out this differentiation. The lack of useful results from the contrast analyses (beyond demonstrating the consistency of the findings) should not deter future researchers from this kind of exploration. It is likely that there are too few studies to work with, and that the studies don't contain sufficient data to perform a valuable contrast analysis. Future studies can embed variables that illuminate the musical treatment, so later analysis can understand which kind of musical instruction is most likely to lead to enhanced spatial skills. It may also be useful to rethink the linear model of transfer presented here, and instead conceptualize spatial skills as one set of mental operations inherent in musical thinking. Can the skills estimated by the spatial tests be reconsidered as reflective, in part, of musical thinking, rather than simply as an outcome effect?—R.H.

CONTRIBUTIONS TO THE FIELD

Distinguished from the "Mozart effect" passive listening studies, these three meta-analyses provide even more robust evidence that active musical training—especially when coupled with music notation—enhances performance on tests of spatial reasoning over at least a two-year period.

Surprisingly, the data across these 15 studies are consistent to the point that varying conditions of music education—such as differences in the amount of parent involvement, use of keyboard or not, length of program, use of expressive movement, inclusion of composition—do not significantly change the results. However, there are some indications that inclusion of notation and the use of one-on-one instruction (vs. group instruction) do increase the effect size significantly.

Results from the meta-analyses suggest also that offering a wide range of music programs in preschools and elementary schools similar to the ones reviewed in this meta-analysis will predict that nearly 70 percent of young children will "show spatial improvement as a result of the music program." Furthermore, this study supports the theory that music might enhance other non-temporal spatial processes such as those that require spatial visualization, rotation, or memory.—L.S.

COMMENTARY

The strong, positive findings reported here have been analyzed meticulously for bias to control for a wide range of methodological threats to their validity. These include the Hawthorne effect, the expectations of the authors, pre-existing differences in the groups, and even the quality of the research designs chosen for the study. There is no doubt in the author's mind as to the causal effect of music instruction on spatial reasoning. In addition, there is little doubt that these findings support the view that pre-wired connections to spatial thinking in the brain are triggered by active engagement with traditional music instruction, regardless of the intent of the music teacher.

Because of the small number of studies included in the meta-analysis, however, it is not possible to conclude that all future music programs will achieve these same results, nor is it possible to assume that these results will last beyond the two years of instruction.

If music can be regarded, as this study suggests, as fertile ground for "teaching for transfer," educators increasingly will have the opportunity to provide a greater range of instruction and teaching strategies geared toward transfer. It seems more than coincidental, for example, that the study that produced the strongest spatial outcomes in this analysis is also the only study that examined the combined effects of teaching spatial skills and music together (Graziano, et al. 1999, summarized in this volume). It is important therefore that future studies determine whether such deliberate integration of music instruction with other domains, such as the combining of spatial-temporally grounded math instruction with authentic and comprehensive music programs will lead to even stronger, clearer, and longer-lasting outcomes of learning transfer across these and other disciplines.—L.S.

"The study provides confirmatory evidence that music making leads to enhanced spatial reasoning skills."

STUDY NAME: **Listening to Music Enhances Spatial-Temporal Reasoning: Evidence for the "Mozart Effect"**
AUTHOR: Lois Hetland
PUBLISHED: The Journal of Aesthetic Education, Fall 2000, 34 (3-4): 105-148

Research Question

Does music listening enhance performance on spatial-temporal tasks?

METHODS

A comprehensive literature search was conducted for published and unpublished studies on music and spatial skills. The initial harvest of 553 studies was found to include 76 with spatial outcomes. Strict inclusion criteria further reduced this set to 26 studies reflecting 36 experiments. First, the author determined if the studies were relevant to the research questions of the meta-analysis. Additionally, the studies had to: (1) use only human subjects, (2) have at least one experimental condition when subjects listened to a musical stimulus, (3) have at least one control condition predicted to not enhance spatial skills, (4) include an outcome measure on at least one spatial task, (5) provide sufficient statistics to compute an effect size, and (6) control for practice effects.

Mozart's Sonata for Two Pianos in D major, K. 448 was the most frequent musical treatment in the collected studies. Other music by Mozart (K. 488), Schubert, Mendelssohn, and Yanni, as well as rhythm and melody alone, were also hypothesized to have spatial effects. Control conditions included silence, relaxation tapes, noises, and music by Philip Glass, Pearl Jam, and others hypothesized to be "non-enhancing" of spatial reasoning. Most of the outcome measures were of spatial-temporal tasks, while some measured non-spatial temporal tasks. Effect sizes (r) were calculated for each task within the selected studies.

Six preliminary analyses compared control conditions to determine if they could be combined into the overall meta-analyses. These preliminary analyses examined relationships between: (1) Mozart K. 448 and silence, (2) classical music and relaxation instructions, (3) silence and relaxation instructions, (4) silence and noise, (5) silence and non-enhancing music, and (6) relaxation and non-enhancing music. Two meta-analyses were then performed. The first meta-analysis examined whether music listening enhances performance on all types of spatial tasks. The second focused on music listening and only spatial-temporal tasks.—R.H.

RESULTS

Results from the preliminary analyses indicated that studies with different control conditions could be combined for the final two meta-analyses. The 36 experiments in the first meta-analysis—that contained music thought to enhance various spatial outcomes—had a mean r of .22 (weighted r = .18). Significance tests indicated that it is highly unlikely that these effects were due to chance, and that similar results are likely in future studies. (Stouffer's Z = 5.77, p < .0001; t of the mean Zr = 5.34, p < .0001). A linear contrast analysis found that music listening enhances performance on spatial-temporal tasks (r = .20) more than on non-spatial temporal tasks (r = .04). The second meta-analysis found a significant effect of music listening on spatial-temporal outcomes (r = .24; weighted r = .19). This was also found to be significant and generalizable (Stouffer's Z = 6.74, p < .0001; t test of the mean Zr, t = 4.84, p < .0001).

Eight linear contrast analyses were conducted to determine the effects of specific moderator variables. Music other than Mozart was found to also enhance spatial-temporal performance. No significant effect differences were found between males and females, or between published and unpublished studies. Certain laboratories were found to produce stronger effects, which may be due to the quality of the studies or other undetermined research conditions.—R.H.

CONTRIBUTIONS TO THE FIELD

The researcher provides a useful review of available literature on the "Mozart effect," that is, the effect of listening to music on spatial-temporal reasoning. Prevailing theories accounting for this phenomenon, such as the trion model of the cortex, arousal, and musical preference, are reviewed. A coded list of gathered research studies provides future researchers with a base for additional investigation, through itemizing the musical treatments and the outcome measures employed by the various studies.

The meta-analysis supplies confirmatory evidence that the so-called Mozart effect is robust and consistent across this set of studies. Music listening appears to enhance spatial-temporal reasoning skills, defined as mental rotation or spatial visualization in the absence of a physical model.—R.H.

COMMENTARY

This meta-analysis, along with the collective work on music and spatial-temporal reasoning it reflects, points to several promising areas for additional research. Effects do not appear limited to Mozart's K. 448, or even to the music of Mozart. Further research with other music may help isolate the most significant musical qualities that influence, or operate alongside of, spatial temporal thinking. We still don't know the particular characteristics of music, or musical thinking, that enhance, interact, or have common elements with spatial temporal reasoning skills. Additional study is indicated to tease out these musical characteristics.

As research continues in this promising area, we may be able to further identify and define the cognitive operations within musical thinking and then understand how these function across other mental domains. It may prove that a categorization scheme that segregates musical and spatial thinking oversimplifies the phenomena observed in these studies. Similar cognitive operations or brain functions may be in play within both of these domains.—R.H.

CONTRIBUTIONS TO THE FIELD

Two meta-analyses of studies confirm the existence of the positive effect of listening to certain kinds of music on immediate follow-up spatial tasks that involve the transformation of mental images without a physical model (first published by Rauscher, Shaw, et al. in 1993). This phenomenon, called the "Mozart effect," has frequently been challenged on the basis of its difficulty of replication and because there are competing explanations for the phenomenon itself.

"This meta-analysis supplies confirmatory evidence that the so-called Mozart effect is robust and consistent across this set of studies."

This analysis, based on a more comprehensive and inclusive set of studies than the most recent meta-analysis of the Mozart effect (Chabris, C., *Nature* 1999 pp. 826-27), reports the highly robust effects of listening to Mozart on various types of spatial reasoning tasks, especially spatial-temporal problems that require a sequence of mental images necessary to solve object-assembly tasks.

The data suggest that the effect is real, yet it can occur with other kinds of music beside Mozart. However, researchers do not yet know conclusively why the effect occurs. The trion model of the cortex (where neurons supposedly are primed by musical processing for spatial tasks) appears more likely to explain the enhanced test scores and brain imaging patterns than the competing "arousal" theory suggested in previous meta-analyses. Yet the author considers the rhythmic aspects of patterns depicted either through aural or visual stimuli as an alternative, yet related, theoretical explanation for the effect.—L.S.

COMMENTARY

The Mozart effect is important for educators, not because it provides another reason for music educators and parents to entice children to listen to classical music, but, as the author points out, because findings from these meta-analyses contradict prevailing views of learning in two areas: brain modularity (the assumption that cognitive capacities are located in discrete areas of the brain) and learning transfer (the assumption that transfer is unlikely and difficult to facilitate across disparate cognitive domains).

The fact that passive listening to music appears to "prime" spatial thinking indicates that neural networks normally associated with one kind of mental activity can readily share the cognitive processes involved in a different activity. Thus learning or thinking in one discipline may not be completely independent of another.

The significance of a learning transfer that occurs with unconscious priming is that there may also be other neurological avenues and facilitative pedagogical strategies for educators and researchers to integrate learning by identifying modes of thinking common to more than one discipline.—L.S.

STUDY NAME: **An Investigation of the Effects of Music on Two Emotionally Disturbed Students'**
Writing Motivations and Writing Skills
AUTHORS: Patrick Kariuki and Cindy Honeycutt
PUBLISHED: Paper presented at the Annual Conference of the Mid-South Research Association,
New Orleans, LA, November 4-6, 1998

Research Question

Can listening to music help motivate emotionally disturbed students to improve their
writing skills?

METHODS

A case study of two fourth-grade boys in a special education class of students classified as "emotionally disturbed" was conducted to determine whether music listening could motivate these boys to improve in writing. The study was divided into four time periods, each lasting about four weeks. In the first and third periods, the boys completed weekly writing assignments without listening to music. During the second and fourth periods, students completed weekly writing assignments while listening to music (through headphones) in a wide range of styles. The writing assignments in the music sessions were related to the type of music heard. Writing was scored for technical skills, creativity, and volume. Researchers also observed the students while writing, and interviewed them about their reactions to the assignments. Students were also given a questionnaire about their attitude about each assignment.—E.W.

RESULTS

Both students improved their writing skill by two letter grades when listening to music. Unfortunately, however, the grades were not broken down by creativity vs. technical skill. Students wrote more words when listening to music. For instance, one student increased his word count from 5 to 40; the other increased his count from 9 to 92! Students also felt more positive about writing when listening to music, and were observed to be more focused when writing to music than when writing without music. Students reported that the music made the writing exciting and helped them stay focused.—E.W.

CONTRIBUTIONS TO THE FIELD

This study suggests that music listening may help emotionally disturbed, special-needs children focus more when completing a writing assignment in school.—E.W.

COMMENTARY

It is not clear who scored the students' writing, nor if the scorers knew whether the writing they were scoring was carried out with or without music. If the researchers themselves did the scoring, and if they did not score the writing blind to whether the writing was accompanied by music or not, it is possible that experimenter bias may have affected the results.

When writing to music, students were asked to write in reaction to the music. When writing in silence, students had no outside stimulus to react to. It is therefore possible that the improved writing during music listening was due to having a stimulus to react to, rather than due to music. Future research should compare music-linked assignments with assignments in which students are given something else specific to react to (such as an autobiographical memory).

Future research should examine whether the positive effects associated with writing found in this case study of two students generalize to other emotionally disturbed students, or to typical children. Future research should examine what kinds of music work best, and which aspects of writing are most helped by music.—E.W.

CONTRIBUTIONS TO THE FIELD

This study employs a design valuable for the study of effects of music listening in the context of language arts activities. It is of value to see that music listening heightened by various activities made such a contribution to the quantity and quality of the written work of two emotionally disturbed students.

The use of music listening as an effective tool for improving emotionally disturbed children's attitude toward writing suggests that music allows children with low levels of motivation to focus on tasks rather than serve as a distraction to the writing process itself.—L.S.

COMMENTARY

This study suggests a cognitive framework that supports the use of music listening as a resource for writing skill development when critical listening brings "interwoven facets of language" into play in the writing process. Interwoven facets such as listening, speaking, reading, and writing are, in the opinions of the authors, stimulated by having the participants learn the music, lyrics, and various parts of the music. In other words, effective music education focused on music listening appears to be a salient factor that supports its utility in the context of other academic work.

Unfortunately, this paper is missing important details that would help readers understand its significance more. For example, we don't know what the qualitative differences look like in the writing samples. Nor do we know what was taken as evidence of the "more creative" writing. These examples would help teachers apply this framework with concrete qualitative results in mind.—L.S.

STUDY NAME: **The Effects of Musical Performance, Rational Emotive Therapy and Vicarious Experience on the Self-Efficacy and Self-Esteem of Juvenile Delinquents and Disadvantaged Children**

AUTHOR: John Roy Kennedy

PUBLISHED: Unpublished Doctoral Dissertation, Department of Music and Dance, University of Kansas, Lawrence, KS, 1998

Research Question

Do performing songs on guitar and singing boost self-esteem and self-efficacy in at-risk youth (in comparison to therapeutic treatments that do not include performance)?

METHODS

Forty-five 8- to 19-year-old males living in residential homes and juvenile detention centers for at-risk youths participated. All were either identified as "at-risk" students or had been arrested for petty or serious offenses. None had experience with the guitar. Five groups were formed: Performance Only, Performance/Cognitive Strategy, Cognitive Strategy, Vicarious, and Control. All received 30-minute weekly guitar instruction, and all but the control group then received 30 minutes of additional instruction depending on the group.

Those in the Performance group received 30 minutes of instruction performance etiquette, strategies for achieving peak performance, memorization, and musical expression. Following this, they gave solo performances to their peers.

Those in the Performance/Cognitive Strategy group received 30 minutes of cognitive instruction (instruction in mental strategies for performing) and musical performance instruction (how to deal with performance anxiety). Following this, they gave solo performances to their peers.

Those in the Cognitive Strategy group received 30 minutes of the same cognitive instruction as the Performance/Cognitive group but were given no chance to rehearse these techniques nor give solo performances.

Those in the Vicarious Experience group received 30 minutes of watching performances followed by discussion of successful and failed performances.

Participants were pre- and post-tested on self-esteem, using the Rosenberg Self-Esteem Scale, and musical self-efficacy (how confident they feel about their musical ability).—*E.W.*

RESULTS

Scores in the Performance and Performance/Cognitive groups improved significantly, but scores in the other groups did not improve.—*E.W.*

CONTRIBUTIONS TO THE FIELD

This study examines social outcomes of music instruction with at-risk youth. The study demonstrated that guitar training coupled with repeated performance experiences improves both musical self-efficacy and self-esteem of these youth.—*E.W.*

COMMENTARY

Only those students who learned to give solo performances showed improvements in self-esteem. This interesting finding suggests that music training improves self-esteem because the opportunity to perform helps youth overcome fears and helps them see that they can succeed. Replication research should ensure that the instruction not be delivered by the experimenter, in order to avoid any unconscious experimenter bias.—*E.W.*

CONTRIBUTIONS TO THE FIELD

This study shows that musical performance and musical performance coupled with cognitive strategies improve self-efficacy (concept of self-capacity) in at-risk youth, whereas the effect of self-esteem (concept of self-worth) was not significant (perhaps due to sample size).

Surprisingly, the use of cognitive strategies alone had no effect on self-efficacy ratings, suggesting that musical performance of music in the popular idiom is a powerful and underused tool for improving the well-being of at-risk youth in our public schools.

This study suggests that mastery of subject matter in musical performance is therapeutic, because it enables the patient to cope more effectively with the environment and acquire social competencies. Consequently this study illustrates the "efficacy of musical education" on the therapeutic goals of the selected population of at-risk students.

In addition, this study reveals that significant therapeutic changes occur through musical performance that do not require extensive previous knowledge of music or music aptitude.

The areas of music therapy techniques related to cognitive and emotional

> "...musical performance of music in the popular idiom is a powerful and underused tool for improving the well-being of at-risk youth in our public schools."

aspects of performance described in this study need to be studied by music educators for the purpose of enhancing the value of their programs in schools.—L.S.

COMMENTARY

The performance tasks and supporting cognitive strategies for performances outlined in this research should be studied carefully for their value to music education and any other aspects of education that rely on performance values.

Not only are the musical performance tasks sequenced skillfully but also the cognitive strategies employed in the study suggest how self-efficacy of any music student would be improved by cognitive strategies such as "having the mind staying in exact step with the music and its physical execution."

The use of performance strategies that limit destructive tendencies of negative self-evaluative judgment would contribute to the goals of inclusivity in public school music programs that otherwise normally weed out students who suffer from performance anxiety.

This study suggests also that improvement in self-efficacy relies also on critical thinking and not on optimal therapeutic conditions alone. This study clearly suggests that applying Rational Emotive Therapy (RET) principles to performance of the song (dealing with errors, preferences, positive thinking in anticipation of chord changes) outweighs the anxiety or discomfort experienced during a vicarious performance. As the author reports, "attending, processing, integrating, and rehearsing information, along with accompanying verbalizations and behaviors, are elements of learning that are effected by self-efficacy expectations in these students."

With regard to the relevance of this study to public education, the author notes also that other research focused on building self-efficacy suggests that musical performance may provide higher levels of motivation to learn in elementary and middle school students with learning problems.—L.S.

STUDY NAME: The Effect of the Incorporation of Music Learning into the Second-Language Classroom on the Mutual Reinforcement of Music and Language

AUTHOR: Anne S. Lowe

PUBLISHED: Unpublished Doctoral Dissertation, 1995, Urbana-Champaign, University of Illinois

Research Questions

When incorporated into an elementary, second-language classroom (French for second-graders), does a music program whose methodology is based on similarities between the structures of music and language reinforce both the learning of music and the learning of the second language?

Does level of academic achievement in French and mathematics affect the degree to which students increase their learning of a second language and of music when music is incorporated into the second-language classroom?

METHODS

Fifty-three second-grade subjects (Control $n = 26$, Experimental $n = 27$) from an elementary school in New Brunswick, Canada (similar academic and socio-economic backgrounds, not further described), were assigned to either control (regular oral-visual drill-type French lessons, taught by a French immersion teacher, and 30 minutes of separate music instruction, taught by a music specialist) or experimental groups. Experimentals received the same "regular" program as the controls (co-planned by the experimental and control group teachers to control for teacher effects), and, in addition, had five, 15-minute music lessons each week, totally incorporated to the French second-language class (it is unclear whether French instruction was consequently reduced by 15 minutes/session). Music instruction focused on music concepts of tonal-rhythmic pattern and form. Language instruction focused on concepts of pronunciation, oral grammar, vocabulary, and comprehension. The integrated music and language instruction was planned and taught daily (duration not specified for French classes) by the regular classroom teacher for a period of eight weeks.

A two-week pilot study was conducted that employed 23 grade two, French immersion students in another school in the district that was not included in the final study. The pilot was used to assess validity and reliability of measures and to assess educational value, format, feasibility, and practicality of the music lessons.

Measures—Multiple measures were used to assess music and language, which avoids a potential bias caused by the form of the test. The pre-/post-test design used tests designed by the study author with the assistance of music and French second-language specialists and criterion-referenced to curriculum objectives. The French tests measured French pronunciation and oral grammar (individually administered) and vocabulary and reading comprehension (group administered). Oral grammar, vocabulary, and reading comprehension tests were hand-scored for number correct, and the pronunciation test was scored blind from audiotapes with average score computed from ratings of a panel of five native-speaking judges (teachers at the school who did not teach the students). The music tests measured tonal-rhythmic pattern and musical form. One part asked subjects to match written notations to melodies, rhythms, and forms played on tapes. This test was scored by hand for number correct. Another section asked subjects to play a given pattern or form on Orff tone bells. Average scores across the five judges (elementary general music teachers in the area) were computed. Academic achievement was tested at pre-test only. The language achievement section, administered orally by the author, tested oral comprehension (through responding with a sentence, demonstrating an action, uttering a word to match an action, and matching written vocabulary words with images). Subjective sections (i.e., all but vocabulary) were audiotaped, judged by five French immersion teachers, and assigned average scores. Vocabulary was administered and hand-scored by the French immersion teachers, and number correct was analyzed. The mathematics test was 75 items that measured numeral dictation, drawing tenths and unities, identifying odd numbers, drawing indicated numerals, and greater than, less than. Mathematics tests were administered and scored by French immersion classroom teachers, and number correct was entered into the analyses. Qualitative data were also collected from the experimental teacher (daily journal and interviews) to assess potential reasons for outcomes.

Analysis—Kuder-Richardson was used to assess test reliability. Pearson product-moment correlations by group, time, and test were calculated to determine which variables covaried. Moderator variables (private piano lessons and three levels of academic achievement) were assessed through t tests and ANOVA. All possible main effects and interactions were assessed through a series of ANCOVAs (group x test time x test—two, four, or six tests—covarying pre-test scores and academic achievement). Scheffe's post-hoc tests were calculated for significant interactions to discover the source of significance in the omnibus tests.

Reporting was clear and detailed, with the exception of amount of time devoted to French and music. We do not know how long the "regular" French classes were, nor whether the experimentals gave up 15 minutes of instruction in French to accommodate the additional 15 minutes of music instruction that was incorporated. Gains in music for the experimental group are not so surprising if music instruction was increased by 45 minutes/week. However, if direct French instruction was reduced for the experimental group, it is quite compelling that French scores increased.—L.H.

RESULTS

The pilot study showed that reliabilities of the French tests were adequate (Kuder-Richardson coefficients ranging from .70 - .99), as were all but the tonal-rhythmic pattern written test ($r = .23$). The author suggests that the tonal-rhythmic pattern test is best combined with the music performance as a composite. Because pilot treatment was so brief (two weeks), it was deemed sufficient that some significant relationships (for form) were found between French and music concepts, so the main study employed French, tonal-rhythm, and form variables.

Private piano lessons did correlate with higher scores on tonal-rhythm pattern reading, but because only a few subjects took private piano lessons, this correlation does not compromise the results. Academic achievement did covary with all tests except tonal-rhythm, so it was employed as a covariate in the main study.

The results of the main analysis suggest that the incorporation of this music program enhanced general French and music skills, and, in particular, oral grammar, reading comprehension, tonal-rhythmic pattern/performance, and form/described (written) concepts.—L.H.

CONTRIBUTIONS TO THE FIELD

This study is a model for research on transfer in the field of arts education. The author carefully reviewed theoretical and empirical literature that identified connections between the structure of music and language, the similar processes of learning and teaching these disciplines, and previous empirical studies linking music and first- and second-language learning. The study was then designed to build on these findings and take a careful next step to extend understanding of a gap in the field: no previous studies had examined learning outcomes in *both language and music* that resulted when music was integrated into language programs.

The study found that learning in both areas was enhanced when music instruction was carefully and deliberately integrated into language instruction in ways that "bridged" areas of structural and pedagogical similarity in music and language instruction, compared with music and language instruction taught separately (not integrated, and without teaching for transfer). This form of music instruction enhanced French oral grammar, pronunciation, vocabulary, and reading comprehension, as well as the understanding of musical concepts related to tonal-rhythmic pattern and form.—L.H.

COMMENTARY

This study suggests that transfer needs to be carefully taught. It can occur when subjects are aligned in structure and/or in methods by which they are taught and learned. It also implies that training in arts and in methods of teaching for transfer is necessary for all teachers who integrate music (or other arts) into their courses. It does not seem necessary for such training to be extensive, however, when teachers have some musical background. It also suggests that student enthusiasm can influence achievement. Parents noticed differences in their children's interest and learning, and this implies that parents could serve as a source of support for such arts programs if they were informed about the rationale for such integrated programs.

It is not clear why the total time/week for music instruction was not held constant for the two groups. Experimentals had 45 minutes more music instruction each week, incorporated into their French classes (five days x 15 minutes per day). It also is not clear whether the time directly spent on French was reduced equivalently.

The author urges caution in interpretation, because groups were not randomized, and because of potential Hawthorne effects (doing better with the introduction of a special program) and teacher effects. In addition, some of the tests were not highly reliable (musical creativity and tonal-rhythmic pattern/written).

The author suggests that future research should vary age and socio-economic levels of subjects, and assess "learning mode dominance." She also suggests (1) developing new and more reliable measures, (2) comparing success of students whose teachers had varying amounts of formal music background, (3) developing programs that focus on other musical concepts such as timbre, articulation, harmony, and expression, (4) focusing on additional language skills such as reading and spelling, and (5) conducting a qualitative study to describe the entire integration process and its elements. She also suggests (6) testing the possibility that music-integration programs may benefit children with attention deficit more than other children. Future replications should be certain to match the duration of music instruction across groups and clearly report that total amount of instructional time per week for each group is equivalent.—L.H.

CONTRIBUTIONS TO THE FIELD

This careful study of music and language learning is very important to music educators, teachers, and researchers interested in the issue of two-way transfer effects between music and language arts. It is particularly important for educators who develop interdisciplinary curricula that focus on learning underlying processes, skills, and structures shared between language and music. Examples of interdisciplinary teaching methods devised in this study demonstrate how music can be "taught for transfer" at the same time for the development of music skill.

That the correlation between pronunciation test scores in language and measures of musical aptitude and instrumental training increases over time illustrates how learning in different areas of study can be enhanced through their interaction.

Furthermore, this study concludes that academic achievement correlates positively with musical achievement—especially with regard to music reading and notation processes. This finding suggests that it will be necessary for music educators to develop programs that foster strong music reading and written notation skills—a worthy goal that is not uniformly supported by instrumental lessons or ensemble studios currently in public schools—if music education is expected to be an effective resource for interdisciplinary approaches to second-language development.—L.S.

COMMENTARY

A literature review (featuring linguistics, musical perception, and speech) carefully outlines links between language and

"...points toward a set of similar brain mechanisms needed for both speech and musical processing."

music through investigating underlying mental processing shared between music and language. Although competing theories of separate intelligences are not discussed fully, much evidence points toward a set of similar brain mechanisms needed for both speech and musical processing.

The focus on cognitive components of reading processes such as "categorical discernment" of sound (phonemic awareness) or sound decoding (phonics) are examined in ways that support the rationale for studying the effects of music education on second-language studies.

Several aspects of music education, such as the focus on rhythmic or pitch (contour) aspects of language processing in vocal music, contribute to commonalities between music and language teaching. The use of songs, not surprisingly, directly enhances pronunciation, grammatical structure, vocabulary, and idiomatic expressions as well as wide variety in speed of delivery, phrasing, and linking of ideas.

Finally the argument is made that interdisciplinary learning should result in students who are better able to see the connections among subject areas and are therefore more likely to understand and remember what they learn. A second-language program that supports two-way learning connections between music and language will most likely serve as a model for interdisciplinary learning across other domains of study.—L.S.

STUDY NAME: **Music Training Causes Long-term Enhancement of Preschool Children's
Spatial-Temporal Reasoning**

AUTHORS: Frances H. Rauscher, Gordon L. Shaw, Linda J. Levine, Eric L. Wright, Wendy R. Dennis, &
Robert L. Newcomb

PUBLISHED: Neurological Research, February 1997, 19 (1): 2-7

Research Question

Does individual instruction on piano keyboards, supplemented by group instruction in singing,
cause long-term enhancement of spatial-temporal reasoning in preschool children?

METHODS

Subjects were 78 preschool children (42 boys and 36 girls) ages 3 and 4, of diverse ethnicity and normal intelligence, who were enrolled in classes from three preschools. Children were assigned to one of four groups: Keyboard (n = 34), Singing (n = 10), Computer (n = 20), and No Lessons (n = 14). Groups were assigned either randomly or as intact classes, depending on school. The study was conducted over a period of two years, but children received either six or eight consecutive months of instruction during that time.

Children in the Keyboard (n = 34) group received 10-minute private keyboard lessons from professional keyboard instructors using traditional methods. Depending on the school, children received lessons either once a week for eight months or twice a week for six months. Although some children received more lessons, no significant effects were found for number of lessons, so the results for both groups were pooled. Lessons focused on pitch intervals, fingering, sight-reading, music notation, and playing from memory. The preschools reserved one hour each day for children in the Keyboard group to practice. In addition, children in the Keyboard group participated daily in 30-minute singing sessions led by a music instructor.

The Computer group (n = 20) received 10-minute private lessons from a professional computer instructor using a personal computer and age-appropriate mathematics and reading software. These lessons were intended to control for hand-eye coordination practice, personal attention, and opportunity for engagement with an activity provided by the keyboard lessons. Children learned how to open the software using basic DOS commands and also learned number recognition, counting, and sentence completion.

The Singing group (n = 10) participated in the same daily 30-minute singing sessions as the Keyboard group but did not receive any additional private instruction. Children in the No Lesson group (n = 14) did not receive any instruction.

All children were pre- and post-tested for spatial reasoning with four tasks from the Performance subtest of the Wechsler Preschool and Primary Scale of Intelligence-Revised (WPPSI-R). The Object Assembly task is designed to measure spatial-temporal skill (i.e., forming a mental image of a completed object and rotating puzzle pieces to match that mental image). The other three tasks used were spatial recognition tasks and included Geometric Design (children match and draw geometric figures), Block Design (children match patterns using colored blocks), and Animal Pegs (children place correctly colored pegs below a series of animal pictures). These latter three do not involve one or more of the skills that define spatial-temporal reasoning: sequencing, mental rotation, matching to only a mental and not a physical image.

One-way ANOVA (for the four training groups) and multiple t tests, with Bonferroni adjustment to protect from the possibility of finding significant results by chance, were used for analysis.—L.H.

RESULTS

Age-adjusted means for pre- and post-tests revealed that children in the Keyboard group improved significantly on the Object Assembly task (pre-test mean = 9.8; post-test mean = 13.41), while children in the other three groups did not ($F_{3,74}$=3.87, p<0.0001). A set of Bonferroni t tests confirmed that mean change scores for the Keyboard group's performance on the Object Assembly task differed significantly from each of the other three groups (p < 0.01). There were no significant differences among Keyboard subjects post-tested within one day of their last keyboard lesson and those post-tested more than a day after the final lesson, which the authors define as a long-term effect. No significant improvement in scores was found for any group on the three spatial recognition tasks.—L.H.

CONTRIBUTIONS TO THE FIELD

This study was the first published, empirical test of the effects on children's spatial abilities caused by active engagement in music instruction (keyboard supplemented with singing). The study has direct implications for instruction with children and should not be confused with the authors' previous study on the "Mozart effect." (That laboratory study demonstrated temporarily enhanced spatial

reasoning abilities for college students after 10 minutes of exposure to a Mozart piano sonata when compared to performance of spatial tasks after listening to silence or audiotapes of relaxation instructions. The Mozart effect study examined how the mind processes information, not how children learn).

The study found enhanced spatial-temporal reasoning for the Keyboard group when compared with students who spent similar time on computer or singing-only instruction, or students who had no extra lessons.—L.H.

COMMENTARY

This study provides compelling evidence that learning to play the piano enhances a particular kind of spatial reasoning—spatial-temporal ability—in preschoolers. Because the effect lasted longer than one day, the results suggest that music instruction may cause long-term structural modifications in regions of the brain that are not exclusive to music processing. The authors speculate that the implications of their findings may be profound, since enhanced spatial-temporal ability may facilitate learning in areas of mathematics and science that rely heavily on spatial-temporal reasoning.

The results are somewhat compromised because the Keyboard group appears to have had up to one hour of additional practice time daily, so instruction time across groups was non-equivalent. In addition, the groups were not randomized at the level of the individual, and they may not have been equivalent before treatment. It is unclear whether singing contributed to the observed spatial enhancement—it did not do so independently, but it may have contributed in combination with piano instruction. A previous pilot study by these authors (1994) found that singing lessons enhanced low-SES children's spatial-temporal reasoning. The conflicting results imply that either or both the structure of the singing program or demographics play some role in producing the effect.

Future studies should continue to explore the specific aspects of music training responsible for the enhancement of spatial-temporal ability and how such increased spatial-temporal skills affect learning in school. They might also examine how such enhancement affects performance on school assessments. Fundamentally, future studies should seek to identify and explore the specific mental processes associated with learning music and spatial reasoning.—L.H.

CONTRIBUTIONS TO THE FIELD

This study suggests that musical training, unlike exposure to music, supports relatively long-term modifications in underlying neural circuitry in regions of the brain not primarily concerned with auditory processing.

This study shows that the effect of comprehensive training in music on tests of spatial ability is relatively long term compared to the short-term effect reported by the authors earlier as the "Mozart effect."

This study establishes that a distinctly comprehensive form of musical performance training on the piano supports a form of temporal-spatial reasoning that enables children to perform better on object assembly tasks that require a combination of skills such as spatial recognition, classification, and finding relationships among patterns in a sequential order—a fundamental process shared among many domains of study (including, but not limited to chess, mathematics, and engineering) and their application to daily life (such as the ability to plan, design, and organize actions, products, or thought).

The validity of these findings is supported by the nature of comprehensive musical training, well-known to conservatory-trained music educators, based on multiple representations of musical knowledge (keyboard, notations, numbers), performance modality (voice, fine motor skills), and symbol processing skills.—L.S.

COMMENTARY

This study reveals that a comprehensive form of musical performance training was employed to produce high performance on object assembly tests. Along with piano and voice instruction, preschool children studied pitch intervals, fine motor coordination, fingering numbering techniques, sight-reading music notation, and playing from memory. As the authors note, keyboard instruction provides a visual-linear representation of the spatial relations between pitches as does singing from notation; physical coordination progressed from one hand to two hands; and children were asked to transpose the fingering patterns to other regions of the keyboard. Thus the independent variable in this study comprises a sophisticated array of teaching practices that will have to be precisely replicated in further studies in other age groups or in school settings.

The results of this study should not surprise music educators who consider the spatial reasoning abilities required by comprehensive musical performance training to be far more complex than those tested in the object assembly task. Music performance skills can be understood in part as a measure of spatial-temporal intelligence. Consequently we should expect musical instruction to make a greater difference in spatial-temporal *performance* test results (such as object assembly tasks) than in the results of simple spatial *recognition* tests.

For educators interested in a deeper exploration of underlying concepts shared between musical skills and mathematics or science, more extensive investigations by researchers on the effect of music education on proportional reasoning (rhythm), hierarchical reasoning (tonal systems), and other forms of systems thinking (composition and analysis) will be welcome.—L.S.

"This study provides compelling evidence that learning to play the piano enhances a particular kind of spatial reasoning—spatial-temporal ability—in preschoolers."

STUDY NAME: Classroom Keyboard Instruction Improves Kindergarten Children's Spatial-Temporal
              Performance: A Field Experiment
AUTHORS: Frances H. Rauscher and Mary Anne Zupan
PUBLISHED: Early Childhood Research Quarterly, 2000, 15, (2): 215-228

Research Question

What is the effect in a public school setting of group music instruction that features learning to play a keyboard instrument on kindergarten children's spatial reasoning?

METHODS

Sixty-two middle-income kindergartners of both genders and diverse ethnicity from two intact classes at two elementary schools in Wisconsin were assigned to either keyboard instruction ($n = 34$) or no music ($n = 28$). In groups of 10 children, the Keyboard group had 20-minute lessons, two times per week for eight months, conducted in an area of their regular classroom. During the music lessons, the children in the control group engaged in "journaling" with their teacher in another part of the classroom. Both groups were pre-tested and re-tested after four and eight months.

Spatial-temporal ability was measured by the Puzzle Solving task (arranging cardboard pieces of a puzzle to create a familiar object) from the McCarthy Scales of Children's Abilities and the Block Building task (reproducing from memory a stair-step structure created and removed by the examiner from 10, 1-inch blocks) from the Learning Accomplishment Profile Standardized Assessment test. The Pictorial Memory subtest from the McCarthy Scales was used to index visual-spatial memory (recalling and identifying previously viewed pictures of objects).

The first analysis used a 2 x 2 x 3 (sex x group x time) MANOVA for each of the three tests. Repeated measures ANOVAs (group x time) were next conducted for each test. A 2 x 2 MANOVA (sex x group) on pre-test scores checked for group equivalence prior to treatment, which was confirmed through post-hoc Scheffe's t tests. Finally, a one-factor (group) MANCOVA (covarying pre-test scores) on gain scores (eight months minus pre-test) was conducted as a check on the previous analyses. Reporting of this study was clear and judicious, with several tables. Reporting would be improved by giving exact p values.—L.H.

RESULTS

The Keyboard group scored significantly higher ($p < .05$) on spatial-temporal measures after only four months of lessons, with greater enhancement demonstrated after eight months of lessons. Pictorial memory tasks did not differ by group at either measurement time.—L.H.

CONTRIBUTIONS TO THE FIELD

This study extends the first author's examination (see Rauscher et al., 1997, summarized in this volume) of the effects of active music instruction (in this case, using piano keyboards) on spatial reasoning tasks. It explores the effect on a new age group (i.e., public-school kindergartners instead of private-school preschoolers), employs keyboard instruction delivered to a group rather than to individuals, and compares spatial-temporal to spatial memory measures.

"...supports the need for further replication and extension into the public school curriculum."

The study found that spatial-temporal tasks (i.e., "tasks that require combining separate elements of an object into a single whole...to match a mental image," p. 216) were enhanced by keyboard training, but pictorial memory tasks were not. There were no gender effects.—L.H.

COMMENTARY

This study suggests that specific types of spatial reasoning (i.e., spatial-temporal) are enhanced by music instruction on keyboards, while another type of spatial ability (i.e., pictorial memory) is not.

The authors are careful not to generalize these positive results to global statements about music's effect on spatial ability and list a series of cautions about interpreting the findings. First, the authors caution that these results should not divert instructional goals toward spatial outcomes, but urge educators to continue to guide the design of musical instruction by learning musical goals such as those set by national music standards. The authors also caution that a Hawthorne effect (positive findings as a result of a new program) is possible because the control group was untreated. However, similar results for the music and no treatment groups on the pictorial memory task counter that threat to a degree. Further, the authors state that because children in the music group engaged in a range of musical activities, including keyboard training, moving to music, singing, reading notation, ear training, music literacy, and solfege (sight-singing), it is not clear which musical component(s) contributed to the spatial enhancement. The authors also remind readers that it is not clear how long the effects last.

Future research should investigate instruction with other age groups, with other socio-economic and geographic groups, and with separate components of music instruction. In addition, the relationship between this particular spatial skill and achievement in mathematics should be further investigated (cf. Graziano, et al. 1999, summarized in this volume).—*L.H.*

CONTRIBUTIONS TO THE FIELD

The educational potential of music training has been broadened through this study of the impact of a comprehensive approach to keyboard performance instruction conducted in a public school classroom.

The speed at which the impact occurs is striking. That such a sharp change in test scores of spatial ability occurs within four weeks suggests a treatment worth implementing in larger-scale school settings.

The authors cite the need for further studies to answer the question as to whether music affects mathematical reasoning (such as ratios and proportion) as it affects spatial-temporal reasoning measured in this study.—*L.S.*

COMMENTARY

As with earlier studies conducted by Frances Rauscher, the treatment on the experimental group is a form of comprehensive musical training that includes a range of musical activities, including keyboard training, moving to music, rhythmic clapping, singing, reading notation, and ear training. It is clear that these activities, taken together, might well support the development of spatial abilities measured by tasks that involve mental imaging and temporal ordering. The overlapping of skills required for comprehensive musical instruction and spatial ability should be seen as a basis for new forms of music and mathematical teaching that involve "relating information entering through one sense mode to analogous information in another mode."

This study suggests a reconciliation between Howard Gardner's view of musical intelligence as a separate domain of reasoning and his later view of musical intelligence as a possible "privileged organizer of cognitive processes" in early education.

While the authors cite brain studies, which support the hypotheses that musical training affects the development of neural pathways relevant to spatial abilities, this study now supports the need for further replication and extension into the public school curriculum.

If the music instruction methods used in this study are available in sufficient detail, they could be extremely useful to educators interested in analyzing the mathematics curriculum according to the neurological constructs of "spatial-temporal" reasoning. Mapping the factors used in these constructs (spatial perception, memory, operation, construction, etc.) onto the mathematics curriculum and the teaching practices of elementary school teachers will contribute to the educational validity and utility of this work.—*L.S.*

STUDY NAME: A Meta-Analysis on the Effects of Music as Reinforcement for Education/Therapy Objectives
AUTHOR: Jayne M. Standley
PUBLISHED: Journal of Research in Music Education 1996, 44(2), 105-133

Research Questions

How effective is "contingent" music (music used as behavioral reinforcement) in facilitating learning and behavior changes in education and therapy settings?

What circumstances affect music's reinforcement value in education and therapy settings?

METHODS

Ninety-eight studies were included in this analysis, with 208 effect sizes computed. Effect sizes for individual studies ranged from $d = 35.44$ to $d = -7.05$—a large range. (Note: negative effects indicate that the control condition was more effective than the music contingency).

The analysis was conducted by standard meta-analytic methods and reports effect sizes by the index called d (which indexes how many standard deviation units the treatment "pushes" the average effect above the mean). The literature search was extensive and included both published and unpublished studies to avoid bias. Inclusion criteria are clearly stated. The sample of studies is well described. Several helpful tables and charts highlight main results clearly.

Factors that may affect validity of results:

(1) Many diverse independent and dependent variables were combined in a single analysis. For example, the main analysis does not differentiate specific academic effects (e.g., outcomes as diverse as achievement in mathematics, reading, general academics, and cognitive music outcomes—such as reading notation and identifying pitches—are combined with attentiveness, color discrimination, and memory for telephone numbers), age of student (studies are combined that work with subjects ranging from 4 to 20 years), or relevant subject characteristics (studies of mentally and learning disabled subjects are combined with "normal" subjects).

(2) The main analysis combines mostly single-subject and small-sample studies, whose effects are systematically larger than those found in between subjects (experimental vs. control) designs. Because study size is not reported for individual studies included in the analysis, it is not clear how well the results generalize to group educational settings.

(3) Measures by which individual studies indexed outcomes are usually not reported.

(4) No inferential statistics are reported, which further limits our ability to generalize from this analysis.—L.H.

RESULTS

The general result is that contingent music ($d = 2.90$; equivalent to $r = .82$) is more effective in promoting education and therapy objectives (all types combined) than other reinforcement techniques ($d = 1.17$, equivalent to $r = .50$).

The analysis examined several moderator variables to explain what conditions contribute systematically to the size of effect:

(1) Using music to increase ($d = 2.97$) or decrease ($d = 2.77$) behavior;

(2) Initiating music as a reward ($d = 2.55$) or interrupting it as a consequence ($d = 3.56$);

(3) Immediate ($d = 3.38$) or delayed ($d = 1.70$) reward with music;

(4) Using music with different ages (highest in infants-4 years: $d = 3.51$ and adults: $d = 4.51$, lower in school-aged children: 5-11 years $d = 2.53$, 12-14 years $d = 1.96$, 15-18 years $d = 1.08$);

(5) Subject ability categories: physically or medially impaired ($d = 2.25$); emotionally impaired ($d = 2.38$), normal ($d = 2.99$), mentally impaired ($d = 3.16$);

(6) Study design (subjects as own controls $d = 3.42$; experimental vs. control groups, $d = 1.62$).

The following outcomes were assessed individually for degree of relationship to various musical "treatments":

(1) educational-academic ($d = 2.18$, mostly achievement in reading and mathematics, not further described)

(2) educational-social ($d = 2.04$, e.g., staying on task, positive interactions, lower noise, and higher attention)

(3) physical rehabilitation ($d = 5.47$)

(4) medical-health ($d = 2.26$)

(5) sports-exercise ($d = 1.39$, e.g., increased duration riding stationary bike)

(6) developmental ($d = 3.40$, including (a) attention/interaction, (b) self-help, (c) behavior in car or bus, (d) stereotopy (e.g., tics, regurgitation, self-stimulation, wandering), (e) complaining, (f) work, and (g) preference variables)—L.H.

CONTRIBUTIONS TO THE FIELD

Through the method of meta-analysis, this study examines diverse results from studies in which music was used as a reward for learning and for behavior changes. To my knowledge, it was the first meta-analysis to address any form of educational outcome in relation to music. Such syntheses of individual studies set the stage for greater scientific precision by establishing base-line effect sizes (that is, an index of the strength of relationship between an educational "treatment" and a measured outcome). The author also clearly defined the value of meta-analyses for policy and future research and encouraged more use of this method within the field. In addition, she described the standard procedures of the technique clearly and in accessible, non-technical language.

The study found contingent music (that is, music used as a reward for desired behavior) to be considerably more effective (by nearly two standard deviations) than other types of reinforcements (e.g., candy, juice, stories, praise) found in previous meta-analyses of non-musical contingencies.

The analysis will be of most interest to therapists and general educators, since most of the studies involve listening to music as a reward rather than learning music or learning through music.—*L.H.*

"This study suggests that contingent music effectively reinforces learning and behavior changes."

COMMENTARY

This study suggests that contingent music effectively reinforces learning and behavior changes. The author's previous meta-analysis of music's uses in medical and dental settings found an effect size slightly greater than one standard deviation for subjects reinforced with music compared with controls. The truly huge effect found in this analysis exceeds even that very large effect.

Several potential criticisms raise questions about the validity of the reported effect. These are ameliorated but not entirely compensated for by analyses of moderator variables (see Methods section).

Future meta-analytic studies should differentiate both independent and dependent variables more precisely and report inferential tests. Future individual studies might benefit from examining the effects of varying a single independent or dependent variable.—*L.H.*

CONTRIBUTIONS TO THE FIELD

This recent meta-analysis of 98 studies shows that researchers in surprisingly diverse fields of application have reported much success using music to effect changes in children's and adults' behavior in and outside of schools. In addition, several experimenters report that the use of music acts simultaneously as reinforcement for social-emotional development, as subject matter, and as an enhancement to academic achievement in other subject areas.

This report focuses on the contingent use of "music initiation, participation, or interruption" as a valuable tool for behavior modification in the normal public school classroom. Studies analyzed in this meta-analysis also reveal that the effects due to contingent use of music compare favorably to other types of reinforcements (food, classroom status, etc.). In addition, the author presents evidence that reinforcement or reward does not negatively impact intrinsic motivation, thus allaying a primary objection to the contingent use of music in classrooms.

Research summarized here suggests strongly that the knowledge of techniques for the contingent use of music should become an important component of the professional development of music educators and music therapists.—*L.S.*

COMMENTARY

The meta-analysis reviewed here takes into account literature from the fields of education (cognitive skills, academic achievement), social-behavioral modification, medical treatment and therapy, social-emotional development, work productivity, and listening preference studies. Analyses of results from studies that use contingency-based music programs hold enormous implications for optimizing classroom management while showing no negative effects on students' academic performance and motivation.

The importance of this meta-analysis is that it (1) organizes a vast body of research that, when seen as a whole, challenges educators to incorporate music in a variety of ways that extend beyond the boundaries of discipline specific instruction, and (2) brings to the forefront the use of music for therapeutic and behavioral objectives that has been largely ignored by classroom teachers, music teachers, and administrators in public schools until this time.

Most important to teachers, careful review of the studies in this meta-analysis suggests that music listening can be adapted creatively to any classroom and that it is applicable across a wide variety of musical, academic, and behavioral objectives.

One example of a practical application of this study for educators is to establish preferences in music listening as a "contingency" for classroom privileges, which, in turn, motivate children to demonstrate desired behavioral changes. For example, an unruly child can gain the privilege of choosing his or her preferred music (1) to be heard during transition from one activity to another, (2) to be heard during a creative writing exercise, (3) to be played during a recreation period, or (4) to accompany any other activity the music or classroom or music teacher deems as appropriate during the school day. Other examples of findings from this study can be applied to public schools. Further research designed to assess how teachers incorporate music listening programs in schools is needed.—*L.S.*

STUDY NAME: **Music and Mathematics: Modest Support for the Oft-Claimed Relationship**
AUTHOR: Kathryn Vaughn
PUBLISHED: Journal of Aesthetic Education, Fall 2000, 34 (3-4):149-166

Research Questions

Is there a relationship between music study and mathematics achievement? Does music instruction cause increases in mathematics achievement? Does listening to background music while thinking about mathematics problems enhance mathematics ability?

METHODS

A search of published and unpublished studies considering the relationship between music and mathematics was gathered. The initial harvest yielded 4,000 references. These were reduced to a set of 25 studies, first by excluding articles deemed to be advocacy pieces or programs descriptions, and then by excluding three other types of studies: (1) when music was used as a reward for high mathematics performance, (2) where musical "jingles" were used as memory aids, and (3) where the studies focused on music and mathematics aptitude rather than achievement. The studies were then assigned to one of three groups: correlational, experimental-music instruction, and experimental-music listening. A separate meta-analysis was performed within each group.

Ten of the twenty studies in the correlational group compared participation in music classes with SAT mathematics performance. These were large studies with over 300,000 subjects each. The other studies had between 34 and 1,969 subjects. Most subjects were high school students. Correlations between mathematics and music study ranged from $r = -.05$ to $.37$. Only six studies were in the experimental-music instruction group with sample sizes from 28 to 128, all from preschool or elementary school. Effect sizes ranged from $r = -.04$ to $.31$. The experimental-music listening group also had smaller sample sizes than the correlational group of studies. There were 15 studies with 10 to 200 subjects. Effect sizes were widely dispersed, ranging from $r = -.18$ to $.82$. These studies compared music predicted to enhance mathematics performance (i.e., classical or "mood calming") with music or sound predicted to interfere (rap, rock, industrial noise).—R.H.

RESULTS

The meta-analysis of the correlational group indicated a significant relationship between music study and mathematics achievement. Students who take music classes in high school are more likely to score higher on standardized mathematics tests such as the SAT. The researcher reported a mean effect size of $r = .15$. When the effect sizes were weighted to account for the large size of the SAT studies, the mean effect was $r = .14$. Significance tests indicated that it is extremely unlikely that these findings are due to chance ($Z = 192.59$, $p < .0001$ and t of the mean $Zr = 4.2$, $p < .0001$).

Analysis of the experimental group indicated that music study appears to *cause* increases in mathematics achievement ($r = .13$, $p = .004$). Curiously, the researcher provides a contradictory interpretation. She first states that students who take music "show higher mathematical achievement as a consequence" of the music classes, and that there is a "small causal relationship…showing that music training enhances math performance." But she then goes on to write, "there is a dearth of existing evidence testing the hypothesis that music training enhances performance in mathematics, and I conclude that the hypothesis has not yet been adequately put to the test."

Listening to some kinds of music may aid performance on mathematics tests. There was a significant, but small, overall mean effect size ($r = .14$, $p = .003$). However, additional analysis did not provide significant results.—R.H.

CONTRIBUTIONS TO THE FIELD

This study helps confirm the relationship between music study and performance on standardized mathematics tests. The analysis adds substance to the widely publicized correlation between music and SAT scores by synthesizing 10 years of SAT analysis with 10 other studies chosen through stringent selection criteria.

The study also provides additional support for the hypothesis that the increases in mathematics scores are not simply correlational, but are due to the music instruction. A meta-analysis of six experimental studies revealed a causal relationship between music and mathematics performance. This is an important contribution, as it indicates several fruitful areas for additional research.—R.H.

COMMENTARY

The study shows positive, unanticipated benefits of music learning that should be of interest to school administrators and policy-makers. Sustained participation in music education programs likely supports the development of thinking skills applicable to mathematical reasoning, which may, in turn, be reflected in mathematics scores. But questions remain for researchers: What is the nature of the relationship between music and mathematics? If music somehow enhances mathematical understanding, how does this come about? Is it due to development of spatial reasoning? What kinds of music instruction might lead to increases in mathematics performance?

Additional research can begin to address some of these

questions. Qualitative studies are needed to describe, isolate, and define the characteristics of music classes and appropriate indicators of learning. Controlled studies should pursue a narrower, sharper approach than those used in the meta-analysis. They might try and measure mediating variables that could provide insight into the mechanism of transfer. They should also investigate the relationships between different types of music study and different types of mathematics learning.—R.H.

CONTRIBUTIONS TO THE FIELD

The method of this study—meta-analysis—is used for the first time to distill and generalize results from a modest number of selected studies that explore the relationship between music and mathematics.

Besides the general positive significant relationships between music and mathematics found in the meta-analysis there are several intriguing findings that emerged out of the broad context of this study.

First, positive correlations between high-stakes standardized mathematics test scores and participation in music ensembles have increased in size and significance over the last decade and need to be investigated for underlying causes. It was disappointing that this meta-analysis study made no attempt to illuminate possible substantive reasons for the consistently strong, positive correlations, particularly with regard to the recent large-sample study cited that claims to control for levels of SES in its research design (Catterall, 1999, and in this Compendium).

Second, this study indicates that the effects of musical instruction on mathematics performance are more significant and much larger in the most recent studies. Are there important clues for why this is so? In one case in particular, the author speculates on the extraordinary possibility that "the combination of music instruction and the particular spatial-temporal mathematics instruction students" received in that study may have led to improved mathematics performance. In other words, the strongest evidence for conditions of causality in this study may be based on the revelation that when authentic music instruction is integrated with mathematical instruction based on spatial-temporal aspects of learning mathematics, the positive association between music and mathematics learning may increase significantly, to the potential benefit of both subject areas.

Third, the results of studying "soothing" background music on test-taking skills in math are mixed, perhaps because the studies themselves are not necessarily conducive to meta-analysis as organized in this study. As educators know, some children need to be soothed to test better, whereas others would benefit more from arousal to perform more productively. What is needed is a much more sophisticated and comprehensive set of meta-analyses focused on the effects that different kinds of music (soothing, arousing, complex, repetitive) may have on various kinds of children (normal, attention-deficit, emotionally challenged) for various purposes (academic, social, behavioral). This meta-analysis perhaps would have been more useful if it had included a more comprehensive set of stud-

ies such as the meta-analysis provided elsewhere in this Compendium (Standley, 1996).—L.S.

COMMENTARY

This meta-analysis provides positive evidence to support the relationship between music and mathematics. The author provides a three-tiered rationale for the close relationship between music and mathematics: (1) musical training in rhythm that emphasizes proportion, patterns, and ratios expressed as mathematical relations, (2) recent studies (cited in this Compendium) that strongly support the connection of music training to spatial-temporal reasoning, and (3) the nature of music and mathematics typically expressed by expert musicians (in this case, Igor Stravinsky). These rationales demonstrate the importance of reconsidering the goals of music education to include: (1) the incorporation of new teaching strategies designed to integrate fundamental concepts in music that are shared with other disciplines, (2) the development of new aspects of teacher training to include awareness of recent research that supports the relationship between musical and cognitive development in other disciplines, and (3) recognition of the importance of musicians continuing to investigate fundamental concepts shared between authentic musical education and other disciplines.—L.S.

"This study helps confirm the relationship between music study and performance on standardized mathematics tests."

Essay:

An Overview of Research on Music and Learning

Larry Scripp

"What we must first seek to answer is whether music is to be placed in education or not, and what power it has...whether as education, play or pastime."

Aristotle

Introduction: Re-examining the role of music in education through research.

Music's place in American schools continues to be uncertain as we begin a new millennium of public education. While the business of producing and selling music thrives commercially, while listening to and making music continues to be of major interest to a large population of youth and adults, and while hundreds of community schools across the nation offer music instruction to those who can afford it, the comprehensive, sequential study of music has yet to be accepted as a core ingredient of public education.

Perhaps one reason policy-makers have been reluctant to support music as a core subject in public schools is that educators, administrators, artists, and parents seem to be divided in their advocacy for music's essential role in public education. On one side, the "essentialists" argue that music should be taught for its own sake. Essentialists maintain that while there exists evidence for several kinds of ancillary benefits from music instruction, music teachers should focus only on the instruction of music's own set of skills and literature and not be responsible for drawing out "extra-musical benefits" from this instruction. By contrast, those sympathetic to the "instrumentalist" point of view believe that music does not exist in a vacuum, that it is connected intrinsically to other subject areas and art forms, and that learning in music inevitably draws on and engages learning processes and fundamental concepts *shared* across many subject areas—often simultaneously.

As research emerges that establishes stronger relationships between music and learning in other areas of the curriculum, advocates from both camps are caught in a complicated bind. While one side worries about pandering to administrators or to school boards that make decisions based primarily on test scores in the academic subjects, the other side worries that, if we ignore aspects of learning transfer between music and other subject areas, music education will remain outside of the mainstream of public education, and thus will survive only as an educational *elective* for the talented or highly motivated few.

Research papers reviewed in this Compendium support a more interactive model of learning in and through music. Although music study takes place in isolation from math and language learning in schools today, research suggests that music functions as a catalyst for cognitive skills and aspects of social-emotional development across disciplines, especially when conditions for transfer are optimized through teaching to principles and processes that engage and deepen learning across disciplines.

Consequently, studies reviewed in this Compendium suggest how music educators and policy-makers may help resolve what increasingly appears to be a false dichotomy between the essentialist and the instrumentalist positions. The gap between these two points of view is beginning to be bridged through research that will be reported here in terms of four major themes.

Theme 1: Meta-analysis studies based on large bodies of research over the last few decades reveal consistently strong, positive relationships between music and learning in other subject areas.

A review of five recent meta-analyses (1995-2000) is included in this Compendium. The emergence of meta-analysis techniques has been particularly helpful in establishing the background context for understanding the impact of music on various cognitive and social-emotional domains. Meta-analysis is a relatively new area of music research, yet it represents an accepted methodology for synthesizing a vast number of extant bodies of literature for the purpose of describing its characteristics and for providing a basis for informed generalization from these data. The use of new statistical procedures to compute effect sizes across similar variables from diverse studies in turn provides insight as to their combined significance, despite differences in research design and populations.

As the reader will discover, there is now a strong body of evidence based on meta-analyses of a broad range of studies, which establishes positive significant associations between music and:

- spatial-temporal reasoning (Hetland 2000a & b),
- achievement in math (Vaughn 2000),
- achievement in reading (Butzlaff 2000), and
- the reinforcement of social-emotional or behavioral objectives (Standley 1996).

While the authors of these meta-analyses caution against over-reaching claims of causal relationships between music and academic

"Research papers reviewed in this Compendium support a more interactive model of learning in and through music."

achievement in language or math, the extensive presence of strong associations between music and other subject areas overwhelmingly is consistent with evidence for positive extra-musical effects of music instruction. Although several studies suggest that explicit attention to teaching for transfer produces stronger results than older studies conducted without this concern, further practitioner research is needed to specify how these links can be best and most consistently achieved through professional development programs for classroom and music teachers in schools.

Theme 2: Generative neurological and cognitive frameworks for learning transfer have emerged from research on music and learning.

> "Music is the effort we make to explain to ourselves how our brains work. We listen to Bach transfixed because this is listening to the human mind."
>
> *Lewis Thomas, U.S. physician, educator, 1979.*

Education research based on neurological and cognitive aspects of music enables educators today to look more precisely, and therefore more responsibly, at the contributions music can make toward teaching and learning across various areas of our public school curriculum. Interest in music listening studies that enhance performance in other forms of cognition (commonly known as the "Mozart effect"), for example, reflects an unprecedented willingness of educators, researchers, and the general public to consider new conceptions of, and inter-relationships among, musical skills, the mind, and the brain.

A meta-analysis of the research on the effect of music listening on spatial-temporal reasoning (Hetland 2000a) provides a neurological—rather than a cultural—orientation for determining music's place in education. The notion that certain forms of music listening appear to prepare the brain for better performance on tasks that require "the ability to transform mental images in the absence of a physical model" is significant, not because it provides another rationale for music appreciation, but because findings from these studies contradict two prevailing views of learning: (1) *brain modularity* (the assumption that cognitive capacities are located in discrete areas of the brain as "separate intelligences") and, its corollary, (2) that it is difficult or counterproductive to promote *learning transfer* across disciplines (as evidenced by the conventional separation between learning music and spatial reasoning math tasks in schools).

The finding that passive listening to music neurologically "primes" spatial-temporal thinking suggests that cognitive processes normally associated with music share neural networks with other kinds of mental activity. Thus we can conclude that "musical and spatial processing centers in the brain are proximal or overlapping and hence linked, rather than being entirely distinct as was predicted by modular theories of the mind" (Hetland 2000a).

While the "Mozart effect" meta-analyses support a model for learning transfer independent of a music education, results from follow-up studies show that authentic and comprehensive musical training—learning to make music and read music in particular—appears to increase further the association between music and various aspects of mathematical reasoning (Hetland 2000b, Rauscher, et al. 1997, Rauscher & Zupan 2000, Vaughn 2000). Meta-analyses reviewed here suggest not only that the effect of musical training in conjunction with mathematical study may benefit greatly from explicit attention to teaching toward this particular aspect of learning transfer (Vaughn 2000), but also that associations between learning music and understanding math are strongest when authentic music instruction is integrated with mathematical instruction based on spatial-temporal or proportional aspects of learning math (Graziano, et al. 1999, summarized in this volume). Results from this study imply that optimal conditions for enhancing learning transfer may depend on new forms of curriculum in both math and music; that is, the design of curricular units that employ fundamental concepts shared by two disciplines (e.g., pro-

"Meta-analyses indicate that there is `a strong and reliable association between the study of music and performance on standardized reading and verbal tests`..."

portional or spatial-temporal thinking included in math and music instruction) may be essential for replicating the success of interdisciplinary learning in public school settings.

Likewise, the relationship between music and language follows a similar pattern in this research. Meta-analyses indicate that there is "a strong and reliable association between the study of music and performance on standardized reading and verbal tests" (Butzlaff 2000), and that success in second-language skill development occurred with the use of music-integrated instruction infused with underlying mental processes drawn from linguistics, musical perception, and speech therapy (Lowe 1995). In this research, the use of songs in second-language instruction directly enhances pronunciation, grammatical structure, vocabulary, and idiomatic expressions as well as encouraging wide variety in speed of delivery, significant phrasing, and linking of ideas.

Less robust effects resulted from studies that employed music lessons or listening sessions not linked with language instruction. This research revealed that relatively superficial aspects of integration, such as the association of lyrics with academic topics or the presence of specific vocabulary in songs, are more likely to affect attitudes *about* reading or writing tasks than to produce positive indications of reading achievement (Andrews 1997, Hallam 1999).

Research on learning transfer between music and other areas of cognition is relevant to educators interested in the contribution of interdisciplinary learning. New levels of meaning become possible in the music-integrated curriculum when competing representations of fundamental concepts, as Dewey might have said, "are grasped in their relations to one another—a result that is attained only when acquisition is accompanied by constant reflection upon the meaning of what is studied."

Theme 3: There is an underlying tension between the "one-way cause and effect" and "two-way interaction" models of research on music and learning.

> Vincenzio [Galileo's father] taught Galileo to sing, and to play the organ and other instruments. . . . In the course of this instruction he introduced the boy to the Pythagorean rule of musical ratios, which required strict obedience in tuning and composition to numerical properties of notes in a scale . . . when Vincenzio filled a room with weighted strings of varying lengths, diameters, and tensions to test certain harmonic ideas, Galileo joined him as his assistant. It seems safe to say that Galileo, who gets credit for being the father of experimental physics, may have learned the rudiments and the value of experimentation from his own father's efforts.
>
> *Galileo's Daughter, Dava Sobel, 2001.*

One-way causal relationships in learning are difficult to determine. The quotation above suggests Galileo received a significant part of his education in an interdisciplinary learning environment richly supported by concepts and learning processes shared among math, physics, and music. However, in this case, it seems no less true to assert that Galileo's instrumental lessons enhanced his understanding of math or physics than to assume that Galileo's interest in his father's scientific experiments improved his musical skill. As is often the case with interdisciplinary learning, conclusions concerning the determination and direction of cause and effect remain problematic.

In addition to the tension between the "essentialist" and "instrumental" points of view mentioned earlier, there exists another tension among researchers who report the undeniable presence of positive associations between learning in music and other disciplines, yet who disagree on the interpretation of these data. The tension arises principally between (a) those who accept strong associations between musical training and academic achievement as evidence sufficient for advancing the conclusion that music enhances learning in other subject areas and (b) those who insist that conclusions about the effect of music on learning in other subjects be drawn only to experimental studies that adhere strictly to standards of "one-way, cause-and-effect" models of analysis. However, in consideration of the research reviewed here, it may be useful to adopt a middle-ground approach: to analyze data from the point of view of "two-way interaction" models of learning across disciplines.

Given the complexity of public school learning environments, many teachers, administrators, and researchers feel it may not be productive to prove that any one form of intervention *causes* learning in another subject. The "two-way interactionist" position is that improvement in learning in either of two disciplines—taught separately or together—suggests that one discipline catalyzes, reinforces, and deepens learning in the other. Thus, academic performance is just as likely to benefit from strong instruction in music, as music is likely to benefit from strong instruction in the academics. Hence it is no longer necessary to position the canons of "one-way proof of causality" against the conclusion that significant, positive correlations between high-quality musical training and math/language achievement reported in every meta-analysis included in this Compendium constitute evidence sufficient to support the integration of music into the core curriculum in public education.

"The 'two-way interactionist' position is that improvement in learning in either of two disciplines—taught separately or together—suggests that one discipline catalyzes, reinforces, and deepens learning in the other."

Theme 4: The use of music as a tool for social-emotional development and behavior modification in schools.

Studies on the effects of music as reinforcement for education and behavioral objectives investigate the use of music listening and music making in academic classrooms. In addition to isolated studies that simply document the effect of different kinds of background music for students responding to writing assignments (Kariuki & Honeycutt 1998, Hallam 1999), a meta-analysis of a wide range of studies suggests that the use of "contingent music" strategies can provide overwhelming positive reinforcement value for behavior in classrooms, on school buses, and in math and reading achievement tests (Standley 1996). Reports from studies that use contingency-based music programs provide strategies for optimizing classroom management and student motivation while showing no negative effects—and several striking indications of positive effects—on students' academic performance and motivation. Perhaps most important to classroom teachers, research demonstrates that contingency plans for music listening and music making can be adapted creatively to any classroom and that they are applicable across a wide variety of musical, academic, and behavioral objectives.

Studies of emotionally disturbed children provide in-depth views of employing music performance and music listening strategies to improve self-efficacy (concept of self-capacity) in at-risk youth (Kennedy 1998, Kariuki & Honeycutt 1998). Improvements in self-efficacy through music rely on critical thinking and not on optimal therapeutic conditions alone. Descriptive data from this research show how musical performance enables patients to acquire social competencies while coping more effectively with this environment. The performance tasks and supporting cognitive strategies outlined in this research should be studied carefully by music educators—not only because they are sequenced skillfully but also because they show how self-efficacy of any music student would be improved by cognitive strategies that limit negative self-evaluative judgment and provide stimulus for creative work in other disciplines (Kariuki & Honeycutt 1998).

Conclusions and Implications

"If the arts help define our path to the future, they need to become curriculum partners with other subject disciplines in ways that will allow them to contribute their own distinctive richness and complexity to the learning process as a whole."

Burton, J., Horowitz, R., and Abeles, H.
"Learning In and Through the Arts: Curriculum Implications,"
in Champions of Change, 1999.

The uncertainty of music's place in education is not due to a lack of research that supports the value of learning in and through music. Research now offers a theoretical basis for, and growing evidence of, the significant effects of learning shared between music and other measures of academic achievement. As a result, music and classroom educators now can embrace learning transfer as a desirable product of interactions between learning in music and academic subjects. From this perspective, fundamental concepts indigenous both to music and math classrooms can become the cornerstone of the music-infused interdisciplinary curriculum. Although music always will exist for its own sake, its unique literature, its particular social and career paths, and as a source of human enjoyment and emotional release—now, bolstered by its value for interdisciplinary learning supported in this research, music can achieve a core status in public education imagined long ago by the ancient Greeks.

Future directions for research in the field of music in education distilled from this Compendium are as follows:
- **Consider levels of musical understanding and skill in cross-disciplinary studies.**
  Virtually all research to date concentrates on the effects of music on other areas of learning and uses *exposure* to musical instruction or listening as an agent to effect change. The validity and practical significance of future research will depend on developing ways to include musical ability factors into research methods so that music educators can assess whether the degree of musical skill makes any critical difference in the level of mathematical or language arts achievement.
- **Develop and validate two-way measures of cross-disciplinary learning effects.**
  New statistical methods need to be developed and refined to test the statistical significance of two-way interactive models of interdisciplinary learning that do not take place in a one-way causal, linear fashion.
- **Determine and examine optimal conditions for cross-disciplinary effects of learning in and through music.**
  Research will benefit from more attention to what constitutes optimal conditions for interdisciplinary instruction, learning, and assessment. Controlling for the quality and comprehensiveness of music teaching and the evaluation of student learning will account for the theoretical as well as practical validity of research in the years to come.
- **Research in music and education should not exist in isolation from studying music's effect on social-emotional development, behavioral modification, or reinforcement of therapeutic objectives.**
  The inclusion of music as a tool for solving social-emotional and behavioral issues that exist at all levels of public education should be addressed by future research. Teachers will not be able fully to understand music's impact on education without knowing how learning in and through music serves as a window onto the interactions among social-emotional issues, behavior modification, and the ability to learn.

"Research now offers a theoretical basis for, and growing evidence of, the significant effects of learning shared between music and other measures of academic achievement."

References

The research reviewed here is organized into four primary points of focus:

I. Music and Language Skills
Butzlaff, R., "Can Music Be Used to Teach Reading?" (*meta-analysis*)
Andrews, L., "Effects of an Integrated Reading and Music Instructional Approach on Fifth-Grade Students' Reading Achievement, Reading Attitude, Music Achievement, and Music Attitude."
Hallam, S.,"The Effects of Background Music on Studying."
Lowe, A., "The Effect of the Incorporation of Music Learning into the Second-Language Classroom on the Mutual Reinforcement of Music and Language."

II. Music, Math, and Spatial Reasoning
Graziano, A., Peterson, M., & Shaw, G., "Enhanced Learning of Proportional Math through Music Training and Spatial-Temporal Training."
Hetland, L., "Listening to Music Enhances Spatial-Temporal Reasoning: Evidence for the 'Mozart Effect.'"(*meta-analysis*)
Hetland, L., "Learning to Make Music Enhances Spatial Reasoning." (*meta-analysis*)
Rauscher, F., Shaw G., Levine, L., Wright, Dennis, W., & Newcomb, R., "Music Training Causes Long-term Enhancement of Preschool Children's Spatial-Temporal Reasoning."
Rauscher. F. & Zupan, M., "Classroom Keyboard Instruction Improves Kindergarten Children's Spatial-Temporal Performance: A Field Experiment."
Vaughn, K., "Music and Mathematics: Modest Support for the Oft-Claimed Relationship." (*meta-analysis*)

III. Music and General Cognitive Development
Bilharz, T., Bruhn, R., & Olson, J., "The Effect of Early Music Training on Child Cognitive Development."
Costa-Giomi, E., "The Effects of Three Years of Piano Instruction on Children's Cognitive Development."

IV. Music, Therapeutic, Social/Emotional, and Behavioral Objectives
Kariuki, P. & Honeycutt, C., "An Investigation of the Effects of Music on Two Emotionally Disturbed Students' Writing Motivations and Writing Skills."
Kennedy, J., "The Effects of Musical Performance, Rational Emotive Therapy and Vicarious Experience on the Self-Efficacy and Self-Esteem of Juvenile Delinquents and Disadvantaged Children."
Standley, J., "A Meta-Analysis of the Effects of Music as Reinforcement for Educational/Therapy Objectives."(*meta-analysis*)

visual arts

STUDY NAME: **Instruction in Visual Art: Can It Help Children Learn to Read?**
AUTHORS: Kristin Burger and Ellen Winner
PUBLISHED: Journal of Aesthetic Education, Fall 2000, 34, (3-4): 277-293

Research Questions

Can reading skills be enhanced by instruction in visual arts?

Meta-analysis 1 studied the cognitive-transfer-of-skill hypothesis: Can art instruction by itself improve reading?

Meta-analysis 2 studied the motivational-entry-point hypothesis: Is teaching reading through art more effective than teaching reading alone?

METHODS

The authors conducted two meta-analyses of studies that test the hypothesis that instruction in the visual arts improves reading. They reviewed over 4,000 individual recorded studies and 41 journals, and sent out invitations to over 200 arts education researchers to submit unpublished research. From this vast amount of work, they selected 10 studies that met their standard of being empirical studies with control groups and that tested the basic hypothesis that some form of visual arts instruction improves some aspect of reading ability. They calculated 13 effect sizes from these 10 studies. Two of the studies required separate effect size calculations because of the nature of the participant groups. Each of these groups was considered as a separate meta-analysis. Meta-analysis 1 focused on nine studies examining cognitive relationships between arts instruction and reading achievement, and meta-analysis 2 included four studies of motivational connections. Eight of the nine studies focused on elementary school subjects from first to fifth grades, and one assessed pre-elementary-aged subjects. Seven studies included average SES students and two assessed low-SES students. Duration ranged from 10 days to one full academic year. Meta-analysis 2 examined four studies comparing art–reading integrated studies with reading instruction alone. Two were reading readiness, and two were reading achievement studies. Three were first- to fifth-grade populations, and one was pre-elementary. Duration ranged widely, as it did for the meta-analysis 1 group, from 27 days to one full academic year.

The study description section indicates that the studies were quite different in nature—duration, population, SES, instructional intensity age level, outcome measure, and grade level. A statistical review of effect sizes in meta-analysis 1 also indicated significant heterogeneity. The fact that both reading readiness and reading achievement measures were used led the authors to separate these two groups for separate analysis.

The studies were coded by two independent judges who disagreed on only one coding. This disagreement was resolved by rechecking the original document.—T.B.

RESULTS

Effect size calculations for the nine studies in meta-analysis 1 do not support the hypothesis that there is a relationship between arts instruction and reading improvement except in the area of reading readiness. The effect sizes ranged from $r = -.3$ to $r = .54$ and the confidence interval spanned zero. For the reading readiness group, however, with an average positive effect size of $r = .25$, the confidence interval ranged from $r = .04$ to $r = .48$ and does not span zero, allowing a conclusion that there is a "small" relationship between visual arts instruction and reading readiness scores. The authors attribute some of this to the fact that reading readiness measures depend to a larger extent than reading achievement measures on visual or figural items rather than linguistic. In their continued study of heterogeneity, the authors were not able to account for all the factors related to reading readiness and concluded that this was an indication of the fact that their sample did not come from a single population of like studies.

Meta-analysis 2's effect sizes were homogeneous, indicating that the studies were similar. The mean effect size was $r = .21$ and the confidence interval range, $r = .03$ to $r = .45$, does not span zero and suggests that the effect sizes would likely be the same in another sample of like studies. The authors conclude that this meta-analysis "revealed a positive, moderately sized relationship between reading improvement and an integrated arts-reading form of instruction. The authors conclude, "...on the basis of the small number of studies found, there is only marginal support for [their] hypothesis."—T.B.

CONTRIBUTIONS TO THE FIELD

The report on these meta-analyses identifies several problems with the research studies they examined ranging from teacher effect issues to control group issues. The identification of research methodology problems in arts education research is a positive contribution to the entire field, but is especially useful for researchers.

The distinction that the authors make between cognitive elements and motivational elements as potential variables in arts education research is also useful for researchers and instructors to consider.

The identification of important design variables is also important for future researchers to consider. Some important variables are missing from this study, and their addition would make its contribution more significant—instructional content elements, especially skills in both the visual arts and reading and motivational or engaging qualities in the visual arts.—T.B.

COMMENTARY

One of the major complaints about meta-analysis as a research technique has to do with the difficulty of finding similar or comparable studies to include. This is particularly vexing to arts personnel who build programs on unique, individualistic, or non-standard arts characteristics and who find it difficult to consider standardization or generalizations about their work. Meta-analysis as a method sometimes exacerbates this response, especially if it groups unlike studies together, because it requires a degree of comparability that unique and individualistic programs do not have, and because it is aimed at greater distribution of results than such programs can support. The authors admit that such is the case here, particularly in their discussion of reading readiness studies in meta-analysis 1. The descriptions of the study design included in the meta-analysis provide ample documentation of the extremes of project characteristics. The authors' appropriate identification of study design weaknesses, such as the teacher effect problem when the authors of seven of the reports, who were aware of the hypotheses being tested, taught the classes, or the failure to provide control groups with alternative treatments, further documents a range of variables in these studies. There is good reason to question the selection of such varied studies for a meta-analysis in the first place. If these are the only studies to merit such attention, it may be best to consider individual study review processes rather than meta-analysis.

The coding categories used in meta-analysis 1 describe the instructional context—length, intensity, SES, integrated vs. separate—but do not present content information, with the exception of identifying "vocabulary" as one topic in reading instruction. The authors report that "these studies did not allow us to determine which skills, if any, might transfer" between visual arts and reading, but they do not say why this was the case. They do say that the type of comparison they conducted in meta-analysis 1 did allow them "...to determine whether extra instruction in the visual arts, taught separately from reading, teaches skills that transfer to reading ability." It's hard to imagine how they could do this when they were not able to identify which skills might transfer.

In spite of their indication that the data in meta-analysis 2 suggest that like studies would have similar results, they also conclude that the results "...cannot be generalized reliably to future studies" (presumably even those that are like studies). They conclude, "It is likely that when reading instruction is integrated with arts instruction, children become more motivated to read," but their discussion does not provide detail about the "motivation" factor that it purports to discuss. If reading is taught "in an engaging way, through art projects," as the authors state, then they should provide details of what constitutes engaging instruction and what aspects of the arts projects are engaging. They should then identify the measures that link this engagement to reading instruction.

The report on meta-analysis 2 also does not distinguish between those studies that used reading readiness measures and those that used reading achievement measures,

> "...the medical/agricultural model upon which these standards for meta-analysis are derived is not necessarily the best one from which to understand the complex endeavor of education or more specifically visual art education."

as the discussion of the first meta-analysis does. The authors point to the fact that reading readiness measures feature figural elements and are perhaps more appropriate for programs that use visual instruction than more linguistic reading achievement measures. This suggests that the issue of selecting or creating appropriate measures when looking at arts-related projects is something that both program designers and researchers should consider. Standardized linguistic-based tests should not be expected to give adequate information about such programs and their effectiveness. It is probably true that more linguistics-based art forms such as drama and narrative writing should also be measured by instruments that use the characteristics of the art forms such as plot, character development, and setting rather than linguistic characteristics such as rhetoric, grammar, and vocabulary.—T.B.

CONTRIBUTIONS TO THE FIELD

The value of this work is its careful and comprehensive review of the entire research field (including published and unpublished work), uncovering 4,133 studies that investigated the effects of visual art on reading.

The research used a widely accepted technique, meta-analysis, allowing the authors to assess the aggregate contribution of multiple studies that employed a range of student reading achievement tests, as well as varied statistical techniques.

The most important contribution, beyond the fact that this is the first systematic review across all the research on this topic, is simply that only a small number of studies met the researchers' standards for acceptable scientific rigor. The clear message is that the field needs more research.

Another important contribution of the research is the finding that art-based reading instruction promotes better reading, largely through the added motivation that art offers for learning. On the other hand, the more indirect connection between the transfer of doing art and increased reading achievement is much harder to document.—B.W.

COMMENTARY

The researchers found only nine studies meeting their strict standards of acceptable research that investigated the relationship between visual art instruction (compared to regular reading instruction) and reading skills and four studies that assessed art–reading integrated instruction with regular reading instruction. The former group of nine studies included a total sample of only 495 students while the latter group of four studies involved only 277 students. So, in almost 50 years of research, only 772 students have been exposed to carefully designed experimental treatments on the learning effects of reading or art–reading integrated instruction. One obvious response is to decry the lack of controlled research in this field.

The more appropriate point is, perhaps, that the medical/agricultural model upon which these standards for meta-analysis are derived is not necessarily the best one from which to understand the complex endeavor of education or more specifically visual art education. The varied contexts in which instruction is delivered, even from classroom to classroom in the same building, make it difficult to meaningfully transfer successes in controlled experimental settings to messy classrooms.

While it is important to understand the value that visual art can add to students' cognitive skills, it is just as important (if not more so) to know the how and why visual art contributes to learning, as well as the organizational and instructional conditions that allow arts learning to help students become more successful students. Thus, the 4,133 studies should also be mined to learn what the many qualitative studies can add to these important questions.—B.W.

STUDY NAME: **The Arts, Language, and Knowing: An Experimental Study of the Potential of the Visual Arts for Assessing Academic Learning by Language Minority Students**

AUTHOR: Karen G. DeJarnette

PUBLISHED: Unpublished Doctoral Dissertation, University of California, Los Angeles, 1997

Research Questions

Can sixth-grade students' understanding of history be assessed through a combination of writing and drawing, and does this kind of assessment reveal more history knowledge than assessments that ask only for writing?

Does the opportunity to show understanding through drawing along with writing particularly help students with limited English skills?

METHODS

Ninety-eight sixth-graders from four world history classes taught by two teachers were randomly assigned to one of two groups. Both groups studied Mesopotamia and ancient Egypt for four weeks each. After each unit, student learning was assessed either by writing alone or a combination of writing and drawing. Thus, each student received both assessments, one for each unit; and half received the writing/drawing assessment for Mesopotamia, and half received this for Egypt. In both assessments students were asked to describe (through words, or words and drawings) important aspects of the region and note the most important people, events, and artifacts and explain why they were important. Responses were scored by the researcher in terms of content knowledge (on a four-point scale) and in terms of interdisciplinary knowledge (on a two-point scale). A second researcher scored a third of the responses, and after disagreements were discussed, 100 percent agreement was reached.—*E.W.*

RESULTS

Students used three types of responses in the writing/drawing assessment. Some students wrote their response and then illustrated it; some first drew and then added words; and some only drew. Drawings included maps and charts as well as illustrations of people, places, events, or objects to convey historical facts. Students achieved higher scores for content knowledge when they both wrote and drew (mean score = 1.99) than when they only wrote (mean score = 1.38). Students also achieved higher interdisciplinary scores (showing that they brought in more information from other subjects, such as geography or religion) when they both wrote and drew, compared to when they only wrote (0.66 vs. 0.22).

Limited-English-ability students (*n* = 20) also scored higher on the writing/drawing assessment (mean score = 1.58) than on the writing alone assessment (mean score = 1.03).

Two limitations should be noted. No statistical tests were reported to determine whether the differences in scores between conditions were significant. And the person who scored all of the data was the researcher, who knew the hypothesis of the study. In future research the scorers should be blind.—*E.W.*

CONTRIBUTIONS TO THE FIELD

This study suggests that students reveal more history knowledge when their knowledge is assessed through a combination of writing plus drawing than when it is assessed through writing alone. This finding held not only for students with limited English skills but for typical students as well. This study shows us that drawing may be one way to reveal what students know but cannot put into words.—*E.W.*

COMMENTARY

This study asks the interesting question of whether the visual arts can complement writing as an assessment tool to reveal what students have learned about another subject, in this case, history.

In future studies, a scorer other than the researcher should be considered, that is, an individual blind to the hypothesis to avoid unconscious bias.—*E.W.*

CONTRIBUTIONS TO THE FIELD

This study argues that allowing students to represent what they have learned visually, in conjunction with a written assignment, can better reveal what they know about a topic than if they simply use words. Thus, the study adds to the growing body of research on claims that alternative assessment influences the quality of student performance and that a mismatch between a student's habitual way of learning and an assessment can give misleading information about the student's level of academic attainment.—*D.C.*

COMMENTARY

Apart from asserting the educational value of having students express what they have learned through writing and drawing, the study claims that there are reliable and valid ways of assessing students' visual representations of content knowledge. The researcher refers to, but does not fully describe, a calibrating process by which she and another rater were able to achieve 100 percent agreement on a sample of the students' work. Because one of the primary obstacles to widespread use of alternative assessments is educators' discomfort with assigning some sort of measurable value to student artwork, studies like this one should provide much more detail about the rating process.—*D.C.*

STUDY NAME: **Investigating the Educational Impact and Potential of the Museum of Modern Art's Visual Thinking Curriculum: Final Report**
AUTHORS: Shari Tishman, Dorothy MacGillivray, and Patricia Palmer
PUBLISHED: Unpublished Report, Museum of Modern Art, New York, NY, 1999

Research Question

When children aged 9 to 10 are trained to look closely at works of art and reason about what they see, can they transfer these same skills to a science activity?

METHODS

A Visual Thinking Curriculum (VTC) was used in which 162 9- and 10-year-olds were trained to look closely at works of art and talk about what they saw in the works. Over the course of a year, these students participated in an average of seven to eight VTC lessons of about 40 minutes each. All of the classes visited the Museum of Modern Art in New York City at least twice.

Prior to participating in this curriculum, students were given an art activity designed to assess how well they could look at and talk about a work of art. They were shown one of two works of art ("Wall with Inscriptions" by Jean Dubuffet and "Liberation" by Ben Shahn) and were asked to write responses to the following two questions: "What's going on in this picture?" and "What do you see that makes you say that?"

After one year of participation in the VTC, children were shown the other picture and were asked the same two questions. Immediately following the response to the art image, students were given a non-art image from the domain of science and asked the same two questions. They were shown a picture of a fossil record of two intersecting sets of animal footprints. The picture was labeled, "Footprints from the Past."

The same Art Activity and Footprints Activity were administered to a control group of 204 students of comparable ages, grades, and socio-economic circumstances as the experimental group.

Responses to the footprint image were scored in terms of amount of reasoning about evidence used. Children who had not experienced the Visual Thinking Curriculum served as a control group. The goal of the study was to determine whether the skills learned in looking at and reasoning about art would transfer to the quite similar task of looking at and reasoning about a non-art image from the discipline of science.—*E.W.*

RESULTS

On the art assessment, children in the control group performed equivalently to children in the VTC at the pre-test, providing evidence that the two groups were commensurate. After a year of the VTC, children achieved higher scores on evidential reasoning in the footprints task than did the control group. They were also less likely to use circular reasoning, and were more aware of the fact that their interpretations were subjective. Thus, the students in the VTC appeared to have looking and reasoning skills acquired from looking at works of art that they then deployed when given a scientific image.—*E.W.*

CONTRIBUTIONS TO THE FIELD

This study demonstrates that the skills learned in looking at and reasoning about a work of art transfer to the task of looking at and reasoning about a biological image. The biological image used here was a picture of a fossil record of two intersecting sets of animal footprints, labeled "Footprints from the Past."

Students trained to look and reason carefully about art showed higher reasoning ability when asked to make inferences about the meaning of the footprint image.—*E.W.*

COMMENTARY

This study presents clear evidence that skills learned through the arts can transfer to science. This is a case of near-transfer: the skills involved in the art domain are very similar to the skills tested in the science domain. In both cases, the critical skill is that of looking closely and reasoning about what is seen.—*E.W.*

CONTRIBUTIONS TO THE FIELD

This study lends weight to the argument that the arts "add value" to what and how students learn beyond specific subject matter attainment, by showing that students' ability to draw inferences about artwork transfers to reasoning about images in other subjects—in this case, science. Thus, engaging in art criticism is a worthy skill to develop, as a tool for developing art appreciation and thinking well in other disciplines.—*D.C.*

COMMENTARY

Although the study primarily addresses whether students can transfer reasoning about works of art to other visual images, the study's methodology hinges directly on two additional issues that are critical to arts education: how educators can determine the level of student performance relative to the arts-related skills in question and what the actual instruction involved looked and sounded like. While the study's stated purpose is central to justifying the use of the arts in education, these latter two issues are integral to helping educators understand how they can implement the arts as essential features of the educational process. It is incumbent on arts education research to spell out carefully the details of how instructors and evaluators handle these matters so as to render arts instruction and integration less opaque.—D.C.

STUDY NAME: **Reading *Is* Seeing: Using Visual Response to Improve the Literary Reading of Reluctant Readers**
AUTHOR: Jeffrey D. Wilhelm
PUBLISHED: Journal of Reading Behavior, 1995, 27 (4): 467-503

Research Question

Can the visual arts be used to help reluctant learning-disabled readers begin to enjoy reading?

METHODS

Two seventh-grade boys who were learning disabled and who were "reluctant" readers were helped in a nine-week session to visualize stories through the visual arts. They were asked to create cutouts or find objects that would represent characters and ideas in the story they were reading, and then use these to dramatize the story. They were also asked to draw a picture of strong visual impressions formed while reading a story. And they were engaged in discussions of how the pictures in illustrated books work along with the words. Students were also asked to illustrate books, and to engage in "picture-mapping," in which they depicted visually the key details of nonfiction texts. The final activity was to create a collage that represented their response to a particular piece of literature.—*E.W.*

RESULTS

The two students became much more sophisticated readers through the course of the nine weeks of visualization training. They took a more active role in reading, and began to interpret text rather than just passively read it. The researcher suggests that visual art provides a concrete "metacognitive marking point" that allowed these readers to see what they understood. It is also possible that because these boys were particularly interested in visual art, the use of visual art in reading made them more motivated to read.—*E.W.*

CONTRIBUTIONS TO THE FIELD

This study is an ethnographic case study that uses ingenious methods involving the visual arts to engage reluctant readers in reading.—*E.W.*

COMMENTARY

This is a hypothesis-generating study. The next step would be to conduct a study with a larger group of students to determine how generalizable the findings are. It would be helpful to know whether this technique works only for students with interest and ability in visual art, or whether it would work for any reluctant reader.—*E.W.*

CONTRIBUTIONS TO THE FIELD

The study demonstrates the value of the arts as an intermediary in the educational process. The author used visual art to engage two students in reading who previously had

"This study is an ethnographic case study that uses ingenious methods involving the visual arts to engage reluctant readers in reading."

been extremely reluctant to do so. The study, therefore, joins others that assert the motivational ability of integrating the arts into instruction in other disciplines.—*D.C.*

COMMENTARY

This study is the kind that can give meaning to research that simply establishes correlations between arts education practices and student achievement. Correlational research suggests promising instructional strategies and activities for educators to use; studies like this one promote understanding about what those actions concretely look and sound like and reveal the meanings those actions have for students. This kind of information is critical to stimulating fruitful educator reflection about how to apply arts education research to new settings.

The next step beyond this study should be to examine the context within which the methods used in this study took place, the kinds of barriers and facilitators schools would face in enacting them, and the kinds of training that the person who works with the students such as those in the case study needs in order to be effective. All three are central to integrating the arts into the everyday school curriculum.—*D.C.*

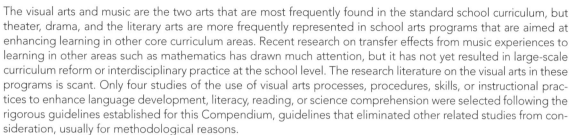

Essay:

Reflections on Visual Arts Education Studies

Terry L. Baker

The visual arts and music are the two arts that are most frequently found in the standard school curriculum, but theater, drama, and the literary arts are more frequently represented in school arts programs that are aimed at enhancing learning in other core curriculum areas. Recent research on transfer effects from music experiences to learning in other areas such as mathematics has drawn much attention, but it has not yet resulted in large-scale curriculum reform or interdisciplinary practice at the school level. The research literature on the visual arts in these programs is scant. Only four studies of the use of visual arts processes, procedures, skills, or instructional practices to enhance language development, literacy, reading, or science comprehension were selected following the rigorous guidelines established for this Compendium, guidelines that eliminated other related studies from consideration, usually for methodological reasons.

These four studies provide the basis for the following discussion. The discussion is not intended to be a critique or dismissal of these studies, but rather an exploration of a significant group of issues they raise that researchers and other professionals in the field need to consider. They open the way for us to reflect on what kinds of studies will best inform both practitioners in arts education and those who consider future research needs in the field of arts education. That such studies exist and that they are being collected for review by all concerned is an important positive marker on the developing path of arts education.

Key Questions for Researchers Investigating Relationships between Visual Arts Elements and Core Curriculum Learning

Drawing is the visual art most included in the studies summarized in the Compendium. Questions that arise when drawing is incorporated in teaching that is aimed at enhancing learning in core curriculum areas include:
- Domain questions such as, "Are we teaching art and the core subject?" "Are we teaching drawing, or are we teaching art?" "How do we distinguish between drawing, mark making, and art making?" "When does drawing become 'art' or 'artistic'?" "Are 'illustrations' art?" "What specific aspects of graphic marks are 'artistic'?" "Are the uses we make of art procedures shaped by or dependent upon their 'artistic' qualities?"
- Authority and validity questions, such as, "Who is to determine when and by what standards a child's scribbles rise to the level of art?" and,
- Teaching and instruction questions, such as, "Is 'teaching' the operative verb?" "If we are not teaching art *per se*, are we simply making 'instrumental' uses of art procedures in the service of other disciplines?" We might also ask what the results would be if we had a more complete teaching balance among the characteristics of all the disciplines being taught, including the arts.

Three of the studies are intended to illuminate instructional practices that promise to improve language or reading capacities, and one relates to teaching science, but none of them promises to improve arts instruction. They all reveal historically troubling aspects of arts in education programming, all related to the tenuous relationship between visual arts instruction and instruction in core curriculum subjects. There are:
- Situational or contextual definitions;
- Balance between instruction in the arts and instruction in the core curriculum subjects when they are taught together;
- Determining when arts instruction is complete and sufficient.

None of the studies describes instructing students in the making of, or understanding of, visual art, but they all describe student use of some element or elements, usually drawing, associated with the visual arts. While the elements described in these research reports may not rise to the level of "art," their association with art is justification for studying their properties and roles in learning situations, primarily because such study prepares the way for further research that can build on the results to isolate or identify "artistic" elements and processes.

Operationalizing Definitions for Specific Situations and Contexts

Defining terms for specific contexts is critical to understanding the elements under examination, especially definitions of what the authors mean by "art." Setting definitions is essential for both those involved in evaluation and assessment of arts learning and those who would use such studies. This is true regardless of the difficulties we have always had defining art and even if the only way we can define it is by describing what art is not—advertising, house painting, illustration. For educators who intend to inform others of the contributions of arts elements to learning in other domains, clear definitions are crucial. If there are to be answers to the questions introduced

> "It is important to remember that research on the impact of 'arts' activities on learning in any capacity—disciplinary or interdisciplinary—requires an attempt to create a working definition of art."

above, they need to be traced back to the practical, context-relevant definitions used by the authors of the papers. In the absence of definitions, most who write about the arts proceed as if there were a common or shared understanding of what is being discussed. The phrase "visual arts" can mean any number of practices, objects, or processes, but it is used in three of the four selected studies as a simple descriptive statement or as a label for the practices of drawing or graphic illustration, without further definition. That most established writers about art and arts education opt for descriptions or illustrations of art rather than definitions is true. Gombrich presents four or five hundred examples of art instead of a definition. It is important to remember that research on the impact of "arts" activities on learning in any capacity—disciplinary or interdisciplinary—requires an attempt to create a working definition of art.

Though he presents his own definition of art, which he admits will disappoint some, Gehlbach (1990) allows that we may not need a single definition of art. Others would argue that there is no single definition of art. It may well be that, as Gombrich states, "There really is no such thing as art. There are only artists." It is more likely that what is meant by "art," like truth, as Pierce (1934) indicates, is "the opinion which is fated to be ultimately agreed upon by all who investigate." For researchers and educators who work in a narrower realm than philosophy, however, there needs to be pragmatic agreement about basic definitions. Gehlbach opts for a communication-based definition:

> Artistic communication…(a) has no specific time reference for appropriate decoding, (b) is displayed for decoding by unspecified individual people, (c) is regarded as different from objects or events as they naturally occur, and (d) is an object of leisure, not related to the survival or physical well-being of the decoder.

He states that, "One may argue that definitions should vary with the context in which they are to be used," and he describes how other forms of instruction such as reading use similarly relativistic approaches to account for different levels of reading fluency. However, he does insist on the need for operational definitions. His definition would be: "appropriate for the purposes of *public* education from a broad cultural perspective"; "*relatively objective*," lending itself to systematic design and experimentation; and "precise enough to discriminate art instruction from all other concerns of general public education."

The Contextual Requirements of Good Research on Good Arts in Education Instruction

Art, which is by most definitions highly situated and contextual, carries these characteristics into instructional settings. As a consequence of this contextual characteristic, operational definitions that limit the terms of related research and define the parameters of instruction are especially useful in arts in education studies. Thus, arts education works against the common flow of instruction, which has historically moved toward generalized distributions of effects across large populations. Lightfoot concludes, "…good teaching, like a good school, is situationally determined, embedded in a context, with a history and an evolution." Researchers who have studied art teaching, searching for those elements that distinguish good arts teaching from good teaching in general, specify that arts teachers focus on those elements of the context that derive from the highly situational personal characteristics of their students, their feelings, thoughts, and life situations outside the classroom. Good arts teachers, say Gray and MacGregor (1986) and Flinders (1989), build their teaching on an understanding and knowledge of their students and their lives to a greater extent than do teachers in other subject areas. There is ample room for additional research to determine whether these teaching characteristics extend to integrated, interdisciplinary, or related instruction that includes the arts.

The need for definition for research and to help educators use research is exacerbated when we extend our specific conceptions of arts instruction beyond the more common arts discipline-based approaches to include instruction for transfer to learning in other subject areas, interdisciplinary instruction, related arts instruction, or integrated instruction. The pertinent issue here is not so much whether the work children are doing in an integrated visual arts/history lesson can be labeled "art," but whether the essential characteristics of the art form are integrated into the instruction with integrity. Explanations of transfer from art experiences to learning in other subject areas, with their constant intertwining of causal effects, demand even more rigorous definitions of the arts elements deemed to be essential to the process of integration. Would the work have more noticeable impact on learning in other subjects if the artistic elements were fully realized? Does work that respects the integrity of the artistic elements have greater or less impact on student learning? The studies examined here make most use of drawing activities. The history of drawing in the public schools of North America has always been problematic for artists and arts educators. "Drawing was introduced into Canadian public schools…linked…with penmanship, utility and mechanical and industrial progress…nothing about creativity… . Drawing was a means of social control and cultural hegemony." If student work using arts elements is thought of as simply illustration, a mechanical act, a utilitarian task without specific artistic or aesthetic dimensions or intentions, is it fair to describe the instruction as "arts-based" or "arts-infused"? If the drawing part of the instruction does not rise to the level of art, is the work an example of "instrumental" uses of the art?

All four reports included in this sample are concentrated on instruction and learning in non-arts content, rather than on instruction in visual art or arts skills. The Tishman report treated here is part of a larger report that probably includes a discussion of arts activities, but the section provided for the Compendium describes "non-art activity" aimed at transfer from a Visual Thinking Curriculum to science. The report talks about "near transfer" to scientific "visual images with a narrative content" and "a surface similarity" to arts images examined by students in class.

The Wilhelm study of two special education students in his regularly scheduled classes who were encouraged to use visual forms of expression rather than verbal to convey their understanding of reading assignments, among those considered here, makes the most of relating instruction using visual elements to the characteristics of individual students. But Wilhelm was primarily concerned with teaching reading. He did not teach the two research subjects to draw or expand their arts knowledge or skills. Though other students in the classes that Wilhem taught who had better language skills were intrigued by the visual work of the two subjects of the study, they did not adopt the techniques for their own work, nor were they encouraged to through instructional activities designed by the instructor.

The DeJarnette study offers definitions of the visual arts as "teaching" and "assessment" tools, but her definitions do not meet Gehlbach's criteria for operationalizing the term "art." Tishman, et al. talk about "visual art," "visual images," and "art activity," but the students in their study indicate that, in their own judgment, the visual material used in their science studies does not qualify as "artistic." For Gehlbach, the absence or inadequacy of definition here would raise critical questions about the connections between visual arts elements and the learning of science that are not answered in the research.

> "Good arts teachers...build their teaching on an understanding and knowledge of their students and their lives to a greater extent than do teachers in other subject areas."

The examples of student work selected for three of the studies examined here are described as drawings and the authors state that "visual arts" elements are used in their lessons, but no one defines the work as art or makes claims for it as art. In the visual thinking skills study, the students themselves state that the visual material that they are applying their thinking skills to is not "art," and the researchers make no contrary claim. For this reader, the absence of such operational definitions leads me to question the fairness of any attribution of language or science knowledge or skills development to the contribution of arts procedures. A related issue is that of whether the procedures selected are uniquely "arts procedures or processes." Making a mark on a piece of paper with a #2 pencil may result in a line or smudge and may be "graphic" in nature, but calling such work "art" or even "artistic" is a stretch. Even producing a representational drawing of an object or artifact, while visual and graphic, may fall far short of being art. The fact that a procedure may be used to make art does not make it an art procedure. Illustration is a very legitimate aim and process, but it is not necessarily art.

Several recent studies [Gray and MacGregor (1986) and Flinders (1989)], including Wilhelm's report among the four studies represented here, have extended the degree to which situational or contextual factors are considered in evaluating or researching school arts education activities. The Education Development Center's studies of the Empire State Partnership Project and the New York Arts Annenberg Project [Baker and Bevan (2000)] have combed contextual variables from among the practices of 130 separate school/cultural agency partnerships, and the researchers there are working to link those variables to instructional practices and student impact. The Burton, Horowitz, and Abeles (2000) *Champions of Change* report incorporated situational data and analysis in an important study that established the importance of considering social "constellations" in determining arts program impact. A whole spate of recent Canadian studies from Ontario, British Columbia, and Calgary are adding detail to the still crudely charted path of arts in education research. Future research will need to extend the mapping of links between discipline characteristics and aesthetic, social, emotional, and cognitive aspects of school contexts beyond what we see in the studies collected for the Compendium.

Balance

The issue of balance is one that affects curriculum content selection, allocations of time and space, and staffing decisions in schools. As an issue of learning and instruction, the balance between discipline-based content, skills taught, and impact on cognition or development is crucial but seldom discussed in the four visual arts studies reviewed here. This researcher's investigations of large-scale school change efforts based on related or integrated arts instruction has seldom found examples of balanced instruction, equal or nearly equal emphasis on the arts and the related discipline. More usually in schools, arts content is not taught as thoroughly as that of other disciplines, and the arts skills students need to produce artistic products are not taught at the same level as the core curriculum disciplines' skills. When new resources such as teaching artists, new arts curricula, or additional specialist teachers are introduced, the balance may shift, but it often shifts away from the core curriculum emphases. A truly balanced instructional program is rare and difficult to maintain. The Wilhelm study illustrates an increasingly common set of balance issues in that the visual elements technique he uses is limited, for the most part, to two students who have identifiable learning disorders, and who benefit from the use of their visual capacities in ways they and the teacher had not anticipated. With increasing use of multiple intelligences modes of instruction, balance may be determined by individual student capabilities and balance may necessarily be an irrelevant concept.

The broader issue of curriculum or content balance is common in the arts education field as well as between arts and other subjects. A completely equitable distribution of time, emphasis, or content among different disciplines is neither possible nor desirable, but neither are completely inequitable distributions. One unfortunate consequence of a constant state of imbalance is resentment on the part of arts educators toward core discipline specialists and arts education advocates who are seen as "using" the arts. Even among the arts, there are issues related to balance in the curriculum. School-based arts education restricts most programs to the static visual arts such as painting and drawing or to music. The performing arts of dance and theater and media arts such as video are not usually included in equal degrees. The balance among the various art forms shifts the other way in arts education programs aimed at relating art to instruction in core curriculum disciplines. A recent statewide convening of over 300 teachers, teaching artists, and school and cultural organization administrators working on curriculum and evaluation for arts education programming that supports core curriculum subjects employed only one, part-time visual arts faculty member among a host of theater, dance, music, and media faculty. Visual arts teachers who attended complained about the absence of resources supporting them in their development of appropriate practices. Music teachers might have raised similar complaints, but none were heard. The instructional programs being designed at this seminar nearly all addressed verbal literacy issues in the schools, and those art forms that used language more prominently were chosen.

Completeness

The issue of developmental aspects of children's drawings has been long and widely discussed. Wilson and Wilson (1979, 1982, 1984), Hatch and Gardner (1993), and Gardner (1980) all view universalistic developmental views of children's graphic development as limited, arguing, instead, for a more complete interpretation that considers many other factors and variables. These researchers look instead at a complex set of interactions among factors, and their work suggests that other researchers should consider a more nearly complete set of elements in arts education. The problem for researchers and educators alike is that of determining just how much is necessary for a complete study. Genetics, culture, skills, emotional disposition, environmental factors, and social and cultural contexts all play roles in the child's development in art, and these factors may interact in entirely idiosyncratic ways from individual to individual. These views, with their inclusion of external context and increased focus on external, social experiences and behaviors, define learning experiences in terms of "events" that:

> …have a quality as a whole. By quality is meant the total meaning of the event. The quality of
> the event is the resultant of the interaction of the experiencer and the world, that is, the inter-
> action of the organism and the physical relations that provide support for the experiences.

The complex reality of such instructional situations, as we see in the studies selected for this discussion, can easily overtax the resources of researchers and research methodology, particularly experimental methodology. The California State University list of minimum proficiencies for arts teachers includes 14 generic competencies grouped as "understandings," "communication and thinking skills," and "values and attitudes," and 34 art competencies identified as "art production," "art history," "art criticism and aesthetics," and "relationships between area of art and connections with life and other disciplines." A question for researchers and audiences alike is "what constitutes the whole?" or at least "what can stand for the whole?" Sharp El Shayeb states that it would be difficult to study all the variables included in the CSU document.

When is instruction in a discipline complete enough? When is a study complete enough to justify faith in its findings? In the case of arts education, perhaps "completeness" needs to be defined at least partially by the accuracy or precision of the connections between arts elements taught and the characteristic elements accepted by the field rather than just by the number of connections made. The national standards for arts education include for the elementary and upper-elementary levels—the levels reported in three of the studies—comparison of relationships in visual, tactile, spatial, and temporal elements, purposes of arts such as communicating, persuading, recording, celebrating, embellishing, and designing. Students at this level are also expected to be able to evaluate their own artwork using established criteria and to compare the roles of art makers in different cultures and times and how their natural environments affected their art.

Would instruction in reading, for example, be considered complete if the students received no skills training? In visual arts instruction it is frequently the case that little skills training is provided before students are asked to begin producing artistic work. "Young children are normally asked…to draw and paint, for example, with no instruction whatsoever in drawing or painting [and they]…spend large amounts of time in activities (e.g., self-expression) for which they lack the requisite prior understanding and skills." (Gehlbach 1990) In projects such as the ones examined in these reports, there was ample room for the children to demonstrate that they had the skills to make art as required and to indicate their understanding of potential effects. Both of these indicators would help evaluate the extent to which art is being taught and learned appropriately along with content and skills in the related disciplines. In the studies reported here, there is no evidence of art skills training.

Are there adequate taxonomies from which the authors of these studies might have chosen arts skills, content, aesthetic responses? Yes. Would their studies have presented a more complete picture of the relationships between arts practices and learning in language areas? Yes. Could the researchers meet the dictates of research methodology, especially those related to controlling the many additional variables in experimental research? Perhaps not. Are we better off for the studies done? Definitely, for they take the beginning steps that are necessary for putting elements associated with the arts into discussions about learning, cognition, instructional strategies, and curriculum content and design. Do we need more complete studies with context-specific definitions of the arts and related elements and control of these elements against the many variables at work in classrooms? Of course.

> "Researchers...need to find ways of counting as appropriate evidence more of the qualitative experience of the arts."

The Path Ahead

Having an opportunity to consider issues related to better arts education programming and instruction, especially in visual arts education, against the backdrop of systematically gathered information has been rare in recent years. The arts in education and all their practitioners need the kind of deliberation these studies support and provide. These researchers have not found all or even most of the answers we need, but they have identified some new paths and helped move our understanding ahead. Researchers need to broaden their definitions of what counts as legitimate and valid investigations or research to include studies that build on and make use of the characteristic elements of the arts. They need to find ways of counting as appropriate evidence more of the qualitative experience of the arts. They need to plant more markers on the paths we explore, but these studies make important beginnings.

Reference

Baker, T. (2001) "Contextual Arts Education Assessment: Counting in Context," Seattle, American Educational Research Association Meeting Annual Meeting.

"New Currency for the Arts in Education: From Change Theory into Promising Practice," in Remer, J. ed. *Beyond Enrichment*. New York: American Council on the Arts, 1996.

and Bevan, B., "School Change through Arts Instruction: Contextual Arts Education in the New York City Partnerships for Arts in Education Program," New Orleans, American Educational Research Association Annual Meeting, April 2000.

Boughton, D., Eisner, E., and Ligtvoet, J. Eds. *Evaluating and Assessing the Visual Arts in Education: International Perspectives*. New York: Teachers College Press, 1996.

Burger, K. and Winner, E. (2000) "Instruction in Visual Art: Can It Help Children Learn to Read?" *Journal of Aesthetic Education*, 34 (3-4), 277-293.

Burton, J., Horowitz, R., and Abeles, H. (2000) "Learning in and Through the Arts: Curriculum Implications," in *Champions of Change: The Impact of the Arts on Learning*. Washington, DC: Arts Education Partnership and the President's Commission on the Arts and the Humanities.

Chalmers, F. Graeme, (1998) "Teaching Drawing in Nineteenth-Century Canada – Why?" in Freedman, K. and Hernandez, F. Eds. *Curriculum, Culture, and Art Education: Comparative Perspectives*. Albany, NY: State University of New York Press.

DeJarnette, K. (1997) "The Arts, Language, and Knowing: An Experimental Study of the Potential of the Visual Arts for Assessing Academic Learning by Language Minority Students," unpublished dissertation, Los Angeles: University of California at Los Angeles.

Flinders, D. (1989) "Voices From the Classroom: Educational Practice Can Inform Policy." Eugene OR: ERIC Clearinghouse on Educational Management, in P. Sharp El Shayeb.

Freedman, K. and Hernandez, F. Eds. (1998) *Curriculum, Culture, and Art Education: Comparative Perspectives*. Albany, NY: State University of New York Press.

Gardner, H. (1980) *Artful Scribbles: the Significance of Children's Drawings*, New York: Basic Books, Inc. Publishers.

"Rejoinder to Steers," in *Evaluating and Assessing the Visual Arts in Education*. Eds. Boughton, Doug, Eisner, Elliot W., and Ligtvoet, Johan. New York: Teachers College Press, 1996.

visual arts

Gehlbach, R. (1990) "Art Education: Issues in Curriculum and Research," *Educational Researcher*. October, 19-25.

Golomb, C. (1991) *The Child's Creation of a Pictorial World*. Berkeley, CA: University of California Press.

Gombrich, E. (1972) *The Story of Art*. Oxford: Phaidon Press.

Gray, J., and MacGregor, R. (1986) "Personally Relevant Observations about Art Concepts and Teaching Activities." Unpublished manuscript, University of British Columbia, Department of Visual and Performing Arts, Vancouver, in P. Sharp El Shayeb.

Hatch, T., and Gardner, H. (1993) "Finding Cognition in the Classroom: An Expanded View of Human Intelligence," in Salomon, G. ed. *Distributed Cognitions: Psychological and Educational Considerations*. Cambridge: Cambridge University Press.

Jenkins, J. J. (1974) "Remember that Old Theory of Memory? Well, Forget It!" American Psychologist, 11, in W. J. Clancy, (1997), *Situated Cognition: On Human Knowledge and Computer Representations*. Cambridge, UK: Cambridge University Press.

Kirshner, D. and Whitson, J. A. (1997) *Situated Cognition: Social, Semiotic and Psychological Perspectives*. Mahwah, NJ: Lawrence Erlbaum Associates, Publishers.

Lave, J. (1988) *Cognition in Practice: Mind, Mathematics and Culture in Everyday Life*. Cambridge, UK: Cambridge University Press.

(1997) "The Culture of Acquisition and the Practice of Understanding," in Kirshner, D. and Whitson, J. A. Eds. Situated Cognition: *Social, Semiotic and Psychological Perspectives*. Mahwah, NJ: Lawrence Erlbaum Associates, Publishers.

Lightfoot, S. (1983) *The Good High School*. New York: Basic Books in P. Sharp El Shayeb.

Mason, R. (1996) "Improving the Quality of Art Teaching," in Boughton, D, Eisner, E. and Ligtvoet, J. Eds. *Evaluating and Assessing the Visual Arts in Education: International Perspectives*. New York: Teachers College Press.

North Carolina State Board of Education/Department of Public Instruction. Visual Arts. Raleigh, NC: North Carolina Department of Public Instruction.

Peirce, C. (1934) *Collected Papers of Charles Sanders Peirce* (Vol. 5) Eds. Hartshorne, C. & Weiss, P. Cambridge, MA: Harvard University Press.

Perkins, D. (1988) "Art as Understanding," *Journal of Aesthetic Education*. 22(1), 111-131.

(1993) "Person-plus: A Distributed View of Thinking and Learning," in Salomon, G. ed. *Distributed Cognitions: Psychological and Educational Considerations*. Cambridge: Cambridge University Press.

Salomon, G. Ed. (1993) *Distributed Cognitions: Psychological and Educational Considerations*. Cambridge: Cambridge University Press.

Sharp El Shayeb, P. (1996) "Good Teaching: Evaluating Art Teaching in the Context of Schools," in Boughton, D., Eisner, E., and Ligtvoet, J. Eds. *Evaluating and Assessing the Visual Arts in Education: International Perspectives*. New York: Teachers College Press.

Tishman, S., MacGillivray, D. and Palmer, P. (1999) *Investigating the Educational Impact and Potential of the Museum of Modern Art's Visual Thinking Curriculum: Final Report*. New York: The Museum of Modern Art.

Wilhelm, J. (1995) "Reading Is Seeing: Using Visual Response to Improve the Literary Reading of Reluctant Readers," *Journal of Reading Behavior*. 27 (4) 467- 503.

Wilson, B. and Wilson, M. (1979) "Figure Structure, Figure Action, and Framing in Drawing of American and Egyptian Children," *Studies in Art Education*. 21 (1), 36-43.

(1982) "The Persistence of the Perpendicular Principle: Why, When, and Where Innate Factors Determine the Nature of Drawings." *Review of Research in Visual Arts Education*. 15, 1-18

(1984) Children's Drawings in Egypt: Cultural Style Acquisition as Graphic Development. *Visual Arts Research*. 10 (1), 13-25.

Winner, E. and Hetland, L. (2000) "The Arts in Education: Evaluating the Evidence for a Causal Link," *Journal of Aesthetic Education*, Vol. 34, Nos. 3-4, Fall/Winter, 1-9.

Wolf, D. (1989) "Artistic Learning: What and Where Is It?" in Gardner, H. & Perkins, D. *Art, Mind & Education*. Urbana, IL: The University of Illinois Press.

Zimmerman, E. (1990) "A Case Study of the Childhood Art Work of an Artistically Talented Young Adult," Paper presented at the 98th Annual Convention of the American Psychological Association, Boston, August.

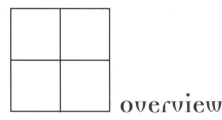

overview

Essay
The Arts and the Transfer of Learning
James S. Catterall

Introduction

The idea that learning in one setting has positive effects "beyond the conditions of initial learning"[1] has engaged cognitive psychologists for at least a century. This should be no surprise. What and how children learn occupy center stage in education research; the impacts on future learning and action deserve an equally prominent place. As one recent review has pointed out, our entire system of formal schooling is built on the assumption that what children learn early on impacts what they learn in later grades; and that what students learn during formal education affects behavior after they leave our schools and colleges.[2] Educators would be quick to agree that skills, attitudes, and work habits surrounding schoolwork rank high among instructional goals—and that for many students such capabilities and orientations accrue over time and by all indications settle in as enduring traits. Debates about the necessary definitions, measures, and designs for inquiry notwithstanding, we refer in these cases to transfer. Transfer denotes instances where learning in one context assists learning in a different context.

Despite the "goes-without-saying" quality of transfer, learning research over the years has failed to corroborate transfer far more often than it has managed to support its existence. The failures are interesting. Children may persist for years studying Latin or rote mathematics under assumptions that general mental discipline will result. Available studies say it does not. Or we might assume that problem-solving strategies learned in one circumstance would naturally carry forward to approaches to solving analogous problems. Things don't always work that way. We might even think that something so specific as learning to judge the area of a rectangle would show up in ability to judge the area of a circle. Not likely, say researchers. Transfer has acquired a tarnished reputation over the years in the realms of learning and developmental psychology—transfer is difficult to achieve, and it is not often found, at least through the methods by which it has been studied. Under the circumstances, it is not surprising that research on transfer lay fairly dormant in recent decades.[3] Why pound one's head against a wall in anticipation of non-publishable research findings?

Arts into the breach

With transfer so assigned to an intellectual backwater, it is only natural that recent worldwide attention to the academic and social effects of learning in the arts has stirred up the academic and artistic communities. A significant chronological marker seems to have been an announcement by researchers at the University of California[4] that was translated by the national media and parents across the nation as "Mozart makes you smarter." Flocks of listeners became curious, active, or agitated in response to the idea. Some academics scurried to replicate and extend the music studies; others took up studies of myriad possible effects of learning in and through other art forms.

Amidst the excitement, skeptics raised their voices. One group was learning psychologists who had reason, according to the traditions of their discipline, to question anything smacking of transfer. Surely, they felt claims such as cognitive development through music, reading achievement through drama, problem-solving through the visual arts, or persistence through dance must be based on flawed research. Or if examined closely, such relationships must be trivial, or not instances of transfer at all, or simply evidence of something else. And the nation's arts educators and artists found themselves in a dilemma as interest in learning through the arts escalated. They feared that the talk of learning mathematics through music or producing increased standardized test scores through the visual arts would demean the higher place of art in society, further shielding the intrinsic worth of the arts from the public eye. At the same time, however, increased interest in the arts was serving to shift public and private resources toward arts education in a significant way. Some artists and arts educators heralded a revival of the arts, for whatever rationale; others felt their callings compromised.

"At the level of neuro-function, learning experiences unequivocally impact future learning experiences."

1 John Bransford and Daniel Schwartz (2000). Rethinking Transfer. Chapter in Review of Research in Education, Volume 24. Washington, D.C.: American Educational Research Association.

2 ibid.

3 This brief overview is based directly on the Bransford & Schwartz characterization of past research on transfer.

4 Shaw et al., 1996

Transfer – a neurological basis

Widely accepted theories of cognition shed light on the transfer debate. At the level of neuro-function, learning experiences unequivocally impact future learning experiences.[5] The main questions are the nature and extent of impacts rather than whether or not effects exist. Experiences reorganize neural pathways, neural receptors, and functioning of specific brain regions such that subsequent experiences are received differently, at levels ranging from trivial or behaviorally undetectable to profound and exceedingly apparent. The experience of hearing a single musical note for the first time provides an illustration—say a well-attacked F sharp from the low register of a contrabassoon. This auditory experience impacts multiple and interacting regions of the brain—those engaged in feelings and attitudes (that sounded good but scared me), memory (I won't forget that), linguistic and rational responses (how did she do that?), autonomous reactions (increased heart rate), to name possible primary responses. When the same note is heard a second time, triggered neural impulses also travel paths among regions of the brain—those involved with cognition, memory, feeling, value, and autonomous response—but in patterns different from those traveled when the note was new. In its first pass, the brain sets up a filing system of sorts for the experience—the reaction on a second hearing may be one of recognition, pleasure or pain of familiarity, discernment, or perhaps rational discourse. Nonetheless, all from a brain restructured by experience.[6]

If a musical note can propel and reorient millions of neurons, the arts experiences described in this Compendium clearly impact the cognitive structures of the children and students involved. To begin, learning in the arts alone should be seen as evidence of cognitive restructuring—the increased expertise of a watercolorist or dancer manifests in neural reorganization. In turn, if altered neuro-function is a consequence of learning in the arts, it is reasonable to think that such neural-conditioning could enhance performance in related skills, either through improved related cognitive functioning or through positive affective developments such as achievement motivation.[7]

Thus we establish a neuro-function argument supporting learning through the arts—the cultivation of capabilities and understandings that occur as "byproducts" or "co-developments" of the changes in cognitive and affective structures brought about by experiences in the arts. More directly, the argument suggests that experiences in the arts create capabilities or motivations that show up in non-arts capabilities.

Transfer in the Compendium studies

This Compendium displays the results of a sizable effort to catalog and describe research on the effects of learning in the arts on academic and social skills. In order to explore the many relationships suggesting evidence of transfer in these studies, it may be useful to provide a detailed portrait of the many arts-related academic and social outcomes that in fact find support in research.

Figure 1 presents just such an inventory. A first reaction might be that a great many academic and social developments have been linked to the arts in accumulated research—65 core relationships by rough count and more if every nuanced outcome variable across all compendium studies were to be listed. Of the relationships shown

5 Bransford, J. et al. (Eds.) How People Learn, Expanded Edition. Washington D.C.: National Academy Press, 2002

6 Damasio, A.R. Descartes' Error: Emotion, Reason, and the Brain. New York: Avon Books, 1995. (First published in 1994.)

7 Sylwester, R. A celebration of neurons: An educator's guide to the human brain. Alexandria, VA: ASCD

Figure 1. Compendium Summary: The Arts and Academic and Social Outcomes

Arts Learning:	Cognitive Capacities and Motivations to Learn:
Visual Arts	
Drawing	Content and organization of writing.
Visualization training	Sophisticated reading skills/interpretation of text.
Reasoning about art	Reasoning about scientific images.
Instruction in visual art	Reading readiness.
Music	
Early childhood music training	Cognitive development
Music listening	Spatial reasoning. Spatial temporal reasoning. Quality of writing. Prolixity of writing.
Piano/keyboard learning	Mathematics proficiency. Spatial reasoning.
Piano and voice	Long-term spatial temporal reasoning.

Music performance	Self-efficacy. Self-concept.
Instrument training	Reading. SAT verbal scores.
Music with language learning	English skills for ESL learners.

Classroom Drama

Dramatic enactment	Story comprehension (oral and written). Character identification. Character motivation. Increased peer interaction. Writing proficiency and prolixity. Conflict resolution skills. Concentrated thought. Understanding social relationships. Ability to understand complex issues and emotions. Engagement. Skill with subsequently read, unrelated texts. Problem-solving dispositions/strategies. General self-concept.

Dance

Traditional dance	Self-confidence. Persistence. Reading skills. Nonverbal reasoning. Expressive skills. Creativity in poetry. Social tolerance. Appreciation of individual/group social development.
Creative dance	General creative thinking – fluency General creative thinking – originality, elaboration, flexibility.

Multi-arts Programs

Integrated arts/academics	Reading, verbal and mathematics skills. Creative thinking. Achievement motivation. Cognitive engagement. Instructional practice in the school. Professional culture of the school. School climate. Community engagement and identity.
Intensive arts experience	Self-confidence. Risk-taking. Paying attention. Persevering. Empathy for others. Self-initiating. Task persistence. Ownership of learning. Collaboration skills. Leadership. Reduced dropout rates. Educational aspirations. Higher-order thinking skills.
Arts-rich school environment	Creativity. Engagement/attendance. Range of personal and social developments. Higher-order thinking skills.

in Figure 1, some links prove to be stronger than others, some less. Some relationships appear in multiple studies, others in only one or two high-quality investigations. The main task here is not to parse this inventory according to comparative strengths of relationships—the essays corresponding to each arts form and the study summaries themselves can assist readers in these purposes. The message of Figure 1 seems first that research has identified a wide variety of academic and social developments to be valid results of learning in or engagement with the arts. Moreover, because the studies chosen for the Compendium met strict criteria for quality of design and their ability to make causal suggestions, Figure 1 suggests the "state of research" on the impact of the arts on academic and social development; the figure at least maps the territory in which effects have been reliably demonstrated.

The Compendium's studies organized and outlined in Figure 1 all show evidence of transfer in the sense that learning activities in the arts have various effects beyond the initial conditions of learning. Virtually all of our studies can be said to fit under such an umbrella; and the myriad ways they can be seen to fit are worth explication. Research on the arts and learning has far transcended the need to test whether or not the arts have impacts with potential manifestations beyond direct learning in the art forms. Of present interest is just what are such manifestations and what can be said of their importance or how they come about. Two somewhat overlapping organizing schemes are useful for considering transfer across the studies in this Compendium. One addresses how similar transferred learnings are to the learnings observed or claimed as their progenitors. The second entails some partitioning between cognitive (skill-based) transfer and affective (motivation-based) transfer.

Similar learnings – near and far. One differentiating quality within the idea of transfer is the degree of similarity between the context in which learning in the arts occurs and the context in which transferred developments are seen and measured. This question closely follows the discussion of transfer and neuro-function above: because specific skill developments impact cognitive structures, similar or closely related skills engaging the same structures may benefit. Some refer to this as a condition of near transfer (very similar contexts). In contrast, skill transfer where the resulting skills bear little similarity to the skills learned (say in the arts) or where they are used in very different situations has been called far transfer (disparate contexts).

These terms are useful more in a heuristic sense than in a substantive sense. While "far" transfer may seem more impressive as a phenomenon in its suggestions of transformed behavior or unexpected effects, any transfer to learning, near or far, is better judged on the veracity of the claimed relationship along with the value of the outcome itself. For example, when reading comprehension skills result from artistic learning that itself involves reading (such as certain classroom drama activities) or when mathematics achievement results from training in music, both outcomes—reading skills and mathematics skills—should be judged in their own right, not at one level of value or another just because the transfer came from near (drama to reading) or far (music to mathematics).

Transfer through motivation. A second way of thinking about transfer from the arts is to distinguish transfer of cognitive or thinking capabilities from transfer of affective orientations, particularly various orientations linked to motivation. Cognitive development of course refers to increased abilities and expertise supporting such developments as academic achievement or social understanding. Affective development refers to the willingness of individuals to put their skills to use: their intrinsic and extrinsic interests in what they are learning, their engagement with tasks at hand, the importance they assign to success, the attributions they make for their success, and the feelings of self-worth generated through effective performance.

Affective gains from the arts find much support. Psychologist Howard Gardner points out that certain learnings in the arts are quite likely to spill over, even if the arts are not in a unique position to make such claims of transfer. In a recent essay on multiple intelligences and the arts, Gardner applauds two different types of transfer from the arts that should be considered foundational. First, in reacting to widespread advocacy for nurturing different intelligences in school in response to his writings, Gardner registers his comfort with the idea, "...because participation in the arts is a wonderful way to develop a range of intelligences in children."[8] A conception implied is that participating and learning in an art form can cultivate awareness, judgment, facility, sensibilities, connoisseurship, and other cognitive attributes that we might associate with artistic or other intelligences more generally. These developments can in turn impact the way children learn or the way they choose to express themselves within the disciplines and perhaps across disciplines. An example is gaining artistic intelligence through progressive learning as a painter. Art skill and artistic intelligence surely are close in kind, yet they may involve some dimension of transfer; intelligence gained is a positive outcome lying beyond the initial conditions of learning to paint or to dance.

Gardner also helps with another notion of transfer in the arts—a sort of transfer that does emerge in the Compendium's studies. Among what Gardner describes as "...the compelling reasons for arts education...are the likelihood that skill and craft gained in the arts help students to understand that they can improve in other consequential activities and that their heightened skill can give pleasure to themselves and to others."[9] This points to instances in which heightened self-concept ("I can succeed on stage") can lead to heightened academic or social

8 Howard Gardner, The happy meeting of multiple intelligences and the arts, Harvard Education Letter, 15/6 (November/December) 1999, 5.

9 Howard Gardner, op. cit.

self-concepts through some mechanism of transfer. Several of our studies included measures of self-concept that were spawned by successful artistic accomplishments and experiences, although Gardner reminds us, correctly, that the arts hold no monopoly on creating transferable feelings of self-worth. Here an important question becomes under what conditions and for whom does success in the arts transfer to success and persistence in school? While success in most anything in school might be assumed to have similar spillover effects, it appears that the arts can attract students who have been pushed away from other opportunities for success in school. Compendium studies showing at-risk and failing students revived by immersion in arts programs offer such suggestions—including that students benefit from engagement inspired by the complexities of the arts in well-drawn programs. Among the relationships shown in Figure 1, learning to perform music, learning in traditional dance, and dramatic enactment emerge in our studies as augmenting general self-concept. It may not be a coincidence that the studies involved are in the performing arts, where demonstrating skills for audiences is an integral component.

The arts and motivation more generally. It is a short step from self-conception to broader ideas of achievement motivation and engagement, and some of the Compendium studies show effects in these areas. Research on self-concept is a component of the larger human development domain of motivation. In this domain, notions of intrinsic and extrinsic interest in schoolwork, levels of cognitive engagement, and attributions made by children for their success or failure in school are central issues. Several of the multi-arts program evaluations summarized in the Compendium, along with specific studies in arts learning, conclude that children are more engaged when involved in artistic activities in school than when involved in other curricular activities. Higher engagement is observed when children integrate the arts and academic learning in programs such as the Chicago Arts Partnerships in Education.[10] Individual studies involving at-risk students frequently characterize their success as a consequence of induced or revived enthusiasm for school attained through the arts.[11] Claims of transfer in the form of higher engagement include observations that children in schools with high levels of arts experiences are generally more engaged and motivated in school. This can be seen as the transfer of attitudes or orientations about school from learning in and with the arts to learning situations more generally. Perhaps children who find parts of their school day satisfying and fun through the arts become more sanguine about the whole school experience.

Arts as curricula for academics. Research studies on drama in education illustrate additional ways that transfer can be considered and observed. One perspective is that the studies in classroom drama tend to focus on what could be called near transfer according to the discussion above. In some cases, the learning studied is so near to learning in the dramatic experience that naming the phenomenon transfer might be called into question. For example, the majority of drama studies in the Compendium connect dramatic enactment with story understanding and reading comprehension. Considering what dramatic play may do to produce such effects conjures suggestions that drama is in fact a curriculum for story and reading comprehension. Witness the Compendium's study designs: young children who act out a story after hearing it read to them ultimately understand the story better—its sequence, its details, its characters—than children who hear the story and then process it through a traditional classroom discussion. In such studies, we might say that dramatic enactment is simply a better way to process a story than a teacher-led discussion; this appears to be the case. As such, when a child's story comprehension is shown to be greater after participation in an enactment than when simply listening to the story, it may be a stretch to call such learning an incidence of transfer. Dramatizing is simply a good way to learn a story. Or when young children write more effectively after acting out a situation, in contrast to receiving a teacher-led lesson, we might say that such dramatization is a better curriculum for topical writing than traditional classroom instruction regarding the topic. But whether or not this should be called transfer is debatable. But an important point should not be lost in the discussion—if story understanding, reading comprehension, and topical writing are valued curricular goals, the drama studies in the Compendium offer suggestions of promising ways to pursue these ends.

Dramatic enactment usually produces an environment focused on interpersonal relations, and here we must acknowledge both opportunities for and evidence of transfer. In drama studies focused on such relations, we see impacts on character understanding, comprehension of character motivation, increased peer-to-peer interactions, increased conflict-resolution skills, and improved problem-solving dispositions and strategies. These outcomes, more than story understanding and writing through classroom drama, seem to be evidence of transfer.

Music and spatial reasoning. Nowhere in the spectrum of arts learning effects on cognitive functioning are impacts more clear than in the rich archive of studies, many very recent, that show connections between music learning or musical experiences and the fundamental cognitive capability called spatial reasoning. Music listening, learning to play piano and keyboards, and learning piano and voice all contribute to spatial reasoning. While

> "…if story understanding, reading comprehension, and topical writing are valued curricular goals, the drama studies in the Compendium offer suggestions of promising ways to pursue these ends."

10 See the summary of the Chicago Arts in Education: Evaluation Summary in this volume.

11 An example is Jeanette Horn's 1992 study, An Exploration into the Writing of Original Scripts by Inner City High School Drama Students, summarized in this volume.

spatial reasoning is not a measure in other music studies, some of the outcomes measured in music research have strong ties to spatial reasoning ability: mathematics, reading and verbal competence, and writing ability. In the vast literature on spatial reasoning (about 3,000 studies in some bibliographies[12]), it is clear that mathematical skills as well as language facility benefit directly from spatial reasoning skills. Some core concepts in mathematics are inherently spatial in character, proportions and fractions as examples. In the case of language development, the relationship is a bit more oblique but nonetheless robust: what we write, what we read, and what we hear involve words that are used and understood in specific contexts. These contexts can be seen as spatial networks involving words with related words, words with their historical backgrounds, words with their social relationships, and words with nearly placed words in expressions. Spatial reasoning is also fundamental to any planning task—a capacity without which we would have trouble organizing our daily lives. The music studies in this Compendium testifying to benefits in the form of spatial reasoning skills are not to be taken lightly. Future studies, including direct neurological studies, are likely to affirm and extend what we see in present research.

Where to from here?

While a great many relationships between the arts and human development have been drawn under the umbrella of transfer, several directions for future research in these traditions seem important. One is a closer examination of "learning in the arts" at the front end of the transfer equation and a closer relationship between transfer research with the more complex and situational views of learning populating the literature in recent years. Another is addressing the clear shortage of transfer studies in the visual arts and dance. And research on the arts and learning might follow the cues of Bransford & Schwartz[13] to test for longer-term impacts on thinking skills and problem-solving dispositions.

More on learning in the arts. Most of the research designs employed in the Compendium studies differentiate average outcomes for students participating in one arts training or arts-related experience versus comparison students without such experiences—classroom drama or not, visual training or not, keyboard lessons or not, or listening to Mozart versus Bach. This assuredly distinguishes learners from those who have had arts training or an arts-related experience and those who have not and sets up conditions in which effects of the arts can be identified. But the Compendium studies generally do not examine learning in the arts within their treatment groups, despite the fact that doing so could significantly increase the power of arts transfer studies. The central point is that transfer of skills from learning in the arts should be more pronounced for students who learn more in the arts. Many designs come to mind: gauging the acquisition of drama skills in a training program across participants to see if high learners gain more in the way of transferred skills; sorting subjects by measures of learned keyboard skills to see if more learning in music associates with higher acquisition of spatial reasoning skills. One suggestion of this design appears in drama studies showing more transferred skill development among those children who spontaneously get out of role to direct or lead a classroom dramatization. These children may be learning more drama and consequently gaining reading or interpersonal skills faster; but they may simply be higher-achieving children within the drama groups to start with—a crucial distinction.

More attention to contemporary views of learning. As just argued, the pursuit of transfer in the Compendium's studies does not at the same time illuminate the nature or degree of learning from which transfer takes place, relying instead on differentiating group treatments or experiential accountings of arts experiences. It is equally evident that current studies on the roles of the arts in academic and social development do not unpack either in fine detail or within comprehensive cognitive models the learning processes accounting for transfer. This point should not be interpreted as an oversight on the part of the researchers—this Compendium contains studies carried out in careful designs that support the relationships argued.

Nonetheless, more thorough understandings of the transfer of learning—from the arts as well as more generally—would require additional and different research. Such inquiry would ultimately need to accommodate growing evidence and beliefs that learning is situational, interactive, and extremely complex. This complexity can be seen in full color in the more completely rendered images of cognitive activity shown in brain scans; it also appears in the models of cognitive scientists attempting to illuminate a full spectrum of influences at play when children learn.

Learning and the role that transfer (by whatever definition) plays are far more complex than simple conceptions allow; we see a range of different words in use to characterize learning such as "parallel," "entangled," "entwined," and "contextual," all of which suggest that not all transfer is alike and that it is not direct. Contextual or situational explanations pose relationships that are key for learning and that will probably begin to define

12 One spatial reasoning bibliography focused on computer science numbers 2700 studies (http://liinwww.ira.uka.de/bibliography/Ai/Spatial.Reasoning.html). Another on-line source organizes spatial reasoning research into broad categories including cognitive and linguistic studies (http://www.cs.albany.edu/~amit/spatsites.html).

13 John Bransford and Daniel Schwartz (2000). Rethinking Transfer. Chapter in Review of Research in Education, Volume 24. Washington DC: American Educational Research Association.

"transfer" as distributed cognition or situational cognition. Processes of transfer would be seen in interactions and relationships of various sorts, and new states of learning, either new knowledge or new understanding, should be seen as the product of these relationships. The implications for this Compendium? While the Compendium research documents valid links between the arts and academic and social abilities, an extended and complementary program of research is needed if we want to understand transfer in its full cognitive glory.[14]

More studies in the visual arts and dance. There are abundant and strong studies supporting transfer from learning and experiences in drama and music, but a significant shortage of studies in the visual arts and dance. The imbalance is considerably wider than the listing in Figure 1 implies. The many relationships shown under drama and music show up in multiple studies. The relationships shown for the visual arts derive from only four studies, and there are about the same number of studies in dance as there are relationships cataloged. Clearly, we know far less about transfer from learning in the visual arts and dance than we do in drama and music. If research is drawn to vacuums, here are two for the taking.

> "...transfer could materialize if researchers would reformulate their theories about transfer and exercise patience in seeking its manifestations."

A higher order of transfer. An enticing contribution of the Bransford & Schwartz review discussed above is the introduction of a formal definition of transfer that contrasts sharply with prevailing conceptions including those seen in the Compendium studies. These scholars argue that traditional studies of transfer have been exceedingly narrow in their search for various direct applications of learning. As such, research to date has been myopic in not asking questions about the degree to which learning experiences might prepare students for future learning or have long-term repercussions on how learners approach any sort of problematic situation. Bransford & Schwartz hypothesize that transfer could materialize if researchers would reformulate their theories about transfer and exercise patience in seeking its manifestations. Transfer may be thought to leap beyond immediate tests of application altogether. The arts and human development generally, and the Compendium's studies particularly, are good candidates for such rethinking. The "preparation for future learning" concept of transfer offers an enticing but relatively unattended prospect that seems tailor-made for research in the arts. Future inquiries into the arts and learning should investigate longer-term developments in how learners approach artistic creation and expression generally; studies also should investigate the possibility that sustained and deep learning in the arts may cultivate habits of mind and dispositions impacting future problem-solving behavior. To some, this represents the Holy Grail of transfer—Transfer with a capital T perhaps. Such potentially powerful Transfer may not occur straightaway, but rather emerge over time. The many contributions of the Compendium's studies notwithstanding, perhaps we have overlooked important evidence of Transfer from learning in the arts by searching at the wrong times and in the wrong places.

157

14 The section on contemporary conceptions of learning draws on discussions and written exchanges with Dr. Terry Baker of the Center for Children and Technology in New York. This author accepts full responsibility for possible misrepresentations or distortions of Baker's contributions.

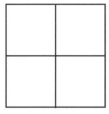

acknowledgments

We are grateful to the National Endowment for the Arts (NEA) and the Office of Educational Research and Improvement (OERI) at the U.S. Department of Education for providing funding for the production of this Compendium. Special thanks to Doug Herbert, director of Arts Education at the NEA, and Rita Foy Moss, research analyst at OERI, for their advice and guidance throughout its development.

During the formative stages of the Compendium we benefited greatly from the wise counsel of the Compendium Advisors listed at the opening of this volume. We are grateful to Michael Timpane of the RAND Corporation for chairing the group.

Lauren Stevenson, research associate at the Arts Education Partnership, was indispensable, serving as assistant Compendium editor, sounding board and adviser on focus and format, and coordinator of production. Peter H. Gerber of the EdDesigns Group assisted greatly by editing summaries and essays and providing counsel throughout. Sara Goldhawk, senior associate at the Arts Education Partnership, gave careful reading to the final proofs. Kathryn E. Ward, former project assistant at the Arts Education Partnership, provided essential administrative support. She also contributed the images of student artists found throughout the Compendium. Jan Stunkard, division coordinator at the NEA, deserves our thanks for her efficient and considerate management of the Cooperative Agreement that funded the production of the Compendium.

First and foremost, of course, thanks are due to the researchers who participated in the Compendium's creation. To those whose original studies are summarized. To James S. Catterall, Lois Hetland, and Ellen Winner for screening, selecting, and summarizing the chosen studies. To James S. Catterall, Terry L. Baker, Karen K. Bradley, Rob Horowitz, Larry Scripp, and Jaci Webb-Dempsey for their summaries and essays. To Dick Corbett, Cynthia I. Gerstl-Pepin, George W. Noblit, Michael A. Seaman, Betty Jane Wagner, and Bruce Wilson for summaries. And to Kristin Burger and Rachel Estrella for systematic searching, and Sean Bennett, Ronnie Cavaluzzi, Lori S. Eisenberg, Rachel Estrella, Joseph Hoffman, Nina Salzman, and Kate Solow for initial drafts of summaries. The Compendium is their collective achievement.